# POLITICAL ADVICE

# POLITICAL ADVICE

## Past, Present and Future

**Edited by**
**Colin Kidd and Jacqueline Rose**

**I.B. TAURIS**
LONDON · NEW YORK · OXFORD · NEW DELHI · SYDNEY

I.B. TAURIS

Bloomsbury Publishing Plc

50 Bedford Square, London, WC1B 3DP, UK

1385 Broadway, New York, NY 10018, USA

29 Earlsfort Terrace, Dublin 2, Ireland

BLOOMSBURY, I.B. TAURIS and the I.B. Tauris logo
are trademarks of Bloomsbury Publishing Plc

First published in Great Britain 2021

Cover design by www.ironicitalics.com
Cover image © starline / Freepik

A catalogue record for this book is available from the British Library.

A catalogue record for this book is available from the Library of Congress.

| ISBN: | HB: | 978-1-8386-0004-4 |
|---|---|---|
| | PB: | 978-1-8386-0120-1 |
| | ePDF: | 978-1-8386-0476-9 |
| | eBook: | 978-1-8386-0477-6 |

Typeset by Integra Software Services Pvt. Ltd.

To find out more about our authors and books visit www.bloomsbury.com
and sign up for our newsletters.

# CONTENTS

# FIGURE

# CONTRIBUTORS

**Ali M. Ansari** is Professor of Iranian History and Founding Director of the Institute for Iranian Studies at the University of St Andrews. He is Senior Associate Fellow at the Royal United Services Institute and is currently on secondment to the Foreign and Commonwealth Office as a Knowledge Exchange Fellow. In 2016 he was elected a Fellow of the Royal Society of Edinburgh. His recent publications include *Modern Iran since 1797*, 3rd updated edition, 2019; *Iran, Islam & Democracy – The Politics of Managing Change*, 3rd updated edition, 2019.

**Colin Burrow** is a Senior Research Fellow in English Literature at All Souls College, Oxford. Before that he was a Fellow of Gonville and Caius College, Cambridge. He does not mix much with politicians, let alone offer them advice, but has written a number of books, including *Shakespeare and Classical Antiquity* (2013) and *Imitating Authors: Plato to Futurity* (2019), and is a frequent contributor to the *London Review of Books*.

**Robin Butler** is a retired British civil servant who sits as a cross-bencher in the House of Lords as Baron Butler of Brockwell. Within the civil service, he worked in Downing Street in various capacities alongside five prime ministers: as Private Secretary to Edward Heath (1972–4) and Harold Wilson (1974–5), as Principal Private Secretary to Margaret Thatcher (1982–5), and as Cabinet Secretary during the premierships of Margaret Thatcher, John Major, and Tony Blair. On retirement he became the Master of University College, Oxford, and was appointed a Knight of the Garter in 2003.

**Sir Martin Donnelly** was a Permanent Secretary in Whitehall for seven years, leading the Department for Business, Innovation and Skills from 2010 to 2016 and then setting up the Department of International Trade. He retired from the civil service in 2017. He started his civil service career in the Treasury in 1980. He has wide experience across government, having also worked in the Foreign Office, Cabinet Office, Home Office, Northern Ireland Office, European Commission, and on secondment to the French Finance Ministry. After leaving government Sir Martin was an Academic Visitor at Hertford College Oxford from 2017 to 2019.

**Esther Eidinow** is Professor of Ancient History at the University of Bristol. Before becoming an academic she worked as a scenario writer, crafting stories for use in strategic planning by national and international organizations. In her current role she specializes in Ancient Greek religion and magic, and has published widely. Her most recent publications include *Envy, Poison, and Death: Women on Trial in Classical Athens* (2016) and *Ancient Divination and Experience* (2019).

**Jim Gallagher** is at the Gwylim Gibbon policy centre in Nuffield College, Oxford, and an honorary professor in the Universities of Glasgow and St Andrews. As a civil servant, he was Private Secretary to two Secretaries of State for Scotland, and head of the Scottish Justice department. He worked in the Cabinet Office, Ministry of Justice, and in two different No 10 Policy Units, for Tony Blair and Gordon Brown. These days, he holds a number of directorships in the commercial and voluntary sectors, and writes mostly about the UK's territorial constitution.

**Rob Goodman** is Assistant Professor of Politics and Public Administration at Ryerson University in Toronto. His academic work has been published in journals including the *American Political Science Review, History of Political Thought,* and *The Review of Politics*. He is the co-author of two books: *A Mind at Play*, a biography of Claude Shannon, and *Rome's Last Citizen*, a book on Cato the Younger and the Roman Republic. He holds a PhD in Political Science from Columbia University, and he was previously a speechwriter for US House Majority Leader Steny Hoyer and US Senator Chris Dodd.

**Colin Kidd** is Wardlaw Professor of Modern History at the University of St Andrews. A former Fellow of All Souls College, Oxford, he is a regular contributor to the *Guardian*, the *London Review of Books* and the *New Statesman*. He has given political advice with regard to the Scottish Question on an informal non-partisan basis. He is a Fellow of both the British Academy and the Royal Society of Edinburgh.

**Jesse Norman MP** is at the time of writing Financial Secretary to the Treasury, responsible for HM Revenue and Customs and national infrastructure policy. He is the author of *Edmund Burke: Philosopher, Politician, Prophet* (2013), and *Adam Smith: What He Thought, and Why It Matters* (2018). He was Executive Director of Policy Exchange in 2005–6, and studied at Oxford (BA, Classics) and at UCL (MPhil and PhD, Philosophy), where he also taught, and is a former Visiting Fellow of All Souls College, Oxford.

**Marius S. Ostrowski** is Examination Fellow in Politics at All Souls College, Oxford, and Max Weber Fellow at the Robert Schuman Centre for Advanced Studies, European University Institute, Florence. His publications include *Eduard Bernstein on Social Democracy and International Politics: Essays and Other Writings* (2018), *Eduard Bernstein on the German Revolution: Selected Historical Writings* (2019), and *Left Unity: Manifesto for a Progressive Alliance* (2020).

**Joanne Paul** is Senior Lecturer in Early Modern History at the University of Sussex. She has published widely on Renaissance and early modern political thought, including books on *Thomas More* (Polity, 2017) and *Counsel and Command in Early Modern English Thought* (Cambridge University Press, 2020), as well as numerous chapters, articles, and edited collections. She has also shared her work in articles for the *Telegraph, Prospect, BBC History Magazine, History Today,* and others, and has made appearances on television and radio. In 2019, she stood as a candidate in the UK General Election for the Green Party in Worthing West.

**Jacqueline Rose** is Senior Lecturer in History at the University of St Andrews. Her first book *Godly Kingship in Restoration England* (2011) won the Royal Historical Society's Whifield Prize. More recently, she has edited *The Politics of Counsel in England and Scotland, 1286–1707* (Oxford University Press/British Academy) and authored various articles on early modern counsel and advice, and is preparing a monograph titled *Kingship and Counsel in Early Modern England*. She is a former Visiting Fellow of All Souls College, Oxford.

**Paul Seaward** is British Academy/Wolfson Foundation Research Professor at the History of Parliament. From 2001 to 2017 he was Director of the History of Parliament; before that he was a clerk in the House of Commons, serving as (among other things) clerk to the Public Service and Public Administration Committees. He has written on parliamentary history, and on politics, political thought, and the writing of history in the seventeenth century, including an edition of Thomas Hobbes's history of the English Civil War, *Behemoth*. He is, with Martin Dzelzainis, joint editor of the Oxford edition of the works of Edward Hyde, earl of Clarendon.

**William Waldegrave** is Provost of Eton College, a member of the House of Lords and a Fellow of All Souls College, Oxford. He was one of the original members of Lord Rothschild's think tank, the Central Policy Review Staff, in the early 1970s, and went on to serve as Political Secretary to the Prime Minister, Edward Heath. In his political career, he sat in Cabinet as Secretary of State for Health, Chancellor of the Duchy of Lancaster (with responsibility for civil service reform and for science), Minister of Agriculture, and Chief Secretary to the Treasury.

# FOREWORD

## POLITICAL ADVISING

### *Lord Butler*

There have been so many issues thrown up by populism in the UK, United States, and other countries that debate about the nature of political advice has not been centre stage. But it emerges as an issue from time to time and is often referred to. When an opportunity arises to reflect on what has been happening, it is certain that one of the questions which will be focused on will be whether present arrangements are fit for purpose or whether they have not only failed to solve, but have actually contributed to, recent difficulties. So it is worth thinking about and discussing this issue as the contributions to this book do.

The final paragraph of Colin Kidd's and Jacqueline Rose's opening overview says that an aim of the book is to provide a bridge between academics in this subject and practitioners. As between those two camps, I certainly belong to the latter. I had the privilege of observing at close range, and participating in, advice to those at the top of government in the UK over nearly forty years, between 1961 and 1998. In the last twenty years I have observed from the outside, without direct access to the content of advice but with some knowledge and experience of how the system works as well as personal acquaintance with many of those involved.

The context and profile of advice to ministers has changed hugely since I joined the Treasury in 1961. At that time there were almost no political or special advisers within government. Those appointed by Lloyd George and Churchill at times of national emergency had left the scene. The men (and a few women) in Whitehall were thought to know best and ministers relied on their advice. But these advisers were largely unknown. Except for occasional hearings before the House of Commons Public Accounts Committee, which were not generally reported, they made no appearances before select committees or in other public fora, and they liked it that way.

The appointment by the 1964 Labour government of Nicky Kaldor and Robert Neild in the Treasury and Tommy Balogh in Number 10 was regarded as radical and threatening to the predominance of civil service advice. It indeed produced some unorthodox (and not altogether successful) innovations like the selective employment tax. But I was secretary of the Treasury's budget committee at the time and I was excited by the way in which Kaldor's and Neild's interventions galvanized the quality of the debate on economic policy. At that early stage of my career, I became a convert to the injection of external advice in order to challenge the established doctrines of Whitehall.

I had an opportunity to take part in a similar initiative in the Heath government which succeeded Wilson's in 1970. I was seconded to the small Central Policy

Review Staff set up under Victor Rothschild in the Cabinet office. The CPRS was expected to correct what was seen as three deficiencies in the processes of Cabinet government. First, it was expected to cause ministers to take a longer view beyond the day-to-day issues which tended to preoccupy them. Its second task was to provide Cabinet ministers with a wider perspective on issues which their departmental colleagues brought before them and on which they would not necessarily have been briefed. The third was to try to prevent ministers from being captured by their departments and to maintain some of the collective purpose with which they had been elected. Robert Wade-Gery, a fellow member of the CPRS, summed all this up as 'injecting some grit into the over-smooth working of the government machine'.

When Harold Wilson returned as prime minister in 1974, the principle of 'spads' had become established. By this time I was the Private Secretary in Number 10 dealing with economic policy. The circumstances following the 1974 general election were traumatic. The civil service Private Secretaries in Number 10, who had been devotedly supporting Edward Heath in dealing with the coalminers' strike which brought down his government, were nervous that our neutrality would not be accepted under a successor determined to reach a settlement with the miners. But Harold Wilson was sufficiently experienced to understand and believe in the professional ethic of the civil service and, although we never achieved a happy modus operandi with Marcia Falkender, under Robert Armstrong's leadership we formed a congenial and effective team with Bernard Donoughue's policy unit and Joe Haines' press office in support of the prime minister.

This stood Wilson and his successor, Jim Callaghan, in good stead in dealing with the economic crises which beset their governments. It also moulded my approach to working with politically appointed special advisers, which I carried through to my role as Principal Private Secretary to Margaret Thatcher and Cabinet Secretary under Margaret Thatcher, John Major, and Tony Blair.

Of course, during that period, the whole context of political debate changed hugely. With the growth of 24/7 media, including the development of social media, political debate became much faster-moving and also more transitory. It created a greater demand for tactical advice. But this is largely froth. It does not obviate the need for good government. Contrary to the belief of some, electors' votes are more likely to be swayed by how they feel about their personal lives than by day-to-day headlines. Ministers still have to make important strategic decisions. So the underlying need for high-quality political advice has not diminished.

If I try to distil the lessons which I learned from my long experience of political advice to ministers, I would suggest the following. First, I believe that if ministers are to be helped to make the best decisions in their own interests and those of the country, they should have input from the widest possible range of relevant perspectives. That should embrace external as well as internal contributions, party as well as civil service, local as well as national. (It is a great help that ministers have constituencies with whom they keep in touch.) This advice should not be obstructed by competition between advisers: it should be a team effort. It should be sympathetic in the sense that it should be based on understanding a minister's objectives and priorities but it should not compromise the facts. And it should recognize and accept a minister's ultimate right to decide.

It is inevitable that times of stress, like the recent ones, should impose strains on relationships between ministers and advisers, and between the advisers themselves. When things go wrong, it is natural (but usually unwise) to look for scapegoats. It is also tempting for politicians who, by the nature of their profession, have strong ideologies to be suspicious of professional civil servants who do not, and to suspect that, if they cannot detect the ideologies of civil servants, it is because they are being concealed. They may even suppose that the civil service is working against them. In my experience, this is invariably wrong. The professional ethos of the civil service, like that of barristers and doctors, is to expend every effort in the interest of their clients, whatever personal views they may or may not have.

If I may express my own view, I believe, on the basis of my experience and observation, that, when the present furore settles down, we will conclude that an all-sources system of political advice, provided that it satisfies the criteria I have described above, has served us well in the past and will continue to do so. Well-informed and disinterested advice from the widest possible range of perspectives will continue to be the foundation for good political decision-making. Bring back Cabinet government.

I hope that this book, with its historical and international perspectives, will make a valuable contribution to the debate.

# ACKNOWLEDGEMENTS

This volume of essays grew out of a one-day conference on Political Advice held at All Souls College, Oxford, on 8 June 2017, as part of the College's public life programme. Although the event was planned and scheduled a full year in advance, by a twist of fate it happened to fall on the day chosen by Theresa May for a snap UK general election. As a result of this fortuitous choice of date, we were, alas, deprived of an appearance by Ed Balls, but unexpectedly gained the services of Lord Butler, who had initially been unable to attend because of a meeting in London, which was later cancelled on account of the election. A salutary reminder that political advice is formulated and delivered in the hurly-burly of shifting real time events; too much advance preparation brings its own risks. We dispatch this volume – at a time when political advice appears in the news on a daily basis – with the characteristic historian's caution about predicting tomorrow's headlines, but with a sense that future events will continue to generate stories about political advice.

The Editors would like to record their appreciation to the Warden and Fellows of All Souls, especially those Fellows who participated in the conference, for their support of this project, both through the conference and through the Fellowships at All Souls during which each undertook work on the volume. They would also like to record a debt to Lucy Kidd who helped with some of the copyediting.

Colin Kidd and Jacqueline Rose
St Andrews
February 2020

## Chapter 1

## POLITICAL ADVICE: PAST, PRESENT – AND FUTURE?

## Colin Kidd and Jacqueline Rose

Political advice has often seemed to be the dowdy neglected sibling of its more glamorous relative, political leadership. Public attention to it began to grow as increasing tensions emerged (particularly during the Blair years) between the conventional career civil service and temporary civil servants, known as special advisers or spads. This alone might have justified a wider and historically informed exploration of the largely unsung phenomenon of political advice. In the intervening years, however, what was once a technical subject, of interest largely to academics and to those inclined towards the less showy inner mechanics of the political process, has outgrown this audience and become the stuff of daily newspaper reports, television news items, and broadsheet analysis. If spads have become the new normal, other political events such as the Trump presidency and Brexit have rendered advice even more contentious, so that within the course of three or four years the question of who advises whom about what has ceased to be a niche topic with little public traction. Far from being overshadowed by the advent of Brexit and Trump, political advice has become an even hotter topic.

During the run-up to the Brexit referendum in 2016, Michael Gove, one of the champions of Leave, denounced the pessimism of 'experts' who questioned the economic wisdom of leaving the European Union. The political turbulence which followed drew in the civil service and the advice it gives government ministers, with a great deal of Brexiteering polemic directed against individual civil servants such as Sir Ivan Rogers, who resigned from his post as the UK Ambassador to the EU, and Olly Robbins, not only Permanent Secretary to the UK's Brexit Department but also Theresa May's advance man, or 'sherpa', in her negotiations with the EU. Indeed, Theresa May's special advisers Nick Timothy and Fiona Hill, figures normally confined to the backrooms of Downing Street, enjoyed a very high profile during the first year of May's government and were then blamed for the disastrous election campaign of 2017, after which Tory MPs forced May to sack them. More broadly, English populists – Nigel Farage of UKIP and the Brexit Party foremost among them – have publicly questioned the integrity of the civil service and its ethos of neutrality. The civil servant who is not for Brexit must be against it, a Remainer indeed, and should be sacked, runs the populist refrain. The backstairs Rosencrantz and Guildenstern class, whose fate in normal times is obscurity, has become a central part of the story. Indeed, when Boris Johnson formed his administration in 2019 he brought in as his chief adviser Dominic Cummings, who had masterminded the Vote Leave campaign in the EU referendum of 2016, and whose role in that campaign had been the subject of a Channel 4 docudrama *Brexit: An Uncivil War*, in which the part of Cummings had been played by the actor Benedict Cumberbatch. This appointment resulted in an unusual amount of media attention, some of it focused on Cummings's particular preferences for Sun Tzu's *Art of War*, game theory and super-forecasting as the basis for decision-making, and his antipathy to what he perceived as a hidebound and unimaginative civil service, which he referred to as 'The Blob'. After Johnson's election victory, Cummings called for radical changes to the functioning of Whitehall, and for more offbeat advisers and quantitatively trained civil servants to counter the hidebound and aridly conventional, arts-based advice supposedly proffered to ministers by the civil service machine. Here, the shadowy world of spads – once the elusive, unaccountable, behind-the-scenes influencers – merges with populist politics: in this instance a spad speaking for the people against the establishment. Spats over spads within Johnson's government boiled over when, in February 2020, Sajid Javid resigned as Chancellor of the Exchequer, refusing to accept a joint No 10-No 11 economic advisory team and stating in his resignation letter how 'crucial' it was for Johnson to have 'people around you who can give you clear and candid advice'. Nor were advisers in Corbynite Labour exempt from attention, given criticisms of the influence of Karie Murphy and Seumas Milne on the party leader.

Political advisers and their modes of advice have now become a key ingredient in the story the media tells on both sides of the Atlantic. Not since the Nixon administration – when, engrossed by the Watergate scandal, the public became familiar with backstairs advisers such as Haldeman, Ehrlichman and Colson; and Nixon's National Security Adviser Henry Kissinger became a global superstar – has the topic of political advice enjoyed such prominence in the media as now during the Trump presidency. Not only have there been a succession of curious appointments – not least of military men – and a relentless churn of White House advisers in key posts – but the media and Trump's Democratic opponents have publicly questioned (like some of his fellow Republicans, more discreetly and anonymously) who was actually getting through to the President and whether the advice given was acted upon. One strain of commentary suggested indeed that Trump – holed up of an evening in front of the television in the personal quarters in the East Wing – was operating largely on the advice proffered by Fox News. Of course, the media also fixated on Trump as a leader. But in this case the leadership style of such an erratic figure inevitably raised questions about political advice. Who were his trusted advisers, and did they have the capacity to frustrate his otherwise untutored caprice? Conversely, on the other side of politics, populist Republicans asked whether their president had been captured by what they referred to as the 'deep state'. Again the question was posed: who was really directing the ship of state? An elected if ill-qualified president or a leviathan bureaucracy whose proper role was to advise him, and otherwise to implement his decisions?

In the White House Trump also resorted to a traditional formula in the history of political advice, reliance – up to a point – on family members as gatekeepers and trusted counsellors, most particularly his daughter Ivanka and son-in-law Jared Kushner. It looked clannish and nepotistic, though there were precedents on a lesser scale from previous administrations, including the Kennedys and the Clintons themselves. Even Dwight D. Eisenhower, a punctilious military man, who took a highly formalistic view of counsel, had when in the White House utilized the advice of his brother, Milton Eisenhower, the President of Pennsylvania State University.[1] Trump's reversion to the dynastic trappings of a traditional 'court' and his seeming addiction to despotic whim and caprice pose another perennial question in the annals of political advice. Can the adviser honestly speak truth to power? Or does the ruler prefer to be surrounded by flatterers and sycophants? Is loyalty in an adviser more important than honesty? Such questions, which have received intense public scrutiny because of the Trump White House, may nevertheless be perennial challenges rather than unprecedented problems – or, at least, episodic rather than unheard of. For, as we shall see, the court analogy is both revealing and misleading, and it is fruitful to think about what advising in a court might have involved.

If court-based advice has often seemed sealed off from the outside world, the rule of populists such as Trump and Boris Johnson brings to the heart of government – and into the focus of external media scrutiny – court-style politics tinged with an anti-expert populism. Does an elite cadre of economists, political scientists, environmental scientists, surgeons general, and chief medical officers really know better than the ordinary person in the street about the workings of the EU single market and customs union, climate change, and the place of vaccination in public health policy? In a democracy should this elite – however well-informed in its advice – frustrate the expressed will of the wider public? Shouldn't the process of decision-making be left entirely to elected politicians who represent the views of the people?

The problem is that government is complex – indeed even in the ancient world was already so complex – that no leader can or could rule entirely on his or her own. Even if a leader were an Einstein rather than a Trump, they still couldn't govern without consulting a whole phalanx of advisers. Leaders – even those who pose as strong men or strong and stable women – have never been able to govern on their own, without advisers or external fonts of advice, including oracles and other portents. Ever since the earliest formation of political communities the realm of political options has proved too complex for a single mind to comprehend or to navigate on its own. Indeed, on closer inspection some of the giants of political leadership turn out to have been the beneficiaries of brilliant advisers. Did Winston Churchill shape Allied success in the Second World War or was this undeniable political genius and master communicator guided towards the best strategy for victory by Field Marshal Alan Brooke and the advisers of his Imperial General Staff, who so often had to confront in Churchill a wilful and wrong-headed amateur general whose knowledge of grand strategy was at times dogmatic, perverse, romantic, and muddled? That is certainly the all-too-persuasive picture which emerges from Alan Brooke's controversial wartime diaries.[2] Political leadership is the public face – in some ways a superficial frontage – of a complex process of advice and behind-the-scenes negotiation, give-and-take, and ongoing interchange between rulers and their advisers.

Whether in history or in politics the Alan Brookes have never, understandably enough, attracted the same degree of attention as the Winston Churchills. By looking first at the multifarious issues with which political advice intersects, then at discussion, analysis, and practice of it, first in the past and then in the modern United States and UK, this introduction shows the significance of the often overlooked role of advisers and officials. It is they who do much of the real work of the ship of state, not only manning the rigging, but sometimes doing the steering and – discreetly – helping to plot the course. And so they, not the leaders, are the central protagonists in this volume.

*I*

In some aspects of political life there is nothing new under the sun. What distinguishes political advice in modernity – at least until the last couple of decades – is its unexplored nature. Yet its central problems seem both distinctively modern and rooted in ancient patterns. Contemporary nuclear and environmental challenges may be unprecedented, but how far does advising in the modern military–industrial complex pose the same challenges as counselling in antiquity? Were earlier eras better at articulating and confronting the perennial difficulties of advising?

Take, for example, the crucial relationship between adviser and leader. The imperative to complement the decision-making role of leaders with the wider wisdom of advisers had, for much of history, a firm foundation in understandings of human nature. From ancient Greece and Rome stemmed the idea that the soul was divided into the passions, shared with animals, and reason, unique to humans. The exercise of reason over the passions provided the self-government that was the prerequisite for good governance of others. This inner psychological governance had an obvious political parallel: rational governors should exercise jurisdiction over the unruly populace. Down the centuries, monarchs could be presented as the rational element of the system – and yet as flawed (and, in a Christian framework, fallen) individuals they too were at risk of succumbing to their passions.

Even in the early modern heyday of the divine right of kings, between the late fifteenth and mid-eighteenth centuries, there was a clear understanding that earthly rulers' juridical omnicompetence did not come packaged with divine omniscience. Good and bad government was therefore organized along an unfamiliar axis, but one which provided a clear dividing line between absolute rule and arbitrary tyranny. The latter was understood in Aristotelian terms as monarchy gone wrong, i.e. rule by one person according to their private interest, whim, and will – it was not having too much power, but abusing it by not governing for the common good.[3] Although usurpation was also treated as a form of tyranny, it was not the one that was most feared. Theorists of divine right or absolutism were obsessed with getting good advice because it was a sign of duly ordered monarchy and prevented tyranny. Jacques-Bénigne Bossuet, tutor to the Dauphin, wrote in the era of the Sun King Louis XIV that monarchy was sacred, paternal, absolute, and subject to reason – ordained by God, caring for its subjects, not to be resisted, and not to breach divine or natural law. Give me the advice you think best for queen and commonwealth, Queen Elizabeth I told her principal minister William Cecil, not that which adheres to my private will.[4] In 1985 Sir Robert Armstrong, head of the Home civil service, quoted Elizabeth's speech as summarizing 'pretty well … what we still expect of our Civil Service and … what we still get out of it'.[5]

Back in the days of Queen Elizabeth I, two solutions could be found to the potential threat of tyranny, and counsel was inherent to both. One picked up the above strain of appealing to monarchs to govern well. Counsel helped supplement an individual's imperfect knowledge and reason with a wider pool of wisdom, experience, and prudence. It was a supporting crutch as well as a virtuous safeguard. It could come from members of institutions – councils, parliaments, and estates – but also from courtiers, tutors, preachers, confessors, lawyers, merchants, and whoever seemed appropriate on the day. Government was limited, but by morality and God's law, and by a small number of 'fundamental laws'. But rulers who ignored good advice and broke such laws were to be punished by God, not by their subjects. The second method of engendering good advice was a constitutionalist route. This required rulers to consult a specific group of advisers, such as members of parliament, leading nobles, or a council appointed and vetted by these. This institutionalized limits on leaders, making them accountable on earth for their errors, and subject to external checks. The second option seems more obviously palatable in the twenty-first century, yet such are the dynamics of governance that rigid institutional requirements rarely produce the best or most effective advice.

The failure of institutionalized and enforced advice has manifested itself in multiple ways. The long history of attempts at restricting advice to groups of councillors who would be appointed or vetted by the nobility or parliament and to whom the monarch had to listen is a history of failure: monarchs almost always ignored or sidelined these as soon as possible. While things were often already going wrong – these suggestions emerged during rebellions or crises – enforced advice failed on a far more frequent basis in the councils that emerged across the increasingly geographically complicated Tudor and Stuart state. Even at the points where the natural monarchical political leader was removed from the scene, for example during royal minority, the obvious solution of more prominent conciliar governance may have failed to provide an effective substitute. As fora for discussion, councils exposed division and disagreement, but may have lacked the ability to reach a decision, or at least lacked a figurehead who carried sufficient political weight to bring everyone fully on side.

Advice, therefore, does not automatically compensate for flawed political leadership. Instead, we need to think about the division of labour in governing. Certain elements in the process of political advice are timeless, circumscribed as they are by the capacities and limits of an individual's concentration span. Any leader can absorb only so much information and counsel, or hold so many meetings with advisers of one sort or another, in the course of a single day. Part of the genius of Churchill's wartime scientific adviser Professor Frederick Lindemann was his ability to condense information, to compile a précis of a précis that conveyed key information and caught Churchill's overburdened attention.[6] No matter how many advisers a ruler has, no matter how many specialists in every field of government, no matter what IT or communications equipment they possess or wealth of information they have at their disposal, the scarcest resource in the realm of counsel is the time available to a ruler and the span of his or her concentration. In 1975, Harold Wilson justified the appointment of political advisers by saying that 'in less hectic days Ministers were their own political advisers' but that this was impossible given 'the burdens of modern government ... the immense volume of papers', the endless succession of meetings.[7] The basic human limits on counsel mean that in today's era of IT and Big Data, some of the essential characteristics of political advice found in classical antiquity retain their purchase. Rulers today have no more time or concentration than their predecessors in antiquity, if anything – in an era of administrative overload, voraciously exhausting schedules and the ubiquitous 24/7 demands of the smartphone and the media – less time for meetings with advisers.

There are also limits to the number of advisers that any one person can consult. Here again there is a vital human dimension to advising. It is ultimately about forging working relationships. Appointing Oliver Cromwell's council in 1654, the House of Commons stressed the 'necessity' of 'some personal knowledge, opinion, and affection between the protector and his council'.[8] 'It is about the chemistry of the core relationship', one spad similarly remarked.[9] Some elusive blend of formal advice and consultation with a trusted team is needed, an issue handled differently, of course, in American and British government. In Britain, conflicts between special advisers and civil servants have resulted in attempts to make the role of the first more formal and rule-bound. The very first requirement of the Government's Code of Conduct for Special Advisers describes spads as complementing the civil service, 'reinforcing' its political impartiality 'by distinguishing the source of political advice and support'. Paragraph 3 requires special advisers to 'establish mutual relationships of confidence and trust' with the civil service, and paragraph 4 explains that special advisers may 'review and comment on – but not suppress or supplant' advice from civil servants.[10]

What balance might be struck between these? Is it sensible to bring on one highly specialized adviser after another, for one performance only, or to build a rapport between the leader and a strictly limited core of advisers, who are therefore, at least in some respects, generalists? Political leaders can only build up relationships of trust with a very small cadre of advisers. Here the modern predicament of political advice resembles older historical patterns. Who has access to the leader? Where do political advisers belong in the state apartments of what are, in effect, modern-day versions of old-style royal courts, even at the head of what are now vast, faceless bureaucratic machines? The architecture of the court – whether in the White House or 10 Downing Street – plays a part, as the contours of courts always have, in determining procedures and protocols of counsel.

References to modern politicians operating a system of court politics conjure up an anarchic world of sinister manipulation, factional personality clashes, or murkily disreputable means of taking advice. Such claims do capture an important element of present-day advising: that access and political intimacy are vital; that political influence decreases with distance; that space matters. The spatial arrangement of the government's headquarters or leader's mansion is inextricably linked to the question of how large a leader's entourage of advisers should be, and the ways in which advice is delivered, whether in cosy, domestic settings, impersonal offices or larger, more formal, palatial halls. 10 Downing Street, for example, comprises three townhouses knocked together into a complex warren of rooms and staircases: a setting that is intimate, unhierarchical, and far from stuffy.[11] How far does the architectural setting determine the nature of the counsel offered? Certainly, the allocation of offices in Downing Street or the West Wing of the White House is crucial to the flow of advice to the leader. It's not simply a matter of who is in the room with the leader for most of his or her working day, but who can pop in easily without going through the hoops of interdepartmental gatekeeping. As advisers tell it, proximity is everything, certainly worth more than notional status, size of office, official title, or even salary. Harold Wilson's political adviser during his 1974–6 administration, Bernard Donoughue, otherwise an impecunious academic, turned down an attractively higher salary and civil service grade, which would have entailed moving into the adjacent Cabinet Office, to preserve his proximity to the prime minister within 10 Downing Street itself. As Donoughue's colleague, Joe Haines, Wilson's press secretary, made clear: 'The Cabinet Office for a Minister, or a Prime Minister's adviser, is what a Mongolian power station is to a Kremlin politician. That door [between 10 Downing St and the Cabinet Office] is always kept locked; access to Downing St. means much more than applying for a key.'[12] Proximity is a necessary if not sufficient determinant of power and influence in the life of an adviser.

Political space plays a rhetorical as well as practical role. Even in earlier court systems, one way to delegitimize advisers was to suggest that they operated in a shadowy backstairs world. Condemning a 'Machiavellian' adviser who worked through 'whisperings and secret suggestions', one Civil War pamphlet complained: 'You shall seldom find him appearing at the Council-Board, but with the king … in his Privy Chamber, the Queen's Bedchamber, the garden, the closet, the close stool or such like places'.[13] We should neither dismiss this as mere caricature nor take on trust the implication that advice given outside the privy council was *ipso facto* invalid. Accounts by perfectly reputable advisers – even by privy councillors – mention giving advice walking in the garden, coming up the backstairs, going into the closet, locking the doors of the privy gallery.

This does not mean that a world of princely courts was one in which advice operated in a political landscape devoid of rules. Some were implicit. Indeed, the most important rule – you can speak freely, once you have been invited to do so – was never formally recorded. But there were other, written rules, and their application was sometimes queried. On the eve of the Civil Wars, part of the trial of the earl of Strafford, Charles I's leading minister, hinged on the rules of advising. Strafford was accused of having advised Charles I to use an Irish army against the English parliament. What exactly had he said? (His words were ambiguous.) Where had he said it – was it a private discourse or at the council table? Was he accountable to parliament anyway? Strafford claimed that nobody would ever be willing to advise the monarch if parliament could prosecute them for a suggestion, which, in the course of debate among advisers, might change anyway and that he was obliged by his oath to speak on all things concerning the king's service.[14]

So in fact there was a set of written rules for (some) advisers: the oath of a privy councillor. Various instantiations of this required true and faithful service, defence of royal authority, that the councillor declare their view 'according to your heart and conscience', not take bribes, advise for the good of the commonwealth, and do all that a good servant ought to do. This job spec is repeated almost unchanged in the present-day oath of a privy councillor.[15] Furthermore, a number of its requirements echo in the government's Code of Conduct for Special Advisors: integrity and honesty (part of the civil service code), confidentiality, declaring gifts, or hospitality.[16]

When considering taking up a post in Ireland, Strafford had wanted to make an annual in-person meeting with the king a condition of accepting the appointment.[17] Access to power is crucial for advice to be effective. The prophet in the wilderness may be admired, but the court astrologer exercises more immediate influence. Confessors, oracles, spouses, lovers, favourites, doctors, and masseurs all offer advice, because they have the crucial advantage of access. They can also act as gatekeepers, filtering out unwanted advisers. No leader can meet every adviser or grasp every micro-specialism. (Micromanagement, after all, didn't help President Jimmy Carter, and it left Philip II of Spain, 500 years before email, drowning in paper.) Yet leaders thought to be governed by their adviser-favourites are scorned. They are, in classical terms, weak tyrants implicitly countenancing the shenanigans of their Rasputins, at risk of provoking rebellion against their court favourites.

Many of the interpersonal questions regarding advice today are questions which for centuries have tantalized observers of advice-giving at courts. Yet, even our own very distinctive problems – borderless environmental issues, nuclear containment, global markets – return us to the question of how a leader can forge relationships with advisers when the technical sub-division of expertise is now such that he or she would need to consult hundreds or possibly thousands of experts to establish a course of action. But this is, of course, impossible, in terms of time and intellectual constraints. A leader's time is finite and so is his or her capacity to foster rapport with advisers. There is an inevitability about advice devolving upon a small inner core of clever generalists which seems to resemble earlier courtly entourages of high counsellors.

But the smaller the entourage the louder the complaints about the secret whispers of overmighty inner counsellors. Secrecy is another cloud which has long hung over processes of political advice. Of course, in the open societies of the modern West, from the Watergate tapes furore to the controversy surrounding Hillary Clinton's private e-mail server when Secretary of State, there have been concerns about unwarranted secrecy, and about how to preserve the necessary confidentiality of advice from legitimate demands for freedom of information. Today it is no easy matter to establish watertight compartments for frank advice which is prey to neither overzealous advocates of open government nor electronic snoopers hunting for injudicious texts and emails. Opacity in advisory processes may seem particularly problematic in democratic contexts. Yet today's issues of trust and accountability have a long pedigree in concerns about secret counsel.

Several centuries ago, secret could be a positive or pejorative term. Councillors – both local and national – were enjoined to discretion and secrecy in their oaths of office, blabbing confidential policy being a timeless political sin. The clerk was sent out of the room when the privy council had its most confidential discussions. In his handbook for secretaries, written in the 1580s, Angel Day emphasized that they were confidential amanuenses – and potential counsellors – while advisory literature for royal secretaries spoke of the importance of keeping papers secure in locked cabinets, with cryptographic notes impossible for outsiders to penetrate.[18] Sometimes secrecy emerged almost by default – the pre-modern government filing system was not designed for easy retrieval. Yet those outside the magic circle of advisers denounced 'secret' counsels, associating them with subversive political doctrines and Machiavellian pretence. Who, other than the ruler, ought to be aware of advice? Should other counsellors be informed of it? Must parliaments be told? The demand for representative, inclusive, transparent consultation conflicts with the need for focus, cohesion, and confidentiality. Even while endorsing discretion, Day still rejected 'private whisperers'.[19] Concern about invisible advisory processes suggests that some rules are being broken. And this is at root a problem that conversations are not always a matter of public record.

The issue of persuasion is another feature of advising which possesses a timeless, human quality. While the spinning of spin doctors seems very contemporary and somewhat pejorative, it has a long and rather more positive history. Assent to a policy cannot be assured. Selling a policy to a ruler has, since ancient times, involved tactics of persuasive speech – of rhetoric. Far from the empty verbiage that the word often signals now, in most periods before the modern age rhetoric was a highly valued skill, with its rules, basic structures and finer points. Eloquence and expressive flair were deployed with the aim of presenting a course of action in the most desirable light. Whether its effect was to sell an already good idea, or to dress up a bad one in a favourable way, was never clear; but it was at least acknowledged as a necessary part of political life. Rhetoric now carries about it a whiff of both the anachronistic and the deceptive. Yet perhaps the rhetorician is not inevitably fated to go the way of the alchemist and the blacksmith. A revival of the redundant art of rhetoric – flattery to the *demos* as a new way of wooing a post-truth public – might yet be on the cards.

Yet there is another unexpected side to this vexed issue. It might sound bizarre and illogical, but one of the most pertinent questions in the field of political advice is the very serious issue of whether the adviser should offer advice at all. Perhaps it should be the main task of an adviser to present a range of options to a ruler. But should that be the limit of an adviser's ambition? Should advisers perhaps try to offer a synthesis of the range of options they discern on a particular topic? Or should they go further and offer their own advice – their personal take on the options – about what the ruler should actually do? There is no clear consensus on this.[20] Furthermore, are there situations in which an adviser can legitimately refuse to advise? Does providing advice that has any chance of being listened to involve unpalatable compromises with one's principles? Service to a prince, Hythloday famously complains in the first book of Thomas More's *Utopia*, is but one syllable removed from servitude.[21]

Famous though this question is, Hythloday asks it from the narrow self-interested perspective of the adviser: what is the point *for him*, rather than for the recipient or the political system as a whole. Nevertheless the political adviser is a figure who has both always been with us, and been tainted in some measure with controversy. As Herbert Goldhamer notes in a wide-ranging survey, 'the political adviser appears in man's earliest surviving documents'.[22] However, Goldhamer also clarifies the thorny distinction between the political adviser and his less problematic counterpart, the official. Officialdom is not dogged with ambiguity in the same way. Whereas the roles of officials are well defined by law or custom, the adviser is protean, assuming a wider variety of roles, sometimes indeed official, but often unofficial.[23] The adviser can range from the favourite of the leader, a friend, a relative, a spouse, a priest, a confessor, a healer, a tutor, a soothsayer, to a more conventional political aide, a speechwriter, pollster, political consultant, civil servant, bureaucrat, economist or scientific specialist.

Repeatedly, the whims of human interaction determine the outcome of an advisory exchange more than formal job titles or role descriptions do. Guy Benveniste remarks on the ironic fate of advice-giving, how the well-thought-out, intensively researched counsel can prove less influential than a few stolen, off-the-cuff remarks. Indeed, here the categories of success and failure for advisers seem less clear cut than they might at first look: 'Failure takes place when experts discover that their reports and recommendations simply gather dust, and excessive success when their tentative advice is translated into hard-and-fast rules which turn out to be undesirable.'[24] There are so many different ways in which things can go wrong for the adviser.

The whiff of controversy surrounding political advice, it transpires, is as old as politics itself. The oldest cliché in political opposition is the trope of the evil counsellor accused of distorting and perverting the benign vision of the ruler. Blaming everything that goes wrong on bad advisers has a long history that goes back for centuries BCE (Before the Cummings Era). Cummings, Hill and Timothy, Campbell, Rasputin, Thomas Cromwell, Sejanus, Achitophel: complaints about evil advisers are the rhetoric of medieval rebels that still echoes on news programmes. Yet there has been an equally strong tradition of explaining the value of good advice. Indeed, political advice is one of the oldest genres in Western literature. It runs back through the mirror of princes literature of the Renaissance and Middle Ages to classical antiquity – to Seneca's *De clementia* (On mercy), addressed to his wayward pupil, the Emperor Nero, and further back still to Xenophon's *Cyropaedia*, which describes the education of an ideal ruler, Cyrus of Persia. Alas, in the case of Nero, he didn't quite get the message; full of fear and resentment in the aftermath of a failed conspiracy on his life, the Emperor – merciful up to a point – ordered his old tutor to kill himself rather than simply having him killed. Such have been the hazards of political advice. Today an adviser rarely risks death, but his or her standing remains precarious: the higher the status the more vertiginous the drop.

Advisory styles that work for one leader may fail to serve another effectively. Just as there is a wide variety of leadership styles, so too therefore the range of forms of advice to rulers is potentially even more variegated. Political advisers have been, historically, as various in their character and aptitudes as there are human needs that need addressing, including the various cognitive needs of leaders. Advice has traditionally come in all shades and kinds, though over the past century or so in the West, the range of counsel seen as appropriate to government has narrowed slightly to policy advisers, scientific advisers, media and IT consultants, speechwriters, pollsters, and advertising agents. There are fewer Rasputins around. Nevertheless, the kind of reassurance that Rasputin offered – spiritual, medical, emotional – is still required. Sometimes rulers get it from unconventional figures, and sometimes our rulers suffer because, notwithstanding the panoply of straightforwardly political advice they receive, they do not get enough warm, friendly tactile support of a less politically focused kind. We should not underestimate the need rulers have for reassurance. Rulers, just as much as common citizens, sometimes feel their confidence in themselves waning.

As one spad reported: 'ministers can feel very isolated … They need a friend whom they can trust, who will find out what is going on in the department'.[25] The idea that friendship and advice go together dates back to the classical world. Cicero's 'On Friendship', written at the close of the Roman republic, stressed the importance of equality of status and virtue: friendship was shared between two good men. Such individuals would 'give true advice with all frankness', a form of speech and behaviour inimical to the flattery necessary under tyranny.[26] The advent of monarchy posed the question of social and political inequality and increased the resonance of the challenge described in a widely read essay by Plutarch, 'How to distinguish a flatterer from a friend'. Can a monarch have friends? Or is a ruler an inherently isolated figure? What about fake friends? Freedom of speech, no longer the right of a democratic citizenry, became a moral imperative in a monarchy. 'A mind of integrity' would recognize that 'lashings by friends' are 'better' 'than the fraudulent kisses of coaxers'.[27] But were recipients always so welcoming? Frank speech was necessary, Plutarch said, but it had to be used carefully, 'intermingle therewith a little praise'.[28]

Nor should we ignore the issue of health in the relationship between rulers and their advisers. Even in modern times the ill health of a leader has created serious problems in governance – and openings for advisers. After Churchill's unpublicized stroke in 1953, the conduct of government was for a while largely in the hands of a civil servant John Colville, Churchill's co-Principal Private Secretary, his superior the Cabinet Secretary Norman Brook, and Churchill's Parliamentary Private Secretary, his son-in-law Christopher Soames, who did not even have proper clearance to see the papers that now came his way and on which he commented so shrewdly. Notwithstanding Churchill's recovery, his energy and powers of concentration were gone, and, as Colville records in his diaries, during the last year and a half of his administration the prime minister largely disregarded public business and the papers that came his way. Colville comments obliquely and with more than a hint of euphemism, that during Churchill's incapacity the distance between the fringes of power (the proper place for a Downing Street civil servant) and the centre of things shortened immeasurably.[29]

There was also a rationale, beyond entertainment value, for the figure of the court jester, who provided a form of institutionalized anti-counsel which pricked the pomposity of accepted wisdom. Long before the notion of 'groupthink' was coined, the office of the court jester licensed a form of dissent – an alternative voice – within the costive formalities of court life. The court jester is not entirely a figure of bygone courts. President Gerald Ford struck up a warm relationship with the official White House photographer, David Kennerly, a dishevelled, free-spirited, hippy-like character, who became a refreshingly outspoken jester-like figure in the Ford White House. As Ford later recalled, a president requires to 'be needled once in a while, if only to be brought down from the false pedestal that the office provides', and Kennerly's 'spontaneous humor and refreshing manner' captured his attention.[30]

Effective advice-giving involves a performance. Since counsel can be an event, a discourse, an institutionally embodied entity, or an enactment of a political relationship; as an exchange between (at least) two individuals, it benefits from the type of interdisciplinary treatment this volume provides. A political drama played out behind closed doors, it has been represented on the public stage too: Polonius, *Sejanus*, *King Lear*, but also in civic pageants that simultaneously represented and provided advice. The producers of Elizabeth I's coronation procession did not need Shakespeare to script advice, presenting the queen with an image of herself as Deborah consulting with her parliament for the good governance of the country, for civic pageantry was an obvious opportunity to advise. Drama offered plausible deniability, a helpfully ambiguous mixture of propaganda and admonition – was the current ruler the butt of criticism or loftily above such mistakes?

Bad advice made for many a story, such as that of Gorboduc, the eponymous king whose well-intentioned desire to take advice results in fratricide and civil war. Avoid the flattering poison hidden in golden vessels, the play warns, and the king urges his advisers to speak plainly. Yet the opening scene that acts out the unwritten rules of advice exposes the difficulty of identifying flattery, for wise advice, correctly presented with a prefatory apology, is rejected.[31] Earlier morality plays, in which characters appeared with helpful names such as 'Respublica' ('Commonwealth'), or 'Good Counsel', drew on this political culture of performed advice. Without a philosopher king, of course, it can all fall apart, as in a cheap pamphlet in which a personified 'Conscience' is thrown out of the court for telling the king his faults. Speaking freely and directly, conscience gains nothing. He is too blunt, 'this troublesome thing … that will be telling His Maiestie of his faults … what a saucy fellow'![32]

If honest advice can often seem rather hopeless, few in the past would have asked conscience 'what hast thou to do with Kings?' We should not neglect the ethical dimension in counsel. Indeed, churchmen long predominated as counsellors of kings, valued of course for their literacy but also for their probity. For much of European history, counsel was as much concerned with doing the right thing – in Christian terms – as it was with the most politically advantageous course of action. Accountability to God was more terrifying than the next ballot box – and without the ability to choose the date for the reckoning. In early modern Europe, for example, it was not always enough for a ruler to feel instinctively that he or she was doing the right thing: it was reassuring when a priest or confessor was able to confirm the religious basis of policy. Perhaps earlier societies were more confident in facing up to the ethical imperatives of counsel and had a different, more sophisticated, toolbox with which to manage it. 'Casuistry', like rhetoric, now carries a whiff of pejorative manipulation about it, but in origin it was a fundamental way of managing moral dilemmas, being the science of how to apply moral precepts in particular circumstances. The structures of counsel in early modern Spain rested on the testing of such moral questions to ensure the ruler's conscience was not compromised.[33] Conscience was public property. Any adviser who took an oath of office was morally bound to the imperatives of that oath and privy councillors who today swear a barely altered version of it are taking one whose main contours were set half a millennium ago, but without the casuistical assistance originally to hand if the multiple demands of the oath come into conflict with one another. Nowadays there is no longer the same imperative, at least in the secular West, for policy to conform to religious orthodoxy. Nevertheless, in a nuclear age the inner need for ethical counsel has not entirely gone away. Indeed, growing concerns about environmental stewardship might see the return of ethical advice in some form or other. How do we support improving diets for a growing population without destroying tropical rainforests or irreversibly depleting fish stocks?

## II

Political leadership occupies a secure place within the study of politics, but what of political advice? Is there a domain within politics – and has there been one in the past – which acknowledges the unsung but vitally important role of the backstairs adviser? The answer, as so often in the humanities, is frustratingly ambiguous: yes and no. Appealing to rulers to govern well by reminding them of the importance of the virtues was embodied in the genre of 'mirrors for princes', *speculum principis*, which was a favoured way of writing about kingship in the Middle Ages. Such works explored the nature and significance of the virtues of justice, wisdom, fortitude, and temperance, alongside piety. In some political works, elaborate analogies were created with the body politic, such as in John of Salisbury's mid-twelfth-century *Policraticus*[34] or with the *Tree of Commonwealth* in Edmund Dudley's early-sixteenth-century book of that name. As late as the 1590s, James VI and I instructed his son in the importance of temperance as well as godliness: dress neither too gaudily nor too coarsely or gravely, avoid excessive eating, drinking, and sleeping.[35] Today, the moralizing dimensions of these works can appear naïve or so utterly commonplace as to say nothing at all.

It was, nevertheless, these sorts of well-established urgings to virtue that Machiavelli subverted in that supposed textbook of political realism, *The Prince*. Advising a new prince on how to hold recently gained and formerly republican territories, Machiavelli insisted that *true* generosity was not magnificence but spending very little in order to keep taxes low, that a prince might need to be feared (although should avoid being hated), and that he must be prepared to break his promises.[36] A book of advice from a disgraced adviser, *The Prince* said relatively little about counsellors – only that the choice of ministers or secretaries indicated the quality of the ruler, that they should be devoted to the ruler's interests, and that the ruler encourage this by rewarding them[37] – but its author's practice of drawing on examples from history reflected a widespread sense that the past was an excellent source of prudence, i.e. practical or applied wisdom, for the examples of the past were a source of experience exceeding that of (but potentially tapped by) the monarch and their advisers.

Readers of Machiavelli were not quite sure whether he was endorsing the practices he described as a model for how to govern or deliberately exposing the prince to evil ways in order to delegitimate monarchy. But what his account highlighted was the ambiguity of what counted as virtue when put into practice. Nearly a century later, Robert Cecil, earl of Salisbury, desperately trying to get a grip on government spending, advised James VI and I that although the king's liberality was a virtue, it was not really liberal to let fiscal prudence slip. Despite its rejection of 'grounds Machiavel[lian]', Salisbury's advice made the same point as *The Prince*.[38]

It was true that an adviser did not need Machiavelli in order to counsel a monarch that the truly virtuous course of action was not the one that necessarily appeared to be so, nor the one that the ruler wanted to pursue. Instead such an adviser needed good training in rhetoric. Because Aristotle's account of virtue as a mean between two extremes or vices remained important, a standard strategy was to redescribe an apparently virtuous course of action as a vice. This technique of moral redescription, or *paradiastole*, can be seen, for example, in the debates in the 1572 parliament over whether to execute Mary Queen of Scots. It might look like mercy to spare her, the bishops told Elizabeth, but in fact this was not merciful to the subject who would suffer if a Catholic monarch succeeded to that throne. Execution was justice, and to proceed with it was not merely Elizabeth's right, but a duty binding on her; here, her parliamentary counsellors sought to make their advice binding.[39]

Still, Machiavelli's book *did* have some relation to a new way of thinking about politics in the late sixteenth and early seventeenth centuries, which may have altered the nature of advice provided from that in the medieval mirrors. Denouncing a (caricatured) Machiavelli as endorsing amorality, many writers still tried to refute him on his own terms – i.e. exploring whether his advice was effective in maintaining power. How should a monarch keep power? Was the morality needed when ruling different from that for ordinary subjects? In an emergency – like a war, or a rebellion, or a Reformation – was the plea of necessity sufficient to override all the normal rules? Could one then tax without consent, or tolerate heresy? And if there were different rules for governing, should these be known only to the ruler and their advisors?

Several different strands therefore came together in the so-called 'reason of state' literature on politics. In maintaining power over the people – who were often treated as inherently unruly and inclined to rebellion – a ruler must maintain their reputation. Ensuring their power was respected might be, in Machiavellian terms, a choice between whether they should be loved or feared; was it best to be virtuous or to look it? What counted as virtue anyway? Rulers and advisors might need to keep their plans secret, especially as they could not rely on other people behaving transparently and honestly. 'He who can't feign, can't reign' ran one popular maxim.[40] Those penning advice literature therefore had to assist rulers to see how they could avoid lying while also surviving in a world of deception. Some endorsed dissimulation (avoiding revealing intent) but not simulation (actively pretending); others both; Justus Lipsius divided 'mixed prudence' into 'light deceit' (necessary practices such as distrust and dissimulation), a middling set of actions to be tolerated (such as lying), and fraud (such as breaking treaties) to be condemned as mere self-interest rather than an aid to the polity.[41] Should a ruler even let their advisers know what they intended? Or should they, as Francis Bacon suggested, remain impenetrably inscrutable when receiving advice?[42] If secrecy did not necessarily acquire a positive spin, it might be recognized as necessary. Engaging in political activity was therefore an initiation into *arcana imperii*, mysteries of state, not fit for general discussion.

During the early modern era there was a gradual shift from reason of state towards a more quasi-technocratic form of governance which paid growing attention to fiscal matters. Nevertheless we should not exaggerate the pace of change, or the lines of demarcation between new and old forms of advice. A hybrid statecraft, attending to the character formation of the ruler, the ethics of counsel and governance, the survival of the state, and political economy not only facilitated the transition to a fiscal-military, commercial, and imperial state, but also contained a telling variety of ingredients.

This history raises the question of what political advice should look like. Clinical analysis of the 'best' policy choice from the most experienced advisers is an attractive theory on paper: appealingly neutral and apparently open-minded, loftily above the partisan political fray. Yet as the chequered evolution of policy science has shown, statecraft has the real world for its laboratory, and is not amenable to a science of advice-giving.

## *III*

The thriving sub-discipline within American political science (and public administration) known as policy analysis or policy science[43] emerged in the course of the twentieth century, and provides a curriculum which caters to the training of today's senior bureaucracy and policy-oriented advisers. However, the subject matter of policy science fails, as some of its own practitioners and leading theorists have pointed out, to cover the whole ground of political advice. It is a sub-discipline which assumes rationality and professionalism in the realm of politics and a technocratic mindset in its supporting cast of advisers and bureaucrats. Indeed, one of the field's leading practitioners, Deborah Stone, claimed, with regret, that such assumptions are part of the very marrow of policy analysis, whose 'mission', she contended, was 'rescuing public policy from the irrationalities and indignities of politics, hoping to make policy instead with rational, analytical and scientific methods'. This, she surmised, was 'an impossible dream', conjured up by academic purists who found politics-as-actually-practised 'messy, foolish, erratic, and inexplicable'. Moreover, rational models of decision-making proved oblivious of the insight that 'policy is more like an endless game of Monopoly than a bicycle repair'.[44] Similarly, one of the earliest overviews of the new field of policy sciences complained that the field-as-constituted was 'politically deodorized', founded on an unrealistic hope of taking the politics out of policymaking.[45] There was, as its internal critics noticed, something sterile and utopian about the new field. Policy science seemed to have relatively little to say about the whims of politicians (and advisers too), the subtle interpersonal dynamics of any group situation and the political externalities – the antecedents of today's populist outrage – that warp sensible solutions to problems.

Indeed, in the 1970s there was considerable disappointment at the achievements of rational, research-based policy. Henry Aaron's *Politics and the Professors* (1978), a wistful retrospective on the evaporation of the optimistic social science consensus which had underpinned the Great Society programmes of the 1960s, concluded that the most basic, primary decision in policymaking – 'whether to commit oneself to the achievement of some goal' – 'largely eludes rational judgment'. A subjective, intuitive element lurked within policymaking that was impossible to evade.[46] Similarly, Aaron Wildavsky's *Speaking Truth to Power: The Art and Craft of Policy Analysis* (1979) distanced itself from the notion that policy was a science with clearly defined goals. Not at all, argued Wildavsky, 'problem-solving' was something of a delusion and was best understood in terms of 'problem succession': you cut off one problem and another sprouts. It was a mistake to construe policy analysis in terms of the quest for solutions. Rational solution mongering was inherently misconceived: 'problems are not so much solved as alleviated, superseded, transformed, and otherwise dropped from view'. Policy analysis, he declared, is an 'art', depending on a sensitivity to constraints rather than on a rational calculation of accessible answers.[47]

The human factor, in all its messiness, prevails in real-life political advice. Advisers as much as politicians find themselves jockeying for position, albeit at a lower and less public level. Nor should we forget the lure of the irrational. Why, over the centuries, have so many political leaders trusted in astrologers, and other cranks and charlatans? Outside the sterile confines of the policy analysis textbook, the contexts and constraints underlying advice-giving mean that sometimes technocratic rationality is difficult to obtain. The real-world permutations of advice-giving are endless. Among our favourite examples is the advice given by Dick Wirthlin, his pollster, to President Reagan shortly after the Iran-Contra scandal broke. He recalls in his memoirs that Reagan contacted Wirthlin while the pollster was still in hospital recovering from an operation, and that he was still groggy from the effects of powerful painkilling medication when he gave advice over the telephone to the President.[48] In the real world, leaders want to hear advice from trusted sources, no matter the condition of the favoured adviser. Political advice is as rich a subject and as diverse as humanity in all its unpredictability and perversity. Policy analysis can only bring us so far.

Nevertheless, policy science, or policy analysis, does go a considerable way towards establishing political advice as a credible sub-field of politics in its own right. The most influential pioneer in this area was the distinguished American political scientist Harold Lasswell (1902–78), a behaviourist, who attempted to synthesize the study of politics with vital adjacent fields such as psychology and communications. Lasswell was fascinated with the intelligence function in policymaking, and attempted to model the various phases in the transformation of raw information into policy recommendation, implementation and its appraisal. Lasswell provided a prospectus for the emerging field of policy science.[49]

The field also received a boost of a very different kind from the revolution effected by Robert McNamara at the Pentagon during his tenure as Secretary of Defense under Presidents Kennedy and Johnson. McNamara's particular proficiency was in mathematics and accounting, which he had taught at Harvard Business School, and in the application of systems analysis to business and administration. Indeed, he regarded all policy issues as being amenable to quantification. At the Ford Motor Company, McNamara led a team known as the 'whiz kids' who reformed the company's procedures, and later became the company's president. McNamara introduced systems analysis at the Pentagon, drawing both on his experience at Ford and on the work of the RAND Corporation, which carried out research and development work for the federal government. McNamara immediately introduced an Office of Systems Analysis into the Pentagon under the supervision of Charles Hitch, formerly of RAND. The systems analysts were responsible for launching a Planning, Programming and Budgeting System (PPBS), by which the Pentagon would exert more direct central financial control over its various quasi-feudal fiefdoms in the army, navy, and air force. During the Presidency of Lyndon Johnson, the methods introduced to the Pentagon were adopted across the federal government. PPBS was ultimately about establishing clear linkages between budgeting and an organization's overall objectives. Its origins lay in microeconomics, especially quantitative decision theory, and utilized the techniques of operations research, cost–benefit analysis and programme budgeting.[50] Thus, in practical terms – and despite Lasswell's midwifery – the new science of policy analysis as it developed within government was the child, not of political science, but of economics. That entailed a certain amount of unhelpful baggage, as economists at that point held a somewhat one-dimensional conception of humanity as rational, profit-seeking beings. Only in time did scholars of politics attempt to reorientate the discipline away from its roots in economics.

In the interim the McNamara revolution became institutionalized in academia, in new curricula, disciplines, schools, and degrees.[51] However, as the field developed, its leading practitioners soon expressed considerable dissatisfaction with its confining contours and unrealistic assumptions. Frank Fisher and John Forester published a collection lamenting the divorce between the new policy sciences and the old arts of rhetoric and persuasion. Not enough attention was being paid to performance and articulation in the delivery of advice. Neither were the policy sciences impersonal; there needed to be relationship building between advisers and advised; otherwise the 'ritualized bargaining' which was a necessary component of effective advising became constrained if not impossible. Rhetoric, Fisher and Forester argued, was not antithetical to analysis, but intrinsic to it. It was folly to ignore or suppress the rhetorical component of policy advising. A reasonable desire for objectivity in analysis did not mean that persuasion was thereby an illegitimate mode of delivery, to be abandoned as besmirching the purity of the discipline. Analysis needed to be 'persuasively gauged', and there was a considerable measure of 'discretion involved in … institutionally staged, organizational performances.'[52] Although the policy sciences had been framed in such a way as to transcend the darkly pejorative realm of Machiavellian counsel, on reflection several of its practitioners sensed that the new science had lost something vital in its separation from the discursive arts associated with Machiavelli, whose spectre hovered over the nascent (and putatively anti-Machiavellian) discipline.[53]

There were other major developments outside the immediate field of policy sciences which were widely influential, especially in the United States, on the limits and dangers of policy advice. The administration of John F. Kennedy provided a particular focus for journalists and psychologists. For a start, Kennedy had made several crucial decisions during his presidency. While he had successfully managed to avoid nuclear war with the Soviet Union during the Cuban missile crisis in October 1962, he had fared spectacularly badly in allowing the Bay of Pigs invasion to go ahead in 1961 and his administration had become entangled in the morass of Vietnam. Moreover, Kennedy's advisers had been drawn from the academic elite at Harvard, Yale and MIT. How did these highly educated men come to perform so badly in office? Two books, both published in 1972, assessed the failings of advice-giving and decision-making in the White House. One was a straightforward journalistic account, David Halberstam's book *The Best and the Brightest*, the other – a more general study of the psychology of decision-making, which nevertheless drew heavily on the mistakes Kennedy and his circle had made – was a pioneering landmark in the study of political advice, Irving L. Janis's study, *Victims of Groupthink: A Psychological Study of Foreign Policy Decisions and Fiascoes*.

Halberstam's study punctured the intellectual razzle-dazzle of the Kennedy crowd. Its highly distinguished members were united in a shared conviction 'that sheer intelligence could answer and solve anything'. Rationality was all. This was unsurprising, for Kennedy's team of advisers oozed braininess. McGeorge Bundy, the National Security Adviser, had entered Yale as an undergraduate with the highest test scores ever, been elected to the national honor society Phi Beta Kappa, achieved similar distinction at Harvard in the Society of Fellows, as a professor in the government Department, and then as Dean. Walt Rostow, Bundy's deputy and later Director of Policy Planning at the State Department, was a similar prodigy, educated at Yale, a Rhodes Scholar at Oxford, a Professor of Economic History at MIT. Robert McNamara, the Secretary of Defense, as we have seen, had enjoyed a hitherto gloriously successful career. Educated at Berkeley and at Harvard Business School, where he had become a professor, McNamara had moved on to Ford, revolutionizing its procedures, before being recruited to implement modern cost–benefit analysis into the Pentagon. None of these brilliant alpha men had known failure until drawn into the quagmire of the Vietnam problem. Their failures, according to Halberstam, were both intellectual and temperamental, deriving from hubris. They could not see that what they thought was a Cold War conflict was primarily an anti-colonial struggle; and as a result they underestimated the determination of the North Vietnamese, who were not simply Soviet pawns. Nor were Kennedy's advisers Asian area studies specialists; rather they attempted as outsiders to apply their rationality and theoretical sophistication to Vietnam as one problem among many which would, like others, yield to rational analysis.[54]

Situated at the intersection of social psychology, political science and history, Janis's work focused on group dynamics during the making of certain key foreign policy disasters, not only the Bay of Pigs and the escalation of the Vietnam war, but also Pearl Harbor and the invasion of North Korea during the Korean War. His subject was not so much the 'mindless conformity' of groups so much as the 'subtle constraints' within any collection of advisers which 'prevent a member from fully exercising his critical powers and from openly expressing doubts when most others in the group appear to have reached a consensus.' There comes a point in some advisory arrangements, Janis argued, when 'strivings for unanimity' override any motivation towards a realistic appraisal of 'alternative courses of action'. Insulating pressures of this sort can result in 'a deterioration of mental efficiency, reality testing, and moral judgment', resulting in an 'illusion of invulnerability', 'excessive optimism' and the downplaying of warnings, as well as – still more insidiously – a self-censorship of any departures from the prevailing consensus. Janis suggested various countervailing procedures that might be deployed to prick groupthinking counsel. Competition provided one route: it should be normal to set up independent evaluation groups to work on the same issue. Occasional outside experts might be invited from time to time to the meetings of the core group. A specific group member might be assigned the role of devil's advocate; though a devil's advocate who was too 'domesticated' and assimilated to group norms, might not prove 'very devilish', and as such little more than 'tokenism'. Nevertheless, it did appear that, during the Cuban missile crisis, Kennedy had specifically assigned his brother Bobby Kennedy to play a devil's advocate role. While psychodramatic role-playing exercises might indeed be more cathartic, as Janis imagined, they hardly seemed very practical. The scheduling of designated second-chance meetings for the airing of doubts might help to concentrate minds. The big problem in the realm of advising, as Janis saw it, was the human proclivity in social settings to succumb, for whatever reason, including modesty and politeness, to a 'concurrence-seeking tendency'.[55]

Janis's work proved highly influential, and the term 'groupthink' entered the wider vocabulary not only of politics but of decision-making at all levels and in other contexts. Some leaders developed their own particular remedies for groupthink. The Israeli Prime Minister Menachem Begin contrived a method of advice-giving which worked against the tendency in advising towards reaching a premature consensus. In discussions with advisers, he deliberately began meetings by asking for counsel from his advisers in reverse order of their seniority. Thus he received unvarnished advice first from his most junior staff, before hearing from his more senior staff, who were presumed to have the stature and self-confidence to disagree with their underlings. Begin himself was an obstinate leader, yet he nevertheless deployed a system which facilitated maximum flexibility in the advice he received.[56]

But might a wariness about groupthink result in overreaction and other kinds of distortion in advice-giving? Quite so, argued Paul Kowert, who thought that a cacophony of competing advice was as likely to lead to 'deadlock' as to enhanced counsel. While some leaders thrived on disagreement and fruitful dissension, others found that the clash of advisers left them 'immobilized', 'overwhelmed by too many conflicting opinions'. Instead of absolute imperatives, there were rather questions of propriety in the field of advice-giving, whether to leaders who favoured the 'open' cut and thrust of freewheeling exchanges or leaders more comfortable with 'closed' groupings and established routines. There were intermediate forms of counsel which might redress the tendencies towards the pathologies of groupthink and deadlock. Might devil's advocacy be institutionalized and routinized in some way, in order to alleviate the problems a closed leader encountered when meetings seemed to descend into structureless disagreement?[57]

What we know of the workings of American presidents and their staffs provides some evidence of the strengths, weaknesses and pitfalls identified by political psychologists. Franklin Delano Roosevelt astutely avoided the dangers of groupthink by commissioning different people to provide advice on the same issue. Competitiveness of this sort was the order of the day under Roosevelt, as was informality. Roosevelt thrived on unstructured face-to-face encounters, and also cultivated irregular advisers, most particularly his friend Harry Hopkins, who was deployed as an unofficial ambassador for Roosevelt during the Second World War. Where Roosevelt was gregarious, Richard Nixon preferred to mull over problems in solitude, or sometimes 'semi-solitude'[58] with a very few trusted aides, often one-on-one. Nixon disliked having to form close working relationships with new people, and also found confrontation and disagreement uncomfortable. Pondering a problem, worrying away at it, while scribbling on a yellow legal pad, more than substituted for the live theatricality of counsel-giving seen in the Roosevelt, Kennedy and Johnson administrations. On the other hand, Kennedy's gifted speechwriter and adviser Ted Sorensen reckoned that 'the interaction of many minds [was] usually more illuminating than the intuition of one.'[59] Indeed, Sorensen wrote a very perceptive and revealing account of advice-giving, based on his first-hand experience of the Kennedy White House. Sorensen saw that there was no all-purpose solution to the problem of counsel. Sometimes group discussions did indeed yield results, but sometimes they created a situation – not least in large 'less flexible' meetings – in which a premium was placed on compromise and consensus. Nor were experts really much help on broader questions of government policy, for they tended to suffer from 'bureaucratic parochialism'. Sorensen was particularly alert to the danger of the president's own interventions. If he committed himself at too early a stage in discussions, then that had the effect of shutting off 'productive debate' among advisers who were afraid to appear disloyal. What worked best for Kennedy were small meetings, to which the president preferred to invite 'only those whose official views he requires or whose unofficial judgment he values.'[60]

Amidst this teeming variety of personal quirks, scholars have tried to taxonomize the forms of political advice-giving in the White House, most notably the competiveness among advisers encouraged by FDR, the collegiality of the Kennedy administration, and the protocol-driven formalism (associated with Eisenhower's Chief of Staff Sherman Adams).[61] Indeed, there is a recognition that the Chief of Staff role has become a necessity, as a gatekeeping funnel controlling the flow of advisers into the Oval Office. The alternative non-pyramidal model – the spokes of the wheel system, by which a President maintains individual contact with a range of advisers, unmediated by a dominant Chief of Staff – was tried for a while by Gerald Ford and then Jimmy Carter,[62] but in both cases was ultimately abandoned as unworkable. As Ford later recounted, he became aware that 'without a strong decision-maker who would help me set my priorities, I'd be hounded to death by gnats and fleas.'[63] The Chief of Staff role has become indispensable in the organization of the White House.[64] More recently political scientists have noticed increasing turnover rates among presidential aides. The reason, it seems, is that the teams of campaign specialists assembled in what is increasingly a candidate-based rather than party-based system of electoral politics are not well-suited to governmental advice, which revolves around bargaining, cooperation and finding common ground, and is as such far removed from campaigning, which focuses on accentuating differences. Presidents tend to reward those advisers who helped them get into office, but then find their loyalty to staff tested in the very different conditions of government.[65]

More recently, political psychologists have identified a more fundamental problem. Philip Tetlock's devastating study, *Expert Political Judgment: How Good Is It? How Can We Know?* (2005), has exposed the fallacy of political expertise. To all intents and purposes there's really no such thing. Tetlock carried out experimental 'tournaments' among legions of political experts of all shades of opinion, from libertarian Right to Marxist Left. Two hundred and eighty-four experts participated in 28,000 predictive exercises, mostly initiated between 1988 and 1995. Such, however, is the intrinsic unpredictability of political outcomes, that Tetlock's army of experts performed no better than the chance equivalent of 'dart-throwing chimps'. Nevertheless, Tetlock did discover that those experts who were most versatile and eclectic in their interests and temperamentally diffident outperformed the more confident, formulaic and decisive, who were imprisoned either in narrowly delimited domains of knowledge or by dogmatically certain worldviews. Yet, of course, a further danger lurks within self-critical thinking of an 'excessive open-mindedness', which can result in confusion.[66]

In certain respects this is all old news, confirmation of what the most sophisticated analysts of politics had always intuited, but could not prove in the bald terms presented by Tetlock's experiments. Henry Kissinger, the most allegedly Machiavellian of advisers in the modern era, saw that the multiplicity of human interactions in politics endowed policymaking with a 'tragic' dimension. Tragedy inhered in unknowability. In his study of the post-Napoleonic concert of Europe, *A World Restored*, Kissinger argued that 'the essence of policy is its contingency; its success depends on the correctness of an estimate which is in part conjectural.'[67] In other words, if policy is a science, it is – ultimately, always has been, always will be – a science of guesswork.

### IV

Notwithstanding common developments in political science, traditions of analysis have followed a somewhat different trajectory in the UK. Here a small corner within political science was devoted to the study of the civil service, whose preeminent practitioner has been Peter Hennessy.[68] Notwithstanding the efforts of Hennessy and others to establish a value-free sub-field within the study of politics, this area of analysis was strongly tinged with polemic and party political concerns. During the 1960s and 1970s a series of radical Labour politicians castigated the civil service as an extension of England's upper class establishment, and as such small-c conservative – indeed almost conventionally Tory – in its prejudices. Richard Crossman's *Diaries of a Cabinet Minister*, which the civil service establishment tried to suppress, let daylight onto the battles between Crossman and his Permanent Secretary at the Ministry of Housing Dame Evelyn Sharp.[69] Less obliquely, Tony Benn and Brian Sedgemore launched scathing attacks on the unconstitutional ways in which the civil service establishment unobtrusively smothered the electoral mandates of Labour governments.[70] In addition, the Oxford economist Thomas Balogh (Harold Wilson's first special adviser) and Lord Crowther-Hunt, an Oxford politics don and senior adviser to Labour on constitutional matters, fumed at the wily unresponsiveness of the civil service to reform, even to the basic requirements of advice-giving in the modern world.[71] After the Northcote-Trevelyan reforms in 1854 the UK civil service had been committed to appointment on the basis of generalist competitive examination. There was no equivalent in the UK to the Ecole Nationale d'Administration established by Charles De Gaulle in 1945 which provided France's senior civil servants with in-depth training in economics, public law and the social sciences. In the UK, by contrast, there were in 1963 only nineteen economists in the entire home civil service.[72] Indeed, here a knowledge of dead languages was no bar to giving advice on the modern world – at times it seemed like the principal requisite. The Report of the Fulton Committee in 1968 had recommended that the civil service reboot itself to meet the demands of a complex, science- and technology-driven society, with more specialist advisers (rather than generalists who were as often as not Oxbridge classicists) and a proper civil service college to meet the training needs of the service. Yet Fulton had not been implemented in full; or rather the civil service, with typical cunning, had gone through the motions of appearing to implement Fulton, but allowed elements of the package to wither and fade.

In more recent decades, critical attention has shifted, almost by a hundred and eighty degrees, from the enormities of the civil service establishment (now idealized as non-partisan) to the emergence of politically appointed temporary civil servants, special advisers (or spads), who are alleged to have diluted the simon-pure ethos of civil service neutrality.[73] The import of a new class of generalists, moreover highly partisan generalists, into the machinery of government has not been an unmixed blessing. The media has focused – ironically and pejoratively – on the supposed fixation of 'spin doctors' with presentational matters and the media, to the exclusion of policy solutions.[74] Particular attention has focused on the highly unusual arrangements associated with Tony Blair's chief special advisers, Alastair Campbell (a former tabloid journalist) and Jonathan Powell, authorized under Orders of the Privy Council to give orders to civil servants. Moreover, as politics itself becomes more of a distinct profession with its own career pathways, so the role of special adviser has become a stepping stone on the route to political office, one taken, variously, by David Cameron, Ed Balls and the Miliband brothers. Advising has become, in certain quarters at least, a kind of apprenticeship for aspirant politicians. Nevertheless, the situation of spads remains a highly ambiguous one, defined with fine shading by Andrew Blick, as 'temporary civil servants of party political association, drawn from beyond the civil service but employed within it'.[75] Indeed, the argument has also been made that spads have, ironically, preserved rather than subverted the neutrality of permanent officials within the civil service, who had found themselves being sucked into party political matters.[76]

The central distinctive feature of advice-giving in the UK is the distinction between the *policy* advice tendered, with political impartiality to elected governments of any stripe, by the civil service, and the *political* advice given by non-civil service political advisers, and, since the 1970s, by spads. But where do we – if we really can – draw the line between nakedly *political* advice and ideologically neutral, non-partisan *policy* advice? This distinction between policy advice and political advice proper is not only a fine one, but hard to maintain in practice, as indeed is the supposed separation between disinterested civil service advice and political decision-making by ministers.

The organizational structure of 10 Downing Street reflects this theoretical distinction between political and policy advice. The Downing Street operation has traditionally been divided into various sectors.[77] The prime minister's key right-hand adviser is, typically, an up-and-coming junior official within the civil service – usually on secondment from the Treasury (of which the prime minister is by designation the 'First Lord'). This official is the Prime Minister's Principal Private Secretary, who heads the Prime Minister's Private Office. The Private Office includes five other civil servants – usually including a couple drawn from the Foreign and Commonwealth Office – who serve as the prime minister's first line of advisers. There is also a Press Office, whose members might be career information officers from the civil service or media advisers specially appointed from outside. Distinct from the Private Office is the Political Office. In 1964 Marcia Williams, Harold Wilson's personal secretary and political adviser as opposition leader, was brought into Downing Street to assist the prime minister on political matters, but was scrupulously paid out of party funds rather than by the government. After this uncomfortable precedent, the civil service became more accommodating, gradually so, of party political advisers based in 10 Downing Street. Wilson later brought in his own political appointee Joe Haines as press secretary. Then when Wilson returned to government after the February 1974 election, he established a Policy Unit in 10 Downing Street under another political appointee, Bernard Donoughue. Although Wilson was accused in the media of running an inner 'kitchen cabinet' of cronies, what might have been the expected lines of estrangement between political appointees and career civil servants did not materialize. Rather Donoughue and Haines found themselves allied in due course with civil service officials against the overweening and capricious power grabs of Marcia Williams, later elevated by Wilson to the peerage as Lady Falkender: the primary axis of division was based on individual personalities, not on categories of adviser.

Job descriptions at 10 Downing St – 'a place of distinct entities but not rigid demarcations'[78] – are, moreover, somewhat notional: what is much more important is getting the work of the prime minster done. By the time Wilson retired in March 1976, Haines's role had mutated from press secretary to that of a more general type of adviser. Not only did he compose most of Wilson's speeches, but Haines also gave counsel on a wide front beyond his supposed remit of press, media and communications.[79]

No Prime Minister has paid as much attention to the machinery of government as Edward Heath. In particular, Heath grappled with one of the central tensions in the field of advice-giving, namely its time horizon. It is difficult for advisers who promote long-term solutions to deep-laid problems to gain traction with political leaders, who focus understandably on the short-term, on the need to gain re-election. Heath's establishment of the Central Policy Review Staff was an attempt to put this right, by institutionalizing long-term thinking and bringing it into the heart of the policy process. The CPRS was a central player in Whitehall under its first Director, the ingenious and flamboyant Victor Rothschild. Yet the CPRS only survived for a decade. Under Rothschild's greyer successor, Kenneth

Berrill, the daring of the CPRS was blunted, and the think tank was gradually domesticated to Whitehall norms. Yet its greyness could not entirely conceal the danger – the electoral risks – attached to daring blue-sky thinking; and in 1983 Margaret Thatcher wound it up. Although Thatcher was more politically successful than Heath, in retrospect it seems that Heath had – for a short period at least – managed to solve one of the most intractable problems that plagues the machinery of government: the fruitful marriage of long-term with short-term counsel. Ironically, Heath spent much of his time in government firefighting a series of crises, which eventually overwhelmed his regime.

There are various other sources of advice available to a British prime minister. First of all, there is the Cabinet, comprising the prime minister's senior party colleagues. Their advice tends, however, to be filtered through the particular policy perspectives of the respective department for which each Cabinet minister is responsible. The prime minister must, however, try to gain an overview of the entire range of government policy, as far as possible uncontaminated by the affliction of departmentalitis. The Cabinet Office, set up to meet the pressures imposed by the First World War on the coordination of policy, is designed to serve the Cabinet and government as a whole, but is the closest entity within the UK system to a synoptic central branch of officialdom. The Cabinet Secretary is the UK's most senior civil servant, typically head of the civil service, as well as head of the Cabinet Office. The Cabinet Secretary can be a very sound source of advice to the prime minister, though the officeholder is also heavily overburdened, owing to the demands of superintending the entire Whitehall machine. Unusually, Sir William Armstrong, head of the civil service under Heath (though not Cabinet Secretary), was so influential, so close to Heath and so deeply associated with his trade union policy, that Armstrong was nicknamed the 'deputy prime minister'. The strain of this dual role at the very limits of Whitehall impartiality took its toll on Armstrong and he suffered a nervous breakdown during the miners' strike of 1973–4 which eventually brought about the implosion of the Heath administration.

During her eleven years as prime minister, Margaret Thatcher relied on advice from various quarters, but over the years as her elderly mentor Willie Whitelaw retired and she fell out with some of her leading ministers, most notably Geoffrey Howe and Nigel Lawson, so her entourage of advisers dwindled to the key members of what had become a 'court' circle in 10 Downing Street. There is nothing surprising in drift of that sort towards an inner circle with whom the leader feels most comfortable. What is astonishing, however, is that the two key members of this court were both supposedly apolitical and impartial civil servants, Charles Powell, an adviser on foreign affairs within her private office (and also notionally junior to her Principal Private Secretary) and her press secretary, Bernard Ingham. Powell and Ingham were retained as Downing Street civil servants long after everybody – including a disconcerted and exasperated civil service machine – realized that the two advisers had crossed the invisible line between neutral civil servant and politicized courtier. Thatcher enjoyed with both Powell and Ingham an enduring rapport. Indeed, it seems that Ingham, in his communications with the press, managed to exaggerate a ventriloquized version of Thatcher's thoughts that in due course alienated her from some of her senior Cabinet colleagues. The process was pernicious. The lines between Thatcher and her neutral advisers, between prime minister and officials, between government and friendship became decidedly blurry. Indeed, Powell's vizier-like ascent destabilized Thatcher's government as a whole in its latter years: not only had he effectively created for himself a non-existent office as de facto National Security Adviser, he had also usurped the place of the Foreign Secretary in the formulation of foreign policy, excluded the Cabinet Secretary and Thatcher's senior ministers from the counsels of the prime minister, assumed a primary role in Cabinet reshuffles and ministerial appointments, and become an acting 'deputy prime minister' in all but name. Even Ingham, his fellow vizier, began to feel the chill of exclusion from an inner circle of two.[80]

Nevertheless, whatever the individual missteps of Ingham and Powell that carried them across the bounds of civil service propriety, their case merely highlights a broader problem facing all civil servants at work in the Downing Street vortex. The rigid demarcation between policy advice and political counsel breaks down easily under the pressures of government, irrespective of any wilful intent on the part of either Downing Street civil servants or prime ministers. Indeed, interviews which the political scientists Kavanagh and Seldon carried out with unnamed Downing Street civil servants reveal a lack of clarity in practice about such distinctions – 'An organisation chart or assignment of fixed spheres of responsibility could not properly describe how we work'; 'Number Ten is a seamless place. You have to take on board the divisions in the party if you are to give good advice to the PM. You can't be too prissy.'[81]

Tony Blair's introduction of the office of Downing Street Chief of Staff, first held by Jonathan Powell, the brother of Charles Powell, as a special adviser, was intended as a clarifying measure. If anything, however, it served further to cloud lines of responsibility among Downing Street advisers. For the role of Chief of Staff seemed to step on the ex officio prerogatives and turf of the Principal Private Secretary. Nevertheless, as in previous administrations, it was not chains of command or organizational charts which largely determined life in the intimate surroundings of 10 Downing Street, but personal temperaments, discretion and camaraderie.

There is, it transpires, no established mode of advising prime ministers, who prefer to receive advice in different ways. Donoughue's diaries of his time running the Policy Unit for first Wilson then Callaghan highlight the vast gulf in approaches of the two Labour prime ministers. While Wilson worked on the hoof, happy to take advice in informal, undeferential, freewheeling exchanges, which were sometimes bruising and bloody – indeed 'almost masochistic', Callaghan was both more sparing of his time and more punctilious about the dignity of his office, insisting on the formalities of appointments for meetings, a written agenda, and sticking to the point in hand.[82] Margaret Thatcher had her own distinctive way of dealing with advisers. First of all, she made no distinction between senior and junior advisers. Everybody was treated the same way: all advice was subjected to a 'howitzer' barrage of objection. If an adviser – no matter how junior – answered back, she would continue to quibble, disagree and interrogate, like a dog with a bone. If the adviser was still standing and still answering back by the end of the session, the advice she had – apparently – rejected was quietly absorbed into her thinking as a robust home truth. As Oliver Letwin, one of her most junior advisers, later a Conservative Cabinet Minister, points out, Thatcher's approach was a 'dialectical method aimed at finding out whether you [the adviser] could stand your ground or whether the ground would give way under your argument if she chucked enough at you and it'. There was not the slightest whiff of 'pomposity' about this procedure, so that no matter how junior the adviser, if he or she could advance advice that withstood her dialectical attacks, then that adviser could speak on equal terms with the prime minister of the UK. The confidence of the ruler was gained not by status or function, but by means of brutal and bloodied intellectual combat.[83]

Nor does advising provide, it seems, an adequate description of what advisers do. There is a famous saying in British politics, first used by Margaret Thatcher when attempting to defuse a serious difference on exchange rate policy between her Chancellor Nigel Lawson and her economics adviser Alan Walters: 'Advisers advise, but ministers decide.' Except that is not entirely true. Sometimes, very often indeed, advisers also decide. This is not a matter of trespass, so much as necessary support. The political scientists Dennis Kavanagh and Anthony Seldon have argued that such are the excessive demands on the individual leader that the key advisers of the British prime minister effectively take decisions on his or her behalf. In effect, they contend, Britain has a 'collective premiership'. Aides – with the blessing of an exhausted prime minister – govern as well as advise. Indeed, the operation of 10 Downing Street bears some comparison, according to Kavanagh and Seldon, with the studio of a great artist like Rubens, where assistants do much of the work attributed to the master. It is vital that they know the prime minister's mind and as such are able to impersonate the leader, in the process, of course, suppressing any personal inclinations that they have which diverge from those of the premier. There is, they contend, 'nothing sinister' in this. It is part of an inevitable process whereby the scale and range of issues faced by a leader overwhelm that individual, no matter how great his or her powers of concentration, stamina, and energy: it's all too much for any human being, and so advisers do not simply advise, they also govern.[84] And the most powerful leaders know how to delegate, how to take advice.

*V*

As should be apparent by now, political advice does not belong exclusively to political science. The importance of advice 'outside the box', of evading the pernicious conformity of groupthink, means that political advice has a curious and unexpected history and its boundaries are hard to pin down. We have noted the unexpected strangeness of some of the most persistent genres of advice, including, for example, medical men from court doctors to less formal healers, from astrologers to subversively counter-cultural hangers-on of one sort or another. Political advice covers an interdisciplinary domain which includes, variously but not exhaustively, political practice and political theory, history, psychology, rhetoric, classics and literature. *Political Advice: Past, Present and Future* attempts to capture some of that range and diversity. It brings several very different voices to bear on the problems of advice and influence, the two-way parasitism of adviser and advised, the nature and idioms of political advice literature, the changing (and sometimes unchanging) nature of expertise, the ever-pressing issue of access and exclusion in the surprisingly cramped spaces occupied by ultimate power-makers, and how that is controlled. Leaders are, ultimately, only exposed to a fraction of the available expert advice potentially on offer, even within their own government machines.

The volume also serves a further ambition, that of bridging the division between the academic analysis of advice and the perspective of the practitioners themselves, whether politicians, special advisers, or civil servants. Thus we have assembled an interdisciplinary team from academic life, but one which is complemented by a variety of practitioner perspectives. The contributors are drawn variously from the civil service proper, from the ranks of temporary political advisers, and from the world of party politics, as well as from various academic specialisms. As their contributions collectively demonstrate, we should take advice in all its multiple manifestations seriously and remember that the search for a universal meta-advice (that is, advice about the best kind of advice) is rainbow chasing. For the first crucial conclusion from this volume is that effective or successful advice is circumstance-dependent: a conjuncture of adviser, advised, rhetoric, time and place. Yet the second is the value of knowing that advice has a propensity to pop up in all sorts of unexpected places. This is more than just an interesting bit of antiquarian research, for a recognition of the diversity and plasticity of advice has important implications for its future. Adaptive flexibility in the face of whatever the political weather throws up may be the best lesson for those giving and taking political advice: past, present – and future.

## Notes

1    Patricia Witherspoon, *Within These Walls: A Study of Communication between Presidents and Their Senior Staffs* (Westport CT: Praeger, 1991), 78.
2    Lord Alanbrooke, *War Diaries: 1939–1945*, ed. Alex Danchev and Dan Todman, new edn (London: Weidenfeld and Nicholson, 2002).
3    Aristotle, *Politics*, III.7, IV.10, V.11.
4    Jacques-Benigne Bossuet, *Politics Drawn from the Very Words of Holy Scripture*, ed. Patrick Riley (Cambridge: Cambridge University Press, 1990); *Elizabeth I and Her Age*, ed. Donald V. Stump and Susan M. Felch (New York: W. W. Norton, 2009), 75–6.
5    Qu. in Peter Hennessy, *Whitehall*, rev. edn (London: Pimlico, 2001), 345.
6    Herbert Goldhamer, *The Adviser* (New York: Elsevier, 1978), 91.
7    Harold Wilson, *The Governance of Britain* (London: Weidenfeld and Nicolson, 1976), 202.

8   Blair Worden, 'Oliver Cromwell and the Council', in *The Cromwellian Protectorate*, ed. Patrick Little (Woodbridge: Boydell, 2007), 90.

9   Qu. in Ben Yong and Robert Hazell, *Special Advisers: Who They Are, What They Do and Why They Matter* (Oxford: Hart Publishing, 2014), 180.

10  https://assets.publishing.service.gov.uk/government/uploads/system/uploads/attachment_data/file/832599/201612_Code_of_Conduct_for_Special_Advisers.pdf. Accessed 10 December 2019.

11  Jack Brown, *No. 10: The Geography of Power at Downing Street* (London: Haus, 2019).

12  Joe Haines, *The Politics of Power* (London: Jonathan Cape, 1977), 217.

13  *A Peece of Ordnance Invented by a Jesuite … with the Help of a Private Engin in the Cabbinet Councell* (1644), 2.

14  John Rushworth, *The Tryal of Thomas Earl of Strafford* (London, 1680), 524–81, 687.

15  Though the demand to counsel for the good of the commonwealth vanished in their period. For these oaths see Jacqueline Rose, 'Sir Edward Hyde and the Problem of Counsel in Mid-Seventeenth-Century Royalist Thought', in *The Politics of Counsel in England and Scotland, 1286–1707*, ed. Rose (Oxford, 2016), 260. For the oath today: https://privycouncil.independent.gov.uk/wp-content/uploads/2016/11/privy-counsellors-oath.pdf. Accessed 10 December 2019.

16  https://assets.publishing.service.gov.uk/government/uploads/system/uploads/attachment_data/file/832599/201612_Code_of_Conduct_for_Special_Advisers.pdf. Accessed 10 December 2019.

17  Perez Zagorin, 'Sir Edward Stanhope's Advice to Thomas Wentworth, Viscount Wentworth, Concerning the Deputyship of Ireland: An Unpublished Letter of 1631', *Historical Journal* 7 (1964): 298–320, at 202.

18  Angel Day, 'Of the Partes, Place and Office of a Secretory', in *The English Secretary* (1599), 102–3, 114; Robert Beale, 'A Treatise of the Office of a Councellor and Principall Secretarie to Her Majestie', printed in Conyers Read, *Mr Secretary Walsingham and the Policy of Queen Elizabeth* (3 vols, Oxford: Clarendon Press, 1925), i. 428; Charles Hughes (ed.), 'Nicholas Faunt's Discourse touching the Office of Principal Secretary of Estate &c, 1592', *English Historical Review* 20 (1905): 499–508, at 502–3.

19  Day, *Secretary*, 116.

20  William Plowden, 'Relationships between Advisers and Departmental Civil Servants', in *Advising the Rulers*, ed. Plowden (Oxford: Royal Institute of Public Administration/Basil Blackwell, 1987), 172–3.

21  Thomas More, *Utopia*, ed. George M. Logan and Robert M. Adams (Cambridge: Cambridge University Press, 1989), 13.

22  Goldhamer, *Adviser*, p. ix.

23  Goldhamer, *Adviser*, p. 3.

24  Guy Benveniste, *The Politics of Expertise*, 2nd edn (San Francisco: Boyd and Fraser, 1977), 21–2.

25  Qu. in Yong and Hazell, *Special Advisers*, 195.

26  Cicero, *Laelius de amicitia*, in *De senectute, de amicitia, de divinatione*, trans. William Armistead Falconer (London: Heinemann, 1923), 162–5, 156–7, 196–7.

27  John of Salisbury, *Policraticus*, ed. Cary J. Nederman (Cambridge: Cambridge University Press, 1990), 20.

28  Plutarch, 'How a Man May Discerne a Flatterer from a Friend', in *The Philosophie, Commonlie Called the Morals*, trans. Philemon Holland (London, 1603), 105, 108, 111–13, 116.

29  John Colville, *The Fringes of Power: Downing Street Diaries 1939–1955* (London: Hodder and Stoughton, 1985), 668–70, 706–7.

30  Gerald Ford, *A Time to Heal* (New York: Harper and Row, 1979), 187–8.

31  Thomas Sackville and Thomas Norton, *Gorboduc or Ferrex and Porrex* (1565), ed. Irby B. Cauthen, jr (London: Edward Arnold, 1970), act I, scene ii, and between the first and second acts.

32  *The Great Eclipse of the Sun* (1644).

33  Nicole Reinhardt, *Voices of Conscience: Royal Confessors and Political Counsel in Seventeenth-Century Spain and France* (Oxford: Oxford University Press, 2016).

34  John of Salisbury, *Policraticus*, 66–7.

35  King James VI and I, *Political Writings*, ed. Johann P. Sommerville (Cambridge: Cambridge University Press, 1994), 50–3.

36  Niccolò Machiavelli, *The Prince*, ed. Quentin Skinner and Russell Price (Cambridge: Cambridge University Press, 1988), chs. 16–18.

37  Machiavelli, *Prince*, ch. 22.

38  Pauline Croft (ed.), 'A Collection of Several Speeches and Treatises of the Late Lord Treasurer Cecil and of Several Observations of the Lords of the Council Given to King James Concerning His Estate and Revenue in the Years 1608, 1609, and 1610', in *Camden Miscellany*, 4th ser., 34 (London: Royal Historical Society, 1987), 245–317, at 284, 278, 289, 302.

39  'Arguments against Mary Queen of Scots … by Some of Both Houses', in *Proceedings in the Parliaments of Elizabeth I*, ed. T. E. Hartley (3 vols, Leicester: Leicester University Press, 1992–5), i. 275, 279–80.

40  Adrianna E. Bakos, '"Qui nescit dissimulare, nescit regnare": Louis XIV and Raison d'etat during the Reign of Louis XIII', *Journal of the History of Ideas* 52 (1991): 399–416.

41  Justus Lipsius, *Six Bookes of Politickes or Civil Doctrine*, trans. William Jones (1594), bk IV, chs 13–14.

42  Francis Bacon, 'Of Counsel', in *The Essayes or Counsel, Civill and Morall*, ed. Michael Kiernan (Oxford: Clarendon Press, 1985), 65, 68.

43  Peter DeLeon, 'The Historical Roots of the Field', in *The Oxford Handbook of Public Policy*, ed. Robert E. Goodon, Michael Moran and Martin Rein (Oxford: Oxford University Press, 2008).

44  Deborah Stone, *Policy Paradox: The Art of Political Decision Making*, 2nd edn (New York: W. W. Norton, 1997), 6–7, 259.

45  H. Hugh Heclo, 'Policy Analysis', *British Journal of Political Science* 2 (1972): 83–108, at 101.

46  Henry J. Aaron, *Politics and the Professors: The Great Society in Perspective* (Washington DC: Brookings, 1978), 179.

47  Aaron Wildavsky, *Speaking Truth to Power: The Art and Craft of Policy Analysis* (Boston and Toronto: Little, Brown and Co., 1979), 2–4, 8–9, 15, 17, 386.

48  Dick Wirthlin, *The Greatest Communicator: What Ronald Reagan Taught Me about Politics, Leadership and Life* (Hoboken, New Jersey: Wiley, 2004), 190.

49  Harold Lasswell et al., *The Policy Sciences* (Palo Alto: Stanford University Press, 1951); Lasswell, *The Decision Process* (College Park, MD: University of Maryland, 1956); Lasswell, 'The Emerging Conception of the Policy Sciences', *Policy Sciences* 1 (1970): 3–14; Lasswell, *A Pre-view of Policy Sciences* (New York: American Elsevier, 1971).

50  Beryl A. Radin, *Beyond Machiavelli: Policy Analysis reaches Midlife*, 2nd edn (Washington DC: Georgetown University Press, 2013), 14–17.

51  Duncan MacRae Jr. and Dale Whittington, *Expert Advice for Policy Choice* (Washington DC: Georgetown University Press, 1997), 5.

52  *The Argumentative Turn in Policy Analysis and Planning*, ed. Frank Fisher and John Forester (Durham NC: Duke University Press, 1993), 1–17.

53  Benveniste, *Politics of Expertise*; Radin, *Beyond Machiavelli*.

54  David Halberstam, *The Best and the Brightest* (1972; New York: Modern Library, 2001).

55  Irving L. Janis, *Victims of Groupthink: A Psychological Study of Foreign-Policy Decisions and Fiascoes* (Boston: Houghton Mifflin, 1972), 3, 9, 197–9, 207, 211–18.

56  Stuart E. Eizenstat, *President Carter* (New York: Thomas Dunne/St Martin's Press, 2018), 510.

57  Paul A. Kowert, *Groupthink or Deadlock: When Do Leaders Learn from Their Advisors?* (Albany, NY: SUNY Press, 2002), 4, 14–15, 18, 21, 23–5, 160.

58  Witherspoon, *Within These Walls*, 93.

59  Theodore Sorensen, *Decision-Making in the White House; The Olive Branch or the Arrows* (1963; New York: Columbia University Press, 2005), 59.

60  Sorensen, *Decision-Making*, 60–70.

61  Richard T. Johnson, *Managing the White House* (New York: Harper and Row, 1974), esp. 3–8, 233–8.

62  Robert Hartmann, *Palace Politics: An Inside Account of the Ford Years* (New York: McGraw-Hill, 1980), 274–83; James Cannon, *Gerald R. Ford* (Ann Arbor: University of Michigan Press, 2013), 204, 263–4; Witherspoon, *Within These Walls*, 11, 120–1, 128.

63  Ford, *Time to Heal*, 186.

64  Chris Whipple, *The Gatekeepers: How the White House Chiefs of Staff Define Every Presidency* (New York: Crown, 2017).

65  Matthew J. Dickinson and Kathryn Dunn Tenpas, 'Explaining Increasing Turnover Rates among Presidential Advisers, 1929–1997', *Journal of Politics* 64 (2002): 434–48.

66  Philip Tetlock, *Expert Political Judgment: How Good Is It? How Can We Know?* (Princeton, NJ: Princeton University Press, 2005), xi, 20–1, 23, 238, 240.

67  Quoted in Niall Ferguson, *Kissinger 1923–1968: The Idealist* (London: Allen Lane, 2015), 310.

68  Hennessy, *Whitehall*.

69  Richard Crossman, *Diaries of a Cabinet Minister: Volume I* (London: Hamish Hamilton/Jonathan Cape, 1975).

70  Tony Benn, *The Case for a Constitutional Civil Service* (Nottingham: Institute for Workers' Control, 1980); Brian Sedgemore, *The Secret Constitution: An Analysis of the Political Establishment* (London: Hodder and Stoughton, 1980).

71  Thomas Balogh, 'The Apotheosis of the Dilettante: the Establishment of Mandarins', in *The Establishment: a Symposium*, ed. Hugh Thomas (London: Anthony Blond, 1959), 81–126; Lord Crowther-Hunt, 'Mandarins and Ministers', *Parliamentary Affairs* 33 (1980): 373–99; Peter Kellner and Crowther-Hunt, *The Civil Servants: An Inquiry into Britain's Ruling Class* (London: Macdonald and Jane's, 1980).

72  Kellner and Crowther-Hunt, *Civil Servants*, 42.

73  Andrew Blick, *People Who Live in the Dark: The History of the Special Adviser in British Politics* (London: Politico's, 2004); Yong and Hazell, *Special Advisers*; Rodney Lowe, 'Grit in the Oyster or Sand in the Machine? The Evolving Role of Special Advisers in British Government', *Twentieth Century British History* 16 (2005): 497–505; Alasdair Palmer, *The Return of Political Patronage: How Special Advisers Are Taking Over Our Civil Service and Why We Need to Worry about It* (London: Civitas, 2015).

74   Nicholas Jones, *Sultans of Spin: The Media and the New Labour Government* (London: Gollancz, 2000).

75   Blick, *People Who Live in the Dark*, 64.

76   Blick, *People Who Live in the Dark*, 19.

77   For the evolution of the advisory system in Downing Street, see Andrew Blick and George Jones, *At Power's Elbow: Aides to the Prime Minister from Robert Walpole to David Cameron* (London: Biteback, 2013).

78   G. W. Jones, 'The Prime Minister's Aides', in *The British Prime Ministers*, ed. Anthony King, 2nd edn (Houndmills: Macmillan, 1985), 72–95, at 92.

79   Robert Harris, *Good and Faithful Servant: The Unauthorized Biography of Bernard Ingham* (London: Faber and Faber, 1990), 80.

80   Charles Moore, *Margaret Thatcher The Authorized Biography: Volume Three Herself Alone* (London: Allen Lane, 2019), 34–5, 157–8, 199, 222–6, 306–11, 324–5, 613; Harris, *Good and Faithful Servant*, 180–1.

81   Dennis Kavanagh and Anthony Seldon, *The Powers behind the Prime Minister* (London: Harper Collins, 1999), 15, 324.

82   Bernard Donoughue, *Downing Street Diary: With Harold Wilson in No. 10* (London: Jonathan Cape, 2005); Donoughue, *Downing Street Diary Volume Two: With James Callaghan in No. 10* (London: Jonathan Cape, 2008); Donoughue, *The Heat of the Kitchen: An Autobiography* (London: Politico's, 2003), 120.

83   Oliver Letwin, *Hearts and Minds: The Battle for the Conservative Party from Thatcher to the Present* (London: Biteback, 2017), 47–50.

84   Kavanagh and Seldon, *Powers*, ix–x, 300.

## Chapter 2

# WHAT WOULD PERIKLES DO, AND WHY IT STILL MATTERS – ASKING THE ANCIENT GREEK GODS FOR POLITICAL ADVICE

## Esther Eidinow

This essay examines the role of divination, especially the consultation of oracles, in political decision-making in ancient Greek culture. It argues that oracular consultation was neither simply a symptom of primitive superstition, nor an empty ritual conducted by an elite to reassure the masses. An examination of the divinatory process – not only how oracles gave answers, but also the ways in which consultants formulated questions – challenges common assumptions about how oracles functioned, and what kind of help their ancient visitors expected. It reveals a variety of possible ways in which divination could assist decision-making at every level of society, and, in particular, on political matters.

The first draft of this essay was delivered as a paper on Thursday, 8 June 2017: the date of a general election in the UK. What followed is yet to be fully represented in historiographical narratives, but perhaps it can be agreed that it was politically turbulent, in a way that has prompted widespread questions not only about the future of the UK as a political entity and its international relations, but also about the future of the democratic system itself.[1]

It seems a suitable time, therefore, to reflect on the culture that gave us *demokratia* in the first place. The ancient Greeks, more specifically the ancient Athenians, are famous for the development of this system of governance. There are relatively obvious parallels that could be drawn between contemporary political developments and the system of government in late-fifth-century BCE Athens. We could focus on the power of rhetoric and sophisticated tools of persuasion for which the Athenians were renowned; or the ways in which the Athenian radical democracy of that period was marked by the rise of the demagogue; or the various responses of different ancient political regimes to challenges to their power. Indeed, there are, it is clear from recent and past engagement with the text of the fifth-century historian Thucydides, many and very different modern parallels to be drawn from reflection on our evidence for the political structures and systems of the ancient Greeks.[2] But rather than revisiting these debates, I want to turn our attention instead to a different set of ancient Greek practices, which also informed their political discussions: divination, especially the consultation of oracles.[3] Such practices may seem very distant from our own culture; indeed, at first sight, they may seem largely irrelevant. But I am going to suggest here that they may prove to be more thought-provoking for our modern political situation than simply retreading more familiar ground, since they draw attention to fundamental processes of inquiry and discussion, explorations of significance, interpretations of meaning, and the far-reaching implications of decisions.

Let me introduce the topic by turning to the main character of my title: the great fifth-century BCE *strategos*, or general, Perikles, and a story from his *Life*, as written by the second-century CE philosopher Plutarch. The episode takes place during a period of political contestation, when Perikles is campaigning against his rival Thucydides, son of Melesias (not the famous historian referred to above). Rather than checking the polls, as a modern politician might do in this situation, the protagonists used a rather different system of forecasting a winner. Plutarch reports a story that a one-horned ram was brought to Perikles from his country estate. It prompted two different reactions: Lampon, who was a seer or diviner, when he saw the horn, declared that, whereas there were two powerful parties in the city, that of Thucydides and that of Perikles, the mastery would finally devolve upon one man – the man to whom this sign had been given. In complete contrast, the philosopher Anaxagoras simply explained the phenomenon by having the ram's skull cut in two, so that he could show how the horn had grown.

At first, it was Anaxagoras's approach that most pleased those watching, but later events seemed to point to another explanation, and this then provoked a different popular reaction. As Plutarch goes on, 'At that time, the story says, it was Anaxagoras who won the plaudits of the bystanders; but a little while after it was Lampon … This was because Thucydides was overthrown, and Perikles was entrusted with the entire control of all the interests of the people.'[4] We can add to this, that it was Lampon that Perikles chose to lead the expedition to re-found a city, Thurii, in South Italy in 444/3 – a crucial element in both his foreign and his domestic policy – and this venture, in turn, also included divinatory activities, as was usual with the founding of a new settlement.

How should we understand the story of Perikles and the ram's horn, and the role of divination within it? Some modern scholars have taken this episode as illustrative of the superstitious tendency of the masses. For example, Donald Kagan notes that 'Pericles, no doubt, preferred the explanation of Anaxagoras', but he had to keep the Athenians happy and 'especially the poorer people' who believed in supernatural signs and portents. 'For them, Lampon was not only a respected public figure but a reassuring symbol of divine approval and guidance.'[5] Kagan's analysis presupposes that such divinatory practices were simply ways of comforting popular fears. They were empty rituals, important to be seen to carry out, but not really a part, in any meaningful way, of the business of government. And, indeed, it would be all too easy to maintain this contrast, and either to assume that 'the cradle of Greek democracy' never really took all that superstitious stuff seriously; or to argue that the Greeks themselves were never free of their fear of the divine and so were unable to act rationally. But, as this essay argues, the answer is messier than that. Here was a society that was like ours, and yet not like ours. In so many ways, it marks the beginnings of many aspects of Western culture, which we think of as rational and scientific. But alongside these important developments, this was a culture that believed that gods spoke to mortals – and they could offer guidance. Within the boundaries of this society, the explanation given by Lampon was meaningful. Other kinds of evidence indicate that this was not an exceptional event: the divine played a far bigger role – and in fact a far more interesting role – in ancient Greek governance than we might at first think, in particular through various modes of divination. As we will see, such activities cannot be written off simply as 'irrational' behaviour, which indulged superstitious fears; far from it, in ancient Greece, divination played a key role in decision-making of most kinds, and in particular political decision-making.[6]

I

We should start by examining what 'divination' comprised. In ancient and modern societies it took and takes many forms, so what follows is by necessity a brief overview. Across ancient cultures, divination was a well-established practice: some of the earliest evidence for this kind of activity comes from ancient Mesopotamia and dates to the twenty-second century BCE.[7] It existed in many different forms: from street-corner shrines to gods, which offered a pair of dice whose throw would locate the 'right' answer to your question from among a list of statements carved nearby;[8] to itinerant diviners, either a *mantis* (that is, a seer) who could read divine signs – whether the liver of a sacrificed animal, or the flight of birds – or a *chresmologos*, who would draw out a suitable verse from a collection of verse oracles.[9] But among such supernatural services, the form of divination perceived to be most reliable tended to take place at oracular sanctuaries, where it was possible to consult a particular god, or hero, or even the dead.[10]

The particular method of divination at oracles also varied: perhaps the most famous took place at Delphi, where the Pythia was inspired by the god Apollo, and spoke her answers to questions in the voice of the god. It is thought that the Pythia spoke in riddling verses, although in fact the evidence indicates that this happens far less frequently than the reputation for this suggests.[11] There has been plenty of academic debate about this idea. For a long time, scholarship explained this phenomenon away by positing that the Pythia – perhaps high on some naturally produced vapours[12] – raved and moaned, and her burblings were turned into coherent, albeit puzzling, verses by male priests, who were either tremendously politically astute or practised psychologists.[13] This characterization was challenged in the 1990s by Lisa Maurizio, who made the crucial observation that 'every ancient source without exception or modification presents the Pythia as issuing oracular responses herself'.[14] Building on this focus on the Pythia's role, more recent work is examining how we might better understand 'the forms of experience, attributed significance, and causal processes involved in Apollo's communication through the Pythia'.[15] This work may also help to illuminate other forms of divination, in which practitioners used particular skills to interpret signs in the environment (for example, the flight of birds), rather than inspiration.[16]

## II

There is ample and varied evidence for specifically political uses of divination. In collecting and analysing this material, I am treating 'political' as a broad category indicating matters 'relating to the support and organisation of a *polis*', in which *polis* is the Greek for a 'city-state', one of the organizational structures of communities (and, of course, the origin of our term 'political'). Perhaps the most straightforward role for divination in this context, and one that seems least puzzling, was its employment in the resolution of questions about the activities of a *polis* that related to the gods and their worship. For example, in the fourth century BCE, the orator Demosthenes tells us that Athens asked at both Delphi and Zeus's oracle at Dodona in northwest Greece (on which more later) about hymns and prayers to Dionysus at the festival of the Dionysia.[17] Closely related to these kinds of inquiries, which were intended to maintain the gods' benevolence towards a community, were questions about unexplained events, especially misfortunes, which had beset a community; for example, the question preserved from the site of Dodona, in which the Dodonaeans ask Zeus 'Whether it is because of the impurity of some man that god sends the storm'.[18] These were closely related because the underlying assumption was, invariably, that these calamities had been caused by the disruption of the relationship between a supernatural figure (god or hero) and a community.

Perhaps closer to the meaning of political as governance were the uses of divination for a community's strategic decision-making. Starting in the late eighth century, as massive changes in state formation were transforming many if not most areas of the Greek world, communities seem to have used divination, especially divination at oracular sanctuaries, to help build consensus around – and lend authority to – difficult state decisions.[19] These included constitutional reforms, whether or not to go to war, public order, and sending out new settlements. But this recourse to divination was not just a result of under-developed government systems trying to manage unfamiliar changes; nor did it recede in the face of growing political sophistication. If we visited Athens in the fourth century BCE, we would find the city sending for oracles in order to help make political decisions;[20] likely storing them for future use, and introducing them into political debates.[21] As we have seen in the story from Plutarch, individuals in high office retained personal seers to advise them;[22] seers were present during the meetings of the Athenian Assembly; and honours were given to seers for their work.[23]

### III

Did people really believe in divination? As the previous discussion suggests, the answer to this question appears to have been: yes. Of course, it also rather depends on what is meant by 'believing' or the nature of 'belief': there is no room to discuss that complex question here, but it is important to raise it, and the questions it introduces, even as we acknowledge that it is certainly the case that divination seems to have exerted extraordinary power for millennia in cultures across the ancient world. Scholarly explanations of this continuous use in ancient Greek culture tend to identify particular functions that it must have served. For example, it has been argued that oracular sanctuaries such as Delphi offered visitors opportunities for sharing useful information, in particular data that was important for planning and preparing new settlements.[24] In turn, processes of divination, more broadly, and oracular consultation in particular could help communities find consensus about difficult decisions. These interpretations are no doubt important factors in understanding different dimensions of the power of divination. But it is also difficult for modern minds to avoid suspicion of a marked gullibility among Delphi's clients. Indeed, scholars have suggested that either the officers of the sanctuary were deceiving their visitors, or they must themselves have been victims of deception.[25] But while we may suspect that some kind of trickery was at play, it is far from easy to find the evidence for it.

Another aspect further complicates our understanding of the operations of oracles: the question of the nature of the oracular responses that visitors received. We have evidence for two models of the oracular consultation process. The first comes largely from the evidence for oracular responses, which are found in literary texts. Usually attributed to the oracle at Delphi, these tend to be in verse and are often relatively lengthy. They are usually part of ancient accounts of the origins of a place or practice; their authority is sometimes reinforced by the unexpected nature of their content. An example is the story of Myskellos of Rhipai (in Achaia), who originally went to the Delphic oracle to find out about his chances of having children, and ended up with the instruction that he must found a settlement at Kroton in South Italy: 'Far-darter Apollo loves you and he will give you children; but first he commands you to found Kroton, a great city amidst fine fields'.[26] This type of response suggests a process in which the interpretation of the answer was a key part of the oracular consultation.[27] The second model of consultation is somewhat more straightforward. It emerges from remarkable epigraphic evidence for the kinds of *questions* that visitors asked at oracles. This comes from Dodona, an oracle of Zeus already mentioned above, which has yielded thousands of lead tablets, inscribed with questions asked not only by state representatives, but also by ordinary men and women – and possibly also slaves.[28] The questions have a distinctive structure, offering a yes/no, or either/or alternatives. Intriguingly, despite the number of tablets showing questions, few answers survive. But where they do, they are very brief, simply confirming one of the two options put forward by the binary structure of the question: for example, one question asks ' … whether it would be better for him and his children and his wife in Kroton?'; the answer is recorded: 'In Kroton'.[29]

Current scholarship is divided on which model of consultation was used at which sanctuary. It is of course possible that both were used, either because different methods of divination were in operation at one site, or because they existed in combination – so that brief answers were gradually turned into verse oracles as narratives developed that described the oracle's outcomes. Whichever answer we prefer, we have to return to what the sheer weight of our evidence seems to indicate: that oracles were used to make important decisions, both by individuals in deciding their everyday business, and by communities for weightier political matters.

*IV*

Let us turn now to practices of consultation. The reasons for this consistent use must lie, at least in part, in the insights that were promised: on the one hand, ample evidence attests to the Greeks' own belief that oracles should be used only to find out information that was hidden to mortal eyes, but was known by the gods; a leader who ignored divine messages risked being seen as politically or personally reckless.[30] But alongside these important religious dimensions, oracular consultation was politically valuable in other ways to do with processes of decision-making.

The evidence for both models of consultation reveals an important aspect of the process of consultation: that is, that it was rare for an individual to go to an oracle without first having a clear idea of what they wanted to ask about. The evidence – both literary and epigraphic – suggests that a consultant had already considered their options when they visited an oracle; its answer was an important part – but only a part – of their decision-making process. This is apparent from a range of different stories that the Greeks themselves told that allude to the 'right' ways to use oracles. To begin with, oracular consultation was not necessarily understood to produce a single right answer. Literary and epigraphic evidence indicates that there were dual consultations – we can identify three kinds: 'serial' consultations, in which related questions on the same subject were asked, one after another, at the same oracular sanctuary; 'simultaneous' consultations, where the same question was posed at the same time at different oracular sanctuaries; and 'successive' consultations, in which the same question was asked at different oracular sanctuaries one after another. There are numerous examples of each kind from across both ancient Greek literature and epigraphy.[31] These dual consultations may offer one answer to modern scholarship's concern with ways in which riddling or ambiguous oracular responses may have worked. It seems it was perfectly acceptable for consultants to check their interpretation of the answer they had received from one oracle by making another consultation (either by asking the same oracle or a different one; and either at the same time or later).

There are ample reasons why someone might check out their concerns with the god more than once: they might be asking about a matter causing them particular anxiety;[32] they might even be afraid that the oracle had been bribed.[33] In situations of political or personal debate, a single oracular statement would be an important focus for the formation of consensus; the addition of a second response would give additional significant weight to an important decision.

Often such secondary inquiries were, the evidence suggests, generated by the interpretation of the first question – which would then require further details in order that action could be carried out. Thus, for example, serial questions occur in accounts of oracular consultations relating to the foundations of new cults, where further information is needed to carry out the instructions of a particular pronouncement.[34] The consultation discussed above – in which Myskellos of Rhipai asks about where he should settle – offers an example of the foundation of a new settlement. Myskellos had to come back to the oracle to ask for directions to the place he had been told in a previous consultation that he was meant to be founding; and, according to the account he was given a third oracle when he still insisted on settling in Sybaris, not far from Kroton in Italy.

Turning to other patterns of multiple consultation, we find that the soldier and historian, Xenophon, thought that simultaneous consultations of oracles would be an appropriate way to seek guidance about foreign policy.[35] And, indeed, there is evidence that on the eve of the Sicilian expedition, Athens consulted Zeus Ammon in Egypt, Zeus at Dodona and Apollo at Delphi.[36] This may have happened at the same time or may be taken as an example of our last kind of consultation: the successive consultation – the visiting of one oracle after another. Similarly, before the battle of Leuktra in 371 BCE, the Thebans appear to have done a similar round-up of oracular consultation.[37] And, in case the literary nature of this evidence suggests that this description of battle preparation may be more imaginative than realistic, there is also evidence for this kind of relationality between oracular sanctuaries in inscriptions that record historical consultations. For example, in a question tablet from Dodona, one Archephon suggests in his question that he has come to ask for Zeus's help, having already been to consult an oracle of Apollo.[38]

To understand the power of divination, as well as thinking about the way questions were asked – and asked again – we also have to consider the ways in which answers were developed. There is the possibility that interpretation of the meaning of an oracle occurred between a diviner and his or her visitor during the consultation: this is well known from anthropological accounts of divination in other cultures.[39] For this to occur, it would not be necessary for the oracle to be in a riddling form: there is some evidence that oracles comprising single written responses were delivered as part of a longer conversation, in which the meaning of the pronouncement was teased out by means of 'a delicate negotiation of meaning' between consultant and the diviner.[40]

It is also possible that interpretation occurred long after the process of divination itself, once the visitor had returned to his or her community with the oracle's response. This may have been a key way for communities and individuals to have explored riddling oracles, in particular if they had to interpret divinatory language full of imagery. We have an example of this in a story that Herodotus reports about a key moment in the Persian Wars, when the Athenians, anticipating the invasion of their city by the Persian army, send ambassadors to consult the oracle at Delphi.[41] What follows includes a serial consultation, of the type described above, and also features an interesting process of interpretation. The first oracle given to the Athenian ambassadors – beginning, 'Why sit you, doomed ones? Fly to the world's end ... ' – instructs them in no uncertain terms to flee their city, which will be destroyed.[42] The ambassadors, unable to contemplate returning home with this message, go back to the Pythia and ask for another oracle. This time the Pythia proclaims a set of verses, which, while riddling, do at least hold out some hope, including the observation that 'the wooden wall only shall not fall, but help you and your children'; and ending with the information:

> Truly a day will come when you will meet him [the foe] face to face.
> Divine Salamis, you will bring death to women's sons
> When the corn is scattered, or the harvest gathered in.[43]

The ambassadors come back to Athens, where a debate ensues about the oracle's meaning. Various interpretations are put forward: for example, there is a debate as to whether the wooden walls mean the thorn-hedge around the city's Acropolis or the Athenian fleet. If the latter, however, the *chresmologoi* argue that the reference to Salamis must indicate where the Athenians will suffer a naval defeat. Finally, it is the general Themistokles who persuades the Athenians of the oracle's meaning – that the wooden walls mean the fleet, but that the reference to Salamis indicates an Athenian victory. This interpretation is followed by the Athenians' victory over the Persians at the battle of Salamis.

There are plenty of questions raised about the likely historical truth of this event. For example, while we can accept that dual consultations were common, it is striking that the Athenians are pictured as seeking a different answer. But for the purpose of exploring processes of interpretation, this is an intriguing account, especially in its description of the way that, once the ambassadors return to Athens, the community continues to debate the meaning of the oracle. We note that the story gives a key role to the general Themistokles in resolving the oracle's true meaning, but, while modern scholars have tended to draw attention to the role of the individual in this story – with Themistokles supplying the answer that no one else can find – the original account may emphasize more the team effort involved.[44] As noted already, while Themistokles provides the insight that 'divine Salamis' foretells the defeat of the Persians, the *chresmologoi* have already argued that the 'wooden wall' is the Athenian fleet.[45] Moreover, Herodotus does not state that Themistokles competed with the *chresmologoi* and beat them: he uses a more circuitous phrase to argue that the Athenians perceived his interpretation as something literally 'more to be chosen'. Thus, while the competitive aspect of the story cannot be denied, there is more than just a single individual involved. The process of interpretation includes not only Themistokles, but also the *chresmologoi*, and even the Athenians, who play an important role by accepting the interpretations given.

## V

Ancient divination could provide an effective tool of political advice in a number of different ways. To begin with, it provided a practical step in a process of decision-making. Whatever type of answer we think was provided as an oracular response, by embarking on a formal divinatory consultation, a person or community had to generate a useful question, and think about the different plausible options for action that might follow. Creating and posing a question was then most likely followed by a number of steps that would further narrow down any possible outcomes – either through additional oracular consultations, or through discussion of the interpretations of the meanings of resulting oracles with relevant stakeholders in the community. Throughout this process, those facing these decisions had to focus on the implications of different interpretations, considering their significance for the community around them.

And this brings us back to the story at the beginning of this essay. Rather than trying to settle for one interpretation or another (as do modern commentators), Plutarch describes the different opinions of Lampon and Anaxagoras in the following way:

> Now there was nothing, in my opinion, to prevent both of them, the naturalist and the seer, from being in the right of the matter; the one correctly divined the cause, the other the object or purpose. It was the proper province of the one to observe why anything happens, and how it comes to be what it is; of the other to declare for what purpose anything happens, and what it means.[46]

In this conclusion, Plutarch was not only drawing an important distinction between the naturalist and the seer, but he was also drawing attention to the central relationship between them, the complementary insights that they provided. Understanding the purpose and meanings with which people endow particular events, activities and objects are an essential skill in many walks of life, but perhaps especially the political arena. For the ancient Greeks, divination, especially oracular consultation, far from being simply an irrelevant expression of superstition, could provide a crucial instrument for exploring prevailing interpretations and reflecting on political advice.

## Notes

1    Roman Krznaric, 'Why We Need to Reinvent Democracy for the Long-term', *BBC Future*, 19 March 2019. http://www.bbc.com/future/story/20190318-can-we-reinvent-democracy-for-the-long-term. Accessed 5 June 2019. 'Lessons from the History of Democracy', *The Economist*, 10 April 2019. https://www.economist.com/open-future/2019/04/10/lessons-from-the-history-of-democracy. Accessed 5 June 2019.

2    As Neville Morley has argued, 'the specter of Thucydides has loomed larger in political discussions over the last few years than it ever has before' (see Neville Morley, 'Why Thucydides?' *Eidolon*, 18 July 2016. https://eidolon.pub/why-thucydides-

55b145152ec3. Accessed 5 June 2019). Some insights into recent uses of his text can be found, for example, at Daniel D. Drezner, 'The Good, the Bad and the Ugly Aspects of Thucydides in the Trump Administration', *Washington Post*, 22 June 2017. https://www.washingtonpost.com/news/posteverything/wp/2017/06/22/the-good-the-bad-and-the-ugly-aspects-of-thucydides-in-the-trump-administration/?noredirect=on&utm_term=.4f13869903f4. Accessed 5 June 2019; and Osita Nwanevu, 'Steve Bannon Boasts about His Love of Thucydides for All the Wrong Reasons', Slate.com, 21 June 2017. https://slate.com/news-and-politics/2017/06/steve-bannon-likes-thucydides-for-all-the-wrong-reasons.html. Accessed 5 June 2019.

3   'The art or practice that seeks to foresee or foretell future events or discover hidden knowledge usually by the interpretation of omens or by the aid of supernatural powers.' See Merriam-Webster Dictionary online. https://www.merriam-webster.com/dictionary/divination

4   Plut. *Per.* 6.3, trans. by Bernadotte Perrin, *Plutarch Lives, Volume III. Pericles and Fabius Maximus. Nicias and Crassus* Loeb Classical Library 65 (Cambridge, MA: Harvard University Press, 1916).

5   Donald Kagan, *Pericles of Athens and the Birth of Democracy* (New York: Macmillan, 1991),129.

6   In what follows, I have drawn on some of my other publications on divination, which are cited in the notes.

7   The Gudea Cylinders record the ritual building of a temple, in which King Gudea seeks permission from the god Ninĝirsu to build a temple, and receives omens in a dream, which must be interpreted. See the discussion in Angela Chapman, 'Gudea and the Gods: Intersecting Policy and Prophecy', *Studia Antiqua* 6 no. 1 (2008), 41–9 https://scholarsarchive.byu.edu/studiaantiqua/vol6/iss1/9. The edict of Theodosius the Great in 385 CE ordered all remaining oracles in the Roman Empire to be closed down. Nevertheless, oracular activity continued: some simply survived (e.g., oracles of Isis at Menouthis, in North Egypt and Philae in South Egypt survived until at least the end of the fifth century CE); others were adopted by new patrons (e.g., at Grand in France, Apollo Grannus was replaced by St. Libaire, who continued to heal people well into the eighteenth century).

8   See Paus. 7.25.10 and Fritz Graf, 'Rolling the Dice for an Answer', in *Mantike: Studies in Ancient Divination*, ed. Sarah Iles Johnston and Peter T. Struck (Leiden: Brill, 2005), 88.

9   The precise distinction between these two categories is much debated by modern scholars, but it seems likely that the former were more likely to have used various techniques of divination, such as reading the entrails of sacrificed animals, while the latter offered readings from collections of oracles, which could be consulted – using some randomizing device, such as a dice.

10  Trevor Curnow, *The Oracles of the Ancient World: A Comprehensive Guide* (London: Bristol Classical Press, 2004) provides an overview of the oracle sites of the ancient world.

11  Lisa Maurizio, 'The Voice at the Center of the World: The Pythias' Ambiguity and Authority', in *Making Silence Speak: Women's Voices in Greek Literature and Society*, ed. A. P. M. H. Lardinois (Princeton: Princeton University Press, 2001), 40, n. 14, suggests that only a third of the oracles we possess are likely to have been ambiguous; however, it is a characteristic that has captured both ancient and modern imaginations.

12  See Darren Lehoux, 'Drugs and the Delphic Oracle', *Classical World* 101 (2007): 41–56.

13  Lisa Maurizio, 'Anthropology and Spirit Possession: A Reconsideration of the Pythia's Role at Delphi', *Journal of Hellenic Studies* 115 (1995): 69–86, provides an overview of the scholarship.

14  Maurizio 'Anthropology and Spirit Possession', 72.

15  Quinton Deeley, 'The Pythia at Delphi: A Cognitive Reconstruction of Oracular Possession', in *Ancient Divination and Experience*, ed. Lindsay Driediger-Murphy and Esther Eidinow (Oxford: Oxford University Press, 2019), 227. See also Esther Eidinow, 'A Feeling for the Future: Ancient Greek Divination and Embodied Cognition', in *Evolution, Cognition, and the History of Religion: New Synthesis. Festschrift in Honour of Armin W. Geertz*, ed. Anders Klostergaard Petersen, Ingvild Sælid Gilhus, Luther Martin, Jeppe Sinding Jensen and Jesper Sørensen (Leiden: Brill, 2018), 447–60.

16  The division of types of divination – inspired or technical – is found in Plato's *Phaedrus* (244) and Cicero *On Divination* (1.6.11–12; 1.18.34; 2.11.26–27; 2.100). While it can be a useful heuristic device, its categories are not as clear-cut as they may, at first sight, seem: see discussion by Michael Flower, *The Seer in Ancient Greece* (Berkeley/London/Los Angeles: University of California Press, 2008), 84–7.

17  Dem. 21.51–4.

18  See Esther Eidinow, *Oracles, Curses, and Risk among the Ancient Greeks* (Oxford: Oxford University Press, 2013), 64.

19  Robert Parker, 'Greek States and Greek Oracles', in *Oxford Readings in Greek Religion*, ed. Richard Buxton (Oxford: Oxford University Press, 2000); also Hugh Bowden, *Classical Athens and the Delphic Oracle: Divination and Democracy* (Cambridge: Cambridge University Press, 2005).

20  *IG* II² 204 ll. 42–54, in which oracles from Delphi are read to the Assembly. The oracles were probably stored with other public documents in the *metroon* (see James P. Sickinger, *Public Records and Archives in Classical Athens* (London and Chapel Hill: The University of North Carolina Press, 1999), 136).

21  Dem. 19.197, 21.52; Dein. 1.78, 98, and Cic. *Div.* 1.43, 95.

22  Plut. *Nic.* 13 implies that the Athenian politicians Nikias and Alkibiades retained personal seers.

23  E.g., *IG* II² 17 + *SEG* 15.84 + *SEG* 16.42 records for example the award of Athenian citizenship to the seer Sthorys of Thasos for the divinatory sacrifices he made before the naval battle of Knidos. Lampon and Hierokles were given permanent dining privileges in the city's Prytaneum, see Flower, *The Ancient Seer*, 122–4.

24  Nassos Papalexandrou, *The Visual Poetics of Power: Warriors, Youths, and Tripods in Early Greece. Greek Studies: Interdisciplinary Approaches* (Lanham, MD: Lexington Books, 2005), 62; and George Forrest, 'Colonisation and the Rise of Delphi', *Historia* 6 (1957): 160–75.

25  Herbert W. Parke and Donald E. W. Wormell, *Delphic Oracle, vol. 1, The History* (Oxford: Blackwell, 1956), 34.

26  Herbert W. Parke and Donald E. W. Wormell, *Delphic Oracle, vol. 2, The Responses* (Oxford: Blackwell, 1956), no. 43; Diodorus Siculus 8.17.1.

27  Catherine Morgan, *Athletes and Oracles: The Transformation of Olympia and Delphi in the Eighth Century BC* (Cambridge: Cambridge University Press, 1990), especially 156–7; Parker, 'Greek States and Greek Oracles', 80; see also Maurizio, 'The Voice', 44. Those that take these accounts seriously have argued that such ambiguity may have protected an oracle from falsification, while others have noted how this quality would have thrown the consultant back on to their own interpretation.

28 Esther Eidinow, '"What Will Happen to Me if I Leave?" Ancient Greek Oracles, Slaves and Slave Owners', in *Slaves and Religions in Graeco-Roman Antiquity and the Modern Americas*, ed. Steven Hodkinson and Dick Geary (Cambridge: Cambridge Scholars, 2011), but see Robert Parker, 'Seeking Advice from Zeus at Dodona', *Greece & Rome* 63 (2016): 69–90.

29 See Eidinow, *Oracles, Curses, and Risk*, 76, no. 5.

30 See Aesch. *Ctes.* 131, where the politician Aeschines accuses his rival, Demosthenes, of ignoring unfavourable omens.

31 See Esther Eidinow, 'Testing the Oracle? On the Experience of (Multiple) Oracle Consultations', in *Ancient Divination and Experience*, ed. Driediger-Murphy and Eidinow, for more in-depth discussion of the examples given here and below.

32 Eidinow, *Oracles, Curses and Risk*, 72–3.

33 Xen. *Hell.* 6.4.7 and Diod. Sic. 15.53. Bribery of the Pythia: Hdt. 6.66.

34 Eidinow, *Oracles, Curses and Risk*, 52–3.

35 Xen. *Poroi* 6.2.

36 Michael Flower, 'Athenian Religion and the Peloponnesian War', in *Athenian Art in the Peloponnesian War*, ed. Olga Palagia (Cambridge: Cambridge University Press, 2003), 10: Plut *Nic.* 13 and 14, Paus. 8.11.12, and Plut. *Mor* 403b and *Nic.* 13, respectively.

37 See Paus. 4.32.5–6.

38 See Eidinow, *Oracles, Curses, and Risk*, 113, no. 4.

39 As summarized by Philip Peek, *African Divination Systems: Ways of Knowing* (Bloomington, IN: Indiana University Press, 1991), 195.

40 As William Klingshirn ('Christian Divination in Late Roman Gaul: The Sortes Sangallenses', in *Mantike: Studies in Ancient Divination*, ed. Sarah Iles Johnston and Peter T. Struck [Leiden: Brill, 2005], 109), has suggested in his description of the use of the divinatory text the Sortes Sangallenses (a late antique Latin lot collection).

41 Hdt. 7.140–144.

42 Hdt. 7.140.2, trans. here and below Aubrey de Sélincourt, revised John Marincola, *Herodotus. The Histories* (London: Penguin Books, 1996 [1954]).

43 Hdt. 7.141.3 and 4, respectively.

44 As I have noted elsewhere, see Esther Eidinow, 'Oracular Consultation, Fate, and the Concept of the Individual', in *Divination in the Ancient* World. *Religious Options and the Individual*, ed. Veit Rosenberger (Stuttgart: Franz Steiner Verlag, 2013), 21–39.

45 As James Evans, 'The Oracle of the "Wooden Wall"', *The Classical Journal* 78 (October–November 1982): 24–9.

46 Plut. *Per.* 6.3. Indeed, this explanation foreshadows more recent ontological approaches to the role of objects in divination. See Martin Holbraad and Morten Axel Pederesen, *The Ontological Turn: An Anthropological Exposition* (Cambridge: Cambridge University Press, 2017), 220–7.

# Chapter 3

## *OBLIQUUS DUCTUS*: INDIRECT POLITICAL ADVICE IN THE RENAISSANCE

## Joanne Paul

'[Morus:] "On the contrary, by the indirect approach you must seek and strive to the best of your power to handle matters tactfully. What you cannot turn to good you must at least make as little bad as you can."

...

[Hythloday:] "As to that indirect approach of yours, I cannot see its relevancy; I mean your advice to use my endeavours, if all things cannot be made good, at least to handle them tactfully and, as far as one may, to make them as little bad as possible ... By their evil companionship, either you will be seduced yourself or, keeping your own integrity and innocence, you will be made a screen for the wickedness and folly of others. Thus you are far from being able to make anything better by that indirect approach of yours."'[1]

After a long period of relative obscurity, in the twenty-first century, the subject of what political advice is and should be has re-emerged with resounding consequences. That is not to say, of course, that political counsel had ever entirely disappeared. Instead, as Andrew Blick put it, advisers had come to 'live in the dark'.[2] As my own recent work suggests, following the debates of the English Civil War and the reorientation of political discourse to the question of sovereignty, counsel 'fade[d] into the shadows of political thought'.[3] In the twenty-first century, we are perhaps paying the price for not giving sufficient attention to what was happening in those shadows, and can look – just in the UK – to the pivotal role played by advice in the unexpected events of the Iraq War,[4] Brexit[5] and the climate emergency[6] for some small glimpse of its impact. In the world of policy analysis, political advice remains a subject of discussion, but it has been nearly five hundred years since this subject was widely considered to be at the centre of political theorizing. There is, therefore, good reason to return to the context of the sixteenth century to aid our thinking about this subject today.

In particular, the questions that Richard Mulgan asked of political advice in the wake of the controversy surrounding the reports of WMDs and the Iraq War are even more relevant over a decade later, and were just as familiar (vocabulary aside) to the sixteenth century:

> What counts as truth or objectivity in advice? Can the very concept of truth or objectivity in politics make sense in a post-positivist world-view? Is politicized distortion or misrepresentation a result of pressure from politicians or self-motivated? Does public attribution of evidence by politicians to supposedly independent officials provide an added pressure towards the politicization of such evidence? Do public servants have an ethical commitment to the accuracy of the public record?[7]

This chapter will investigate only one aspect of the first of these questions, by exploring sixteenth-century debates surrounding the 'indirect' approach to political advice-giving. At the heart of these disputes was the question of truth, and the balance that must be maintained by political advisers between truth and – to borrow Mulgan's phrasing – 'the concerns of their political masters'.[8]

Thomas More, in his *Utopia* of 1516 – arguably the best known of the texts on counsel published during the English 'monarchy of counsel'[9] – gives over much of the crux of his 'dialogue of counsel'[10] to a discussion of what has in modern times been translated as the 'indirect approach' (*obliquus ductus*). This term is mentioned no fewer than three times (above) in only a few pages at the climax of the first book and shortly before the transition into the discussion of the island of Utopia in Book II. Attempts to understand fully what More meant by *obliquus ductus*, however, are rare,[11] despite the repetition of the importance of this concept, for More's work and the 'discourse of counsel' in which he was participating.[12]

There are a variety of ways this phrase, *obliquus ductus* in the original Latin, might have been interpreted even in More's own time; like much in *Utopia*, More's use of it remains vague and ambiguous. Thinking through the various interpretations of *obliquus ductus* nevertheless helps us explore a number of the strategies for dealing with the Renaissance 'problem of counsel', which may have some resonance with the issues of today. Ranging from the use of rhetorical techniques to outright deception, meanings associated with *obliquus ductus* are all part of the humanist model of counsel, in which the counsellor leads his prince towards virtue, often by whatever means necessary. This model would be outright rejected towards the end of the Renaissance, by writers such as Hobbes, in favour of the subjection of counsel to sovereignty, and a more straightforward delivery of practical fact-based advice. Standing in opposition to the 'railing' associated with what was termed *parrhesia*, that is frank speech, *obliquus ductus* presents an alternative – and more roundabout – way of presenting truthful and virtuous advice, which for many in the Renaissance (as for More's interlocutor Hythloday) opened too wide a door to outright deception and a politics devoid of truth. Attempts to shut that door have only served to push counsel into the shadows of political thinking, with significant consequences for the post-truth politics of the twenty-first century.

*I*

It is now widely acknowledged that the period from the end of the Wars of the Roses to the English Civil War saw a shift of focus to counsel as a central concept of political discourse.[13] This 'monarchy of counsel', as J. G. A. Pocock put it, brought with it a 'problem of counsel', a phrase first coined in reference to the subject of Book I of More's *Utopia*, and now applied widely in the period in question.[14] The problem of counsel was well known and discussed in the period, as Erasmus puts it in reference to the advice of Martin Luther:

> [Luther] should spare the dignity of rulers, for if they are inopportunely insulted or admonished they do not improve, but rather become embittered and sometimes stir up dangerous storms. As a result, the critic loses his authority and sometimes his life, and the advice its effect. While it is never lawful to oppose the truth, still it is sometimes expedient to conceal it at the right time.[15]

As Erasmus explains, inappropriate advice risks two possible consequences: (1) making the situation the adviser seeks to rectify worse (or at the least not making any change) and (2) a loss of position and perhaps even life, in which case the adviser loses his ability to advise in future. It is thus a problem not just of a threat to the individual, but also of one to the continued status of good advice in that court. Erasmus here turns to well-timed concealment of the truth as the solution to this problem of counsel, and there is much to say on that topic.[16] The other much-propounded solution, and the one to which More turns in *Utopia*, is changing the rhetorical tone of the advice and, in the end, adopting the 'indirect approach' or *obliquus ductus*. Like Erasmus's advice, this too could mean a significant compromise on truth.

There is one more element that must be added, in addition to the discourse and problem of counsel, and that is the 'paradox of counsel'.[17] Monarchs were expected to receive counsel, or else risk being thought tyrants and even being overthrown (as the example of Richard II had demonstrated).[18] Contrastingly, however, such a condition of legitimacy could potentially undermine a monarch's authority, especially if it was expected not just that he or she hear advice but also that he or she act directly on it. To put it another, starker, way: 'if counsel is obligatory, it impinges upon sovereignty. If it is not, it then becomes irrelevant and futile'.[19] The first wave of humanists of the Northern Renaissance generally erred on the side of avoiding the second consequence, and not minding much if their advice meant that the sovereign was not quite so sovereign. Counsel and the counsellor, for these humanists, served to mitigate the lottery of hereditary monarchy and to impart republican principles into a decidedly un-republican context.[20] The humanist 'model' of counsel, then, saw the prince as led or even ruled by his or her counsellors' prudence or reason. Dangers might come from corrupt counsellors, to be sure, but there was little worry on the part of the humanists that this took away from the prince's own sovereignty. Both these issues gained traction through the course of the sixteenth century and erupted in dramatic fashion in the context of the English Civil War.[21]

Returning to More's early-sixteenth-century context: to argue that the prince ought to be led, by all the impressively strong techniques of humanist rhetorical training, to virtue by his counsellors, was hardly shocking to More and his contemporaries. It was at the boundaries of this truism, however, that debate arose. Could a humanist counsellor, dedicated to virtue and truth, use deception to achieve those aims in order to avoid the problem of counsel? This is the question at the heart of More's discussion of the *obliquus ductus*, which by the sixteenth century already had a long history.

## II

As with so much in More's *Utopia*, the three references to *obliquus ductus* in the dialogue of counsel in Book I are not throwaway remarks, but rather make reference to a rich classical tradition and its Renaissance recovery. As Lucia Carboli Montefusco has pointed out, the rhetorical *ductus* first appears in the three-part rhetorical handbook of Consultus Fortunatianus, a fourth- (or possibly fifth-) century rhetorician.[22] Fortunatianus followed Quintilian in much of his work, though he added the discussion of *ductus*, used but not elaborated upon by Quintilian, and its relationship to openness or *verum* in the first book of his treatise.[23] *Ductus* can be defined a number of different ways, but speaks to the path or direction the speaker takes in his speech, often in relation to how honest or open he chooses to make it: the 'directions of cause' (*conduções da causa*).[24] We can think of *ductus* as a sort of aqueduct (and Fortunatianus's follower Martianus Capella stated this connection explicitly): the speaker makes the path, and the listeners – the water – follow it towards the goal he had set out.[25]

Fortunatianus gives a number of different versions of what the *ductus* can be: *simplex* ('what he says is what he really means'), *subtilis* ('the orator does not really want what he seems to be pleading for'), *figuratus* ('if fear pushes him to avoid the explicit mention of the crucial point') and finally *obliquus* ('because of fear the speaker might not be willing to show his *verum consilium*').[26] Notably, in the case of *obliquus ductus*, Fortunatianus gives the example of 'pleading against a tyrant who, after resigning from his tyranny, applies for a public office' [*Tyrannus deposuit dominationem sub pacto abolitio[n]is. uult petere magistratum*].[27] In order to prevent him from attaining it, the orator chooses a strategy (or *consilium*: 'the faculty of judgement which enables the orator to gauge and respond successfully to the circumstances in which he is speaking') for planning his path or *ductus* that is not based on truth.[28] *Concilium* can, of course, be translated as counsel, or even advice, but in the context of classical rhetoric tended to relate more to the orator's own judgement in setting out his *ductus*. If the cause of the dispute relates to the past, then the *concilium* will be true and the *ductus* simple, if it relates to the present or future, a less straightforward path will be required. Finally, if it produces fear, then the speech will take on the *obliquus ductus*.[29] The connection, therefore, to the problem of counsel is not a difficult one to make, and the idea of the *ductus* was consistent with a humanist model of leading the counselled prince.[30]

There are two sources for this discussion in the Renaissance. The first, highlighted by Mary Carruthers, comes through the tradition of medieval monasticism. Adopted by Augustine and his followers, the *ductus* becomes associated with prayerful meditation: a path to God and tranquillity.[31] The second was mediated by the Cretan scholar George of Trebizond, writing in the fifteenth century.[32] George of Trebizond reorganizes the categories of paths set out by Fortunatianus, placing *obliquus ductus* under the larger umbrella of *figuratus ductus* and giving it a more precise definition (paraphrased by Virginia Cox): 'when [the orator] wants to persuade [the audience] of the opposite of what he is saying, and at the same time adopts an oblique approach to his ostensible case'.[33] This work, his *Rhetoricorum libri quinque*, was well known in the early sixteenth century, and there is little reason why More would not have encountered it, at the very least at second hand. More's friend and collaborator Erasmus had asked to see the text in a letter of 1500, and in 1516, the year that *Utopia* was published, he writes to Guillaume Budé, one of the humanists to contribute a letter to the publication of *Utopia*, that he had studied George's work.[34] Andrea Frank has even suggested that this longest of the paratextual letters is an example of rhetorical indirectness.[35]

These ideas were picked up in Renaissance Venice by the humanist Ermolao Barbaro in discussion of the mismatch between an academic rhetorical education and the demands of a republican civic life, a theme that sits very close to the themes of More's 'dialogue of counsel', which contrasts 'academic philosophy' with a 'more civil philosophy'.[36] Barbaro praises the technical aspects of oratory, not the moral ones, and focuses on *consilium* and *ductus* (as well as *insinuatio*) as a means to think through the issue of dealing with 'morally unpalatable' topics rhetorically, even if towards the defence of truth.[37]

### III

There is only one text other than *Utopia* in which Thomas More uses the term *obliquus ductus*: his *History of King Richard the Third*, written in the same period as *Utopia* (roughly 1513 to 1519) but not published until after his death. Like *Utopia*, *Richard the Third* deals with the theme of counsel, but presents a dystopian vision of counsel gone wrong, at least until the end of the text, when its redemptive power is alluded to.

The phrase is employed explicitly in the context of the propagandistic persuasions of one of Richard III's men: Doctor Shaa. At a 'sermon at Poules Crosse', Shaa is asked to 'encline the peple to the protectours ghostly purpose' by alleging that the sons of Edward IV were bastards, and therefore not eligible to take the crown.[38] He is even allowed to suggest that Edward IV was illegitimate. Given, however, that this could imply that Richard's own mother committed adultery, he must ensure that 'yᵉ point should be lesse & more favourably handled, not euen fully plain & directly, but that yᵉ matter should be *touched a slope craftily*, as though men spared in yᵗ point to speke al the trouth for fere of his displeasure'.[39] The key phrase here is 'touched a slope craftily', as it appears to be a rendering of *obliquus ductus*. *Richard the Third* was written more or less simultaneously in English and Latin, with neither finished. By all appearances, More went back and forth in his writing, sometimes beginning with the Latin, sometimes with the English.[40] There are even moments where we might be able to detect from which of the two versions More was translating. This description of Shaa's speech might be one of them, as More has the difficult task of attempting to translate *obliquus ductus*: 'sed eum locum obloquo ingrediendum ductu, atque arte tractandum, velutique timide'.[41] Here, the *obliquus ductus* or 'a slope craftily' is a technique used by a spin doctor for a tyrant to convince the people of the illegitimacy of a legitimate claimant to the throne. This is an interesting choice, if we recall the definition of the *obliquus ductus* noted above; the description of its use directly related to the fear of a tyrant. By using this technique, Shaa – and More – identifies Richard III as such a tyrant who, although he has not been thrown out of public office, is seeking election to it. Although employed to dubious ends, the technique itself is not sinister, as Shaa is only feigning the *obliquus ductus*, having been instructed to use it by the tyrant.

There is another instance in the text that might allow us to see the 'indirect approach' in action: when the figure of John Morton, who also appears in *Utopia*, uses his rhetorical ability to right the wrong caused by Richard III's tyrannous usurpation.[42] Notably, he does this by stoking the pride and ambition of the Duke of Buckingham to rebellion. Whether Morton is using the technique remains an open question, as More's Latin text does not extend as far as the English here, so we cannot check for the appearance of the phrase. In More's words, Morton 'craftely sought y^e waies to pricke [Buckingham] forwarde taking alwaies thoccasion of his coming & so keeping himself close w^tin his bondes, that he rather semed him to follow hym then to lead him'.[43] Had More translated this into the Latin, could this have been another instance of the *obliquus ductus*? There is reason to believe that the 'craftely sought … waies' of Morton are another example and translation of the *obliquus ductus*, and that Morus's suggestion in *Utopia* is thus a genuine one; Morton is presented as almost single-handedly saving the kingdom in *Richard the Third*, and he does so by, arguably, employing this rhetorical technique in his counsel. Deceptive techniques and a compromise on truth, therefore, become essential to the commonwealth-redeeming act of political advice-giving, not a threat to it.

## IV

The example of More's *Richard the Third* demonstrates two important points. First, that recovering an understanding of the *obliquus ductus* involves thinking carefully about translation. Second, that humanists were aware that this approach could be used for dubious purposes as well as honourable ones.

So, how are we to translate *obliquus ductus*? More's contemporary and fellow writer on counsel, Thomas Elyot, translates *obliquus* as 'contrary to straight' and *ductus* as 'ledde' in his *Dictionary* of 1540: More's 'a slope' therefore seems consistent, as does the notion of indirectness, though both miss the 'craftily' also associated with the term.[44] The English State Papers from the period are full of references, usually pejorative ones, to indirectness – usually some form of 'indirect means' or 'practices' – at times associating it with 'crafte'.[45] A letter from the Privy Council in 1545 connects the 'indirect meane' to 'grop[ing] the fox', an image with decidedly Machiavellian connotations.[46] The phrase is just as often applied, however, to the suspicions of ambassadors or other political actors as it is used to encourage such practices on the part of the English, and comprises part of an arms race of deception that defines late Tudor politics.

Perhaps it is for this reason that when Ralph Robinson came to translate *Utopia* in 1551 and 1556, he chose to translate *obliquus ductus* as 'with a crafty wile and a subtle train' (Robinson had a tendency to provide two phrases in the English for one in the Latin), all three times that it appears.[47] As Dominic Baker-Smith has suggested, this 'sounds closer to Machiavelli than to More', though the suggestion that Robinson 'lose[s] the thread' here is perhaps unfair.[48] Robinson was translating in a context where elements of Machiavellianism were present. There is also the puzzle of accounting for the use of 'craft' in reference to Morton's approach at the close of *Richard the Third*, which, if not an example of *obliquus ductus*, is certainly not a condemnation of it. This pairing of terms, 'wile' and 'train' – both meaning a trick or lie, with roots in hunting and trapping – also appears in Foxe's *Book of Martyrs*, where they are once again used positively; it is a 'godly trayne & wile', not a sinister one.[49] Therefore, even in the context of Machiavellianism and translated into terms more explicitly associated with outright deception, the *obliquus ductus* (or something like it) could still be employed in a positive sense. The determining factor was the end of the counsel, not the means of giving it.

V

There remain, however, a number of contemporary critiques of this approach, which are worth outlining. The first is expressed by Hythloday's objection: the suspicion of such advice and its uncomfortable relationship to truth. As others have shown, *parrhesia*, or frankly speaking, was much lauded in the Renaissance, though most did not advocate it in its purest form, stripped of rhetorical ornamentation.[50] Even Elyot, who presents two *parrhesiastes* in the form of Pasquil in *Pasquil the Playne* and Plato in *The Knowledge Which Maketh a Wise Man*, allows for arguments for the tempering of the frank presentation of truth to power. Pasquil, for instance, is a 'railing' *parrhesiastes*, but is forced to be, as he has been barred from the court of his master.[51] Likewise, though a truth-speaker, before presenting his advice to the tyrant Dionysius Plato waited until an opportune moment presented itself, when his words would have the most effect, and then only presented his advice through an oration praising good kingship, not directly condemning his master's tyranny.[52] Most others, including Erasmus and More, as well as Baldassare Castiglione in his *Courtier*, condemn unembellished truth-speaking as bringing about, rather than avoiding, the problem of counsel. Castiglione, for instance, rejects the unadorned counsel of the 'grave Philosopher' who would show a prince 'plainlie and without enie circomstance the horrible face of true vertue and teache them good maners and what the lief [sic] of a good Prince ought to be, I ame assured they wolde abhorr him at first sight, as a most venimous serpent or elles they wolde make him a laughinge stock, as a most vile matter'.[53] To 'bende' the prince to virtue, the courtier must use all of the skills available to him to 'purchase him the good will and allure unto him the minde of his Prince, that he maye make him a free and safe passage to comune with him in every matter without troubling him'.[54] The arguments from pure *parrhesia* tend to be, as they are in *Utopia*, presented by an interlocutor in a dialogue, who is then shown the error of his ways.

Of more significance is another objection, associated with the above but not present in More's text. This is the rejection of the model from which the *obliquus ductus* emerges and in which it forms a central component. The humanists had clung to the assumption that the well-educated, experienced humanist ought to lead his prince to virtue through rhetorical means, one of the most notable being the indirect approach. The association of this, however, with duplicity in the context of a political discourse saturated with suspicion of Machiavellian self-interest, brings the entire model into question. The Machiavellian model of counsel reversed that of the more orthodox humanists, suggesting that counsellors ought to be dependent on their prince's prudence, rather than the other way around. This was particularly worrying in the English context, where the second half of the sixteenth century saw a minor and two women (Edward VI, Mary I and Elizabeth I) on the throne, all of whom were seen to be especially vulnerable to being misled by self-interested counsellors, and yet more in need of advice and guidance than an adult male monarch.[55]

The epitome of this rejection is expressed by Thomas Hobbes, following the intense debates over the source and content of viable political counsel in the opening decades of the seventeenth century.[56] Hobbes wishes to see a politics stripped of rhetoric and considers one of the biggest threats to the commonwealth to be the manipulation of words and their meanings.[57] Counsellors are recast, not as educated individuals who lead a wayward prince to virtue through indirect paths by the overwhelming force of their rhetoric, but as conduits for factual information about political realities. This is perhaps best demonstrated in Hobbes's own counsel, intended for Charles I in late 1643 or 1644, in which he presents knowledge of the situation of other states and the passions of men in a straightforward proposal, which is devoid of rhetorical structure.[58] Although he suggests that persuasive speech be used to move the passions of others to abandon a course that endangers the commonwealth, he as an adviser does not use any himself.[59] This is consistent with what he says on the topic in *Leviathan*, an advisory text which is nothing if not direct. Counsellors ought to hold the same position as 'Memory and Mentall Discourse' does in a man, but whereas for a man 'the naturall objects of sense … work upon him without passion, or interest of their own', men do have their own ends and passions, which if inconsistent with those of the counselled can lead the latter astray.[60] This is most clearly expressed in his – ironically passionate – condemnation of the misinterpretation of counsel in chapter 25 of *Leviathan*: 'How fallacious it is to judge of the nature of things, by the ordinary and inconstant use of words, appeareth in nothing more, than in the confusion of Counsels, and Commands'.[61] Here, Hobbes makes special mention of those who use 'exhortation' in their counsel, appealing to the 'common Passions, and opinions of men' by use of 'Similtudes, Metaphors, Examples, and other tooles of Oratory' in order to persuade a case which emerges 'from his own occasions'.[62] Instead, disapproving of roundabout rhetorical attempts to lead the prince through trickery and 'craft', Hobbes believed that 'the best Counsell ... is to be taken from the generall informations, and complaints of the people' which did not stand 'in derogation of the essentiall Rights of Soveraignty'.[63] It is Hobbes who set the agenda for 'modern' political discourse: a discourse focused on sovereignty and with little official space for political advice.

*VI*

Hobbes's solution to the paradox of counsel, which seeks to reject the humanists' answer to the problem of counsel, in fact solves very little. The insistence that political advice ought simply to relate straightforward political realities does not actually translate into unbiased objectivity in practice. How much an 'indirect approach' is employed by today's political advisers would be almost impossible to determine, which is in many ways the point. Political advising is, and has long been, a muddled mess, full of problems, paradoxes and inherent tensions – one of the most pressing being around the relationship between 'truthful' advice and advice that gets the job done. Relegating it to the 'shadows' has not worked. Headache that it may be, it is time to bring political counsel back into the light of theoretical scrutiny and to the centre of political discourse.

*Notes*

1    Thomas More, *The Yale Edition of the Complete Works of St. Thomas More: Utopia*, ed. Edward Surtz and J. H. Hexter, vol. 4 (New Haven: Yale University Press, 1965), 99–103. Latin: "'sed obliquo ductu conandum est, atque adnitendum tibi, uti pro tua uirili omnia tractes commode." ... "Nam obliquus ille ductus tuus non uideo quid sibi uelit ... quorum peruersa consuetudine uel deprauaberis, uel ipse integer atque innocens, alienae malitiae, stultitiaeque praetexeris, tantum abest ut aliquid possit in melius obliquo illo ductu conuertere". Compare: "'Instead, by an indirect approach, you must strive and struggle as best you can to handle everything tactfully – and thus what you cannot turn to good, you may at least make as little bad as possible" ... "As for that 'indirect approach' of yours, I simply don't know what you mean ... Either they will seduce you by their evil ways, or, if you remain honest and innocent, you will be made a screen for the knavery and folly of others. You wouldn't stand a chance of changing anything for the better by that 'indirect approach'". Thomas More, *Utopia*, ed. George M. Logan and Robert M. Adams (Cambridge: Cambridge University Press, 2002), 36–7.

2 Andrew Blick, *People Who Live in the Dark: The History of the Special Adviser in British Politics* (London: Politico's Publishing, 2004).

3 Joanne Paul, *Counsel and Command in Early Modern English Thought* (Cambridge: Cambridge University Press, 2020), 216.

4 See, for instance, Richard Mulgan, 'Truth in Government and the Politicization of Public Service Advice', *Public Administration* 85, no. 3 (2007): 569–86.

5 See, for instance, Geoffrey Evans and Anand Menon, *Brexit and British Politics* (Cambridge: Polity Press, 2017), preface; Karin Forss and Linnea Magro, 'Facts or Feelings, Facts and Feelings? The Post-Democracy Narrative in the Brexit Debate', *European Policy Analysis* 2, no. 2 (2016): 12–17.

6 See for instance: Sonja Boehmer-Christiansen, 'Global Climate Protection Policy: The Limits of Scientific Advice: Part 1', *Global Environmental Change* 4, no. 2 (1994): 140–59; Hans von Storch, 'Climate Research and Policy Advice: Scientific and Cultural Constructions of Knowledge', *Environmental Science & Policy* 12, no. 7 (2009): 741–7; Susan Owens, 'Learning across Levels of Governance: Expert Advice and the Adoption of Carbon Dioxide Emissions Reduction Targets in the UK', *Global Environmental Change* 20, no. 3: *Governance, Complexity and Resilience* (2010): 394–401.

7 Mulgan, 'Truth in Government', 570.

8 Mulgan, 'Truth in Government', 570.

9 J. G. A. Pocock, 'A Discourse of Sovereignty: Observations on the Work in Progress', in *Political Discourse in Early Modern Britain*, ed. Nicholas Phillipson and Quentin Skinner (Cambridge: Cambridge University Press, 1993), 395–6.

10 J. H. Hexter, 'Thomas More and the Problem of Counsel', in *Quincentennial Essays on St. Thomas More: Selected Papers from the Thomas More College Conference* (Boone: Albion, 1978), 55–66.

11 I have only been able to identify a handful of attempts: More, *CW: Utopia*, 373–4; Dominic Baker-Smith, 'On Translating More's *Utopia*', *Canadian Review of Comparative Literature/Revue Canadienne de Littérature Comparée* 41, no. 4 (2014): 500–1; Michael Foley, 'The Difference Theology Makes: A Reflection on the First Margin Note in Thomas More's Utopia', *Moreana* 54 (Number 207), no. 1 (2017): 74. None draw the connections discussed in what follows.

12 John Guy, 'The Rhetoric of Counsel in Early Modern England', in *Tudor Political Culture*, ed. Dale Hoak (Cambridge: Cambridge University Press, 1995), 292–310.

13 See for instance Guy, 'Rhetoric of Counsel', 292–310; Jacqueline Rose (ed.), *The Politics of Counsel in England and Scotland, 1286–1707, Proceedings of the British Academy* (Oxford: Oxford University Press, 2016); Paul, *Counsel and Command*.

14 Hexter, 'Thomas More and the Problem of Counsel', 55–66.

15 Erasmus, *Erasmus and His Age: Selected Letters of Desiderius Erasmus*, ed. Hans J. Hillerbrand (New York: Harper and Row Ltd, 1970), 160.

16 A theme considered frequently in Paul, *Counsel and Command*.

17 Judith Ferster, *Fictions of Advice: The Literature and Politics of Counsel in Late Medieval England* (Philadelphia: University of Pennsylvania Press, 1996), 39–40; Paul, *Counsel and Command*.

18 Paul, *Counsel and Command*, 8.

19 Paul, *Counsel and Command*, 1.

20 Paul, *Counsel and Command*, 15–16.

21 See Paul, *Counsel and Command*, chapter 7.

22 Lucia Calboli Montefusco, 'Ductus and Color: The Right Way to Compose a Suitable Speech', *Rhetorica: A Journal of the History of Rhetoric* 21, no. 2 (2003): 113.

23 Mary Carruthers, *The Craft of Thought: Meditation, Rhetoric, and the Making of Images, 400–1200* (Cambridge: Cambridge University Press, 2000), 78.

24 Virginia Cox, 'Rhetoric and Humanism in Quattrocento Venice', *Renaissance Quarterly* 56, no. 3 (2003): 657; Carruthers, *Craft of Thought*, 78; Izabella Lombardi Garbellini, 'Tradução e comentário da Arte Retórica de Consulto Fortunaciano' (Thesis, Universidade de São Paulo, 2010), 14.

25 Carruthers, *Craft of Thought*, 78.

26 Montefusco, 'Ductus and Color', 120. There is also *mixtus*, when 'the orator combines two of these different ways to plead a case'.

27 Montefusco, 'Ductus and Color', 120.

28 Cox, 'Rhetoric and Humanism', 656–7. In this, Fortunatianus is apparently expanding upon Quintilian's discussion of figures in Book IX of his *Institutio Oratoria*, where he allows for 'circuitous and indirect methods' [*deverticulum et anfractus*] and 'indirect insinuations' [*obliquus sententia*], while also deriding them as the purview of the weaker orator; Quintilian, *Institutio Oratoria*, IX, 2: 78, 79, 94.

29 Garbellini, 'Tradução e comentário', 29.

30 Notably, one of the ways of leading listeners through one's chosen *ductus*, especially if it is not simple, is to add (in Fortunatianus's words) *modus* or (in Capella's) *color*. 'Colours' in rhetoric often refer to rhetorical figures and in the Renaissance more specifically to a particular rhetorical figure: *paradiastole* or 'rhetorical description', the attempt to recast a perceived vice as a virtue, or vice versa; see Quentin Skinner, 'Paradiastole: Redescribing the Vices as Virtues', in *Renaissance Figures of Speech*, ed. Sylvia Adamson, Gavin Alexander and Katrin Ettenhuber (Cambridge: Cambridge University Press, 2007), 149–65.

31 Carruthers, *Craft of Thought*, 80.

32 Cox, 'Rhetoric and Humanism', 657–8.

33 Cox, 'Rhetoric and Humanism', 658.

34 John Monfasani, *George of Trebizond: A Biography and a Study of His Rhetoric and Logic* (Leiden: Brill, 1976), 318 n. 3.

35 Andrea Frank, 'Humanist Guillaume Budé's Artful Rhetoric: Responding in Kind to Utopia', *Moreana* 54 (Number 208), no. 2 (2017): 204–24.

36 Cox, Rhetoric and Humanism', 652–94; More, *CW: Utopia*, 99.

37 Cox, 'Rhetoric and Humanism', 658–9.

38 Thomas More, *The Yale Edition of the Complete Works of St. Thomas More: History of King Richard III*, ed. Richard S. Sylvester, vol. 2 (New Haven: Yale University Press, 1963), 59.

39 More, *CW: Richard III*, 59. This is in contrast to the point about Edward's children, which 'should be openly declared & inforsed to the vttermost'. Italics added.

40 Alison Hanham, 'The Texts of Thomas More's Richard III', *Renaissance Studies* 21, no. 1 (2007): 62–84.

41 More, *CW: Richard III*, 59, 237.

42 I have suggested that this is the case elsewhere: Paul, *Counsel and Command*, 29, though the matter is very much up for debate.

43 More, *CW: Richard III*, 91–2.

44 Thomas Elyot, *The Dictionary* (London, 1538), sig. Pii$^{v}$.

45 'Instructions geven by the Kinges Highnes to his trusty clerc and counsaillour Maister William Knight, Doctor of the Lawe, the Kynges Ambassadour with the Lady Margaret, touching certeyn matiers to be treated and done with the Duc of Burbon, as folowith' in *State Papers Published under the Authority of his Majesty's Commission: King Henry the Eighth, 1830–1852. Vol. 6: Part V: Foreign Correspondence, 1473–1527*

(London: Her Majesty's Stationery Office, 1849 State Papers Online, Gale. Cengage Learning, 2019).

46    TNA, SP 1/202, fo. 149.

47    Thomas More, Francis Bacon, and Henry Neville, *Three Early Modern Utopias Thomas More: Utopia/Francis Bacon: New Atlantis/Henry Neville: The Isle of Pines*, ed. Susan Bruce (Oxford: Oxford University Press, 2008), 42–3.

48    Baker-Smith, 'Translating More's *Utopia*', 501.

49    'The Acts and Monuments Online'. https://www.dhi.ac.uk/foxe/index.php?realm= text&gototype=&edition=1570&pageid=303&anchor=wile#kw. Accessed 20 December 2019.

50    See David Colclough, *Freedom of Speech in Early Stuart England* (Cambridge: Cambridge University Press, 2005).

51    Thomas Elyot, *Pasquil the Playne* (London, 1533); see Arthur E. Walzer, 'Rhetoric of Counsel in Thomas Elyot's Pasquil the Playne', *Rhetorica: A Journal of the History of Rhetoric* 30, no. 1 (2012): 1–21.

52    Thomas Elyot, *Of the Knowledeg Whiche Maketh a Wise Man* (London, 1533); see Arthur E. Walzer, 'The Rhetoric of Counsel and Thomas Elyot's Of the Knowledge Which Maketh a Wise Man', *Philosophy and Rhetoric* 45, no. 1 (2012): 24–45.

53    Baldesar Castiglione, *The Book of the Courtier*, ed. Virginia Cox, trans. Thomas Hoby (London: J. M. Dent & Sons Ltd/Everyman's Library, 1994), 298–9.

54    Castiglione, *The Courtier*, 299.

55    See Paul, *Counsel and Command*, chapter 5.

56    Paul, *Counsel and Command*, chapter 7.

57    Quentin Skinner, *Reason and Rhetoric in the Philosophy of Hobbes* (Cambridge: Cambridge University Press, 1996).

58    Noel Malcolm, 'An Unknown Policy Proposal by Thomas Hobbes', *The Historical Journal* 55, no.1 (2012): 145–60, at 146–7.

59    Paul, *Counsel and Command*, 208.

60    Thomas Hobbes, *Thomas Hobbes: Leviathan: The English and Latin Texts*, ed. Noel Malcolm (3 vols, Oxford: Oxford University Press, 2012), 404.

61    Hobbes, *Leviathan*, 398.

62    Hobbes, *Leviathan*, 400.

63    Hobbes, *Leviathan*, 548.

## Chapter 4

# HOW NOT TO DO IT: POETS AND COUNSEL, THOMAS WYATT TO GEOFFREY HILL

## Colin Burrow

Everyone knows what a political special adviser looks like. Spads wear smart suits and smart shirts (usually monochrome) without ties. Sometimes, however, they try to remain invisible, cultivating reputations as attack dogs ready to savage the enemies of their paymasters.

But SPADs could also participate in a rather different kind of dogfight. The SPAD 7, produced by a company called the Société Pour L'Aviation et ses Dérivés, was a biplane first deployed in 1916, when its capacity to go into a fast steep dive offset its relative lack of manoeuvrability – and an ability to duck, dive, and flee is a skill often displayed by political spads too. The dubious history of the Société Pour L'Aviation et ses Dérivés also contains a lesson for the political kind of spad. The company was originally called the Société de Production des Aéroplanes Deperdussin. Unfortunately, Monsieur Deperdussin was arrested for fraud in 1913. This led to the rapid rebranding of the company so that it could retain the familiar acronym SPAD whilst erasing from memory the dodgy name of Deperdussin. Spads remain experts at obliterating unpleasant details from their pasts, whilst carrying on just the same.

This fortuitous overlap of acronyms underlies the first line of a characteristically dense poem by the late Professor of Poetry at Oxford, Sir Geoffrey Hill:

Spads have their own advisers; bank Gnome-Rhônes;
The dogfights a spectacular peril;
Ilyria peers skyward, dodges bones.[1]

These lines are characteristic of Geoffrey Hill in that they appear to be second cousin to a crossword clue. The main key to unlock them is of course that coincidence of acronyms between political spads and early-twentieth-century French biplanes, though it also helps to know that Gnome-et-Rhônes manufactured aero-engines. So the first line implies that political spads breed their own nest of political advisers; but the pun on the biplanes (which Hill confirmed to me in a letter he wrote shortly before he died) is matched by a pun on 'bank', which is of course what aeroplanes do when they turn. It is also what capitalists do with the profits of war. Hill suggests that spads in the political sense breed more spads, and both the political and the aeronautical kinds of spads bank and swoop all the way to the bank.

This poem is characteristic of Geoffrey Hill's attitudes to political advice in his writing from the 1990s until the early 2000s. During this period of his career he frequently presented himself as a prophet of liberty who excoriated the political state of the present. *Canaan* (1996) contains a group of poems addressed 'To the High Court of Parliament', which are dated November 1994. These poems were inspired by Hill's rage (expressed through his favoured mixture of the gnomic and the comic) at the Criminal Justice and Public Order Act of 1994, which received royal assent in November. Sections 34 to 39 of that Act allowed inferences to be drawn from the silence of suspects. This prompted Hill to write about the links between bad counsel, political tyranny, and language. And in a series of volumes over the next decade, Hill presented himself as a political adviser-cum-prophet to the British nation. He aligned his rhetorical stance explicitly with that of John Milton – who had of course presented his attack on prepublication censorship in *Areopagitica* of 1644 as a speech to parliament, even though at that date Milton was not even remotely close to being a Member of Parliament. We can be certain that no politician listened to Hill's advice, if such it can be called. Hill was convinced that the very medium of language is so clotted with contamination that what sounds like a clear and direct message is likely to be a debased falsehood. This means that his 'advice' can sound like fulminating obscurity. But his rage is deeply relishable. Within that wonder of Victorian Gothic, the Houses of Parliament, MPs do their venal business:

> None the less amazing: Barry's and Pugin's grand
> dark-lantern above the incumbent Thames.
> You: as by custom unillumined
> masters of servile counsel. (p. 235)

Hill's compacted and satirical way of offering counsel to the nation had deep historical roots. Although he presented himself as an eccentric crank (p. 279), his attitudes towards political advice and advisers grow from a clearly discernible poetic tradition. This tradition I will explore through three indicative examples from the period 1530 to 1667.

*I*

There is some dispute about what happened to the nature of political advice during Henry VIII's break with Rome in the 1530s. Geoffrey Elton put this decade at the heart of the 'Tudor Revolution in Government'.[2] He argued that the period from 1536 to 1539 marked the rise of the Privy Council in its modern form, and that this changed the nature of political advice. Recent and persuasive work by John Watts and others has shown how many of the things Elton said were new were in fact not new, and that in many respects political counsel in the early sixteenth century carried on as it had done from about the first half of the fourteenth century.[3]

However, literary representations and historical actualities do not always coincide. There were striking literary innovations in the 1530s in the ways in which counsel was represented by poets. These literary changes do not simply vindicate Elton's larger thesis about administrative reform in the period or refute Watts's arguments for continuities. But what they do illustrate is that in the 1530s a significant number of people who were trained to speak both to and for their monarch were placed in exceptionally uncomfortable positions as a result of Henry VIII's 'great matter', or the royal divorce and the subsequent break with Rome. One consequence of the 'great matter' was that the king enlarged his customary council. As Richard Rex has argued, this was not so that he could get more and better political counsel:[4] Henry VIII could scarcely be described as the greatest listener ever to have occupied the throne of England. Rex argues that Henry enlarged his council during his 'great matter' so that he could persuade as many people as possible to go along with the divorce. The enlarging of the council, however, coincided with the exclusion from it of several people who thought they should have the ear of the king.

Being excluded from counsel, or being on the edges of a circle of political advisers, was in Tudor England a powerful stimulus to writing. The dialogue about counsel in the first book of Thomas More's *Utopia* (1516) was written from the point of view of a person about to take up office closer to the court. But ejected counsellors could also write about political advice. Sir Thomas Elyot's *Pasquil the Plain* (1533) is a meditation on counsel from the viewpoint of someone excluded from it. Elyot was abruptly replaced by Thomas Cranmer as ambassador to the Holy Roman Emperor in 1533, probably as a result of Elyot's reluctance to support the royal divorce. In *Pasquil the Plain*, Pasquil – the statue in Rome to which satirical attacks on the powerful could be pinned – speaks frank words of counsel which are ignored. Meanwhile the wily master of silence and suggestion Gnatho (whom some commentators have identified with Thomas Cranmer) obtains the ear of the powerful because of his skill at not saying what his political master did not want to hear. In Elyot's *Pasquil the Plain* the frank speaker – that traditional adviser to princes – becomes a satirist whose 'undiscrete libertie in speche' results in his counsel no longer being heard by his ruler.[5] He laments that 'my playnnes is so well knowen, that I shall never come unto privie chambre or galeri', the spaces in which confidential advice was murmured into the ears of rulers in this period.[6]

So while the 1530s may not have brought about structural changes in the ways in which political advice was conducted, they did bring about shifts in the ways in which political advice was represented. The figure of the frank speaker condemned to the margins of political life, and thus unable to deliver counsel to his monarch, became one of the major literary personae of the later Henrician period. And the rise of that persona enabled literary innovation. Probably in around 1538, Sir Thomas Wyatt wrote a verse epistle to Sir Francis Bryan. This was one of the very earliest English poems known to be overtly modelled on the Epistles of Horace. Wyatt drew on Horace's persona of bemused and withdrawn virtue to structure his own response to the political environment of the 1530s. Both Wyatt and Bryan had acted as ambassadors during periods in which Henry attempted to break apart a potential alliance between the French King Francis I and the Emperor Charles V. Both men were famous for their plain speaking and wild living. Wyatt had to bail Bryan out of a massive gambling debt of £200 in Nice in June 1538. Both men had been intimate to varying degrees with the king in the happier days of the 1520s, and Bryan for his loose tongue and morals was known to his friends as the 'Vicar of Hell'.[7] Wyatt's epistle to Bryan merges together the plain, honest speech of a good counsellor with needling sarcasm: the opening line says 'Francis dear boy, if you're going to spend money like water you simply have to earn it':

> A spending hand that alway powreth owte
> Had nede to have a bringer in as fast,
> And on the stone that still doeth tourne abowte
> There groweth no mosse: these proverbes yet do last,
> Reason hath set theim in so sure a place
> That lenght of yeres their force can never wast.
> When I remember this and eke the case
> Where in thou stondes I thowght forthwith to write,
> Brian, to the, who knows how great a grace
> In writing is to cownsell man the right. (1–10)[8]

The main joke here is that a counsellor is in need of counsel. But its sharpest barb is an invisible intertextual one. The poem is loosely based on Horace's Epistle 2.5, in which Teiresias, summoned from the underworld, offers advice to Ulysses (2.5) 'missis ambagibus', without any ambiguity, on how to get rich. Wyatt models his own voice of counsel on that of Horace's Teiresias, a prophet who counsels men how to do wrong. This enables Wyatt to offer plain speaking and direct advice, as it were from the underworld, to a man known as the Vicar of Hell who knows 'how to counsel men the right'. And that advice is 'political' in a narrowly pragmatic sense: marry a rich widow, he says. Sell your daughter. That's how to get on. Bryan insists that he wants to keep his honest name. Wyatt responds by saying that Bryan can keep his 'free tongue' (87) if he wishes. But the consequence will be that he will have to learn to live with poverty.

One of the books read by Elyot, Wyatt, and probably also by Bryan was Castiglione's *Book of the Courtier* – a copy of which that arch-political adviser and spad to end all spads Thomas Cromwell, who was Wyatt's patron and protector, seems to have owned.[9] In the last book of this guide for courtiers about how to conduct themselves in court Castiglione expounds the final end of the courtier. That end is to become a virtuous, free-speaking counsellor. He should acquire skill at masks and tourneys and at plain speaking so that he can inform a monarch 'franckly of the trueth of every matter meete for him to understand, without fear or perill to displease him'.[10] This is a classic statement of the humanist view of the role of the counsellor or political adviser. He is eloquent and frank; he possesses virtue and effortless verbal artistry; he is a friend to the ruler; and he uses that intimacy to prevent tyranny.

Wyatt's Horatian epistles are grounded in this ideal of 'free speech', which was central to early modern conceptions of counsel. It should be remembered, however, that 'free speech' of the kind imagined by Castiglione did not mean 'a legally protected right to express personal opinions without punishment'. Rather, it is what the Greeks (and the rhetorical tradition generally) called *parrhesia*, or a figure of speech which overtly declares the speaker's frankness. This figure, as Quintilian (9.2.28) noted, was potentially duplicitous: it could also be used to conceal flattery beneath a display of plainness.[11] That potential for duplicity within the 'free' speech of a counsellor runs through Wyatt's poem to Bryan. It displays what we might call the failed counsellor syndrome, in which a counsellor who is no longer able to give advice to a monarch uses the virtues of free and frank speech in a deliberately duplicitous manner. Wyatt 'plainly' advises another failed counsellor to pursue courses of action that are plainly immoral, and while he does so he privily reminds his addressee of his moral and practical failings. The apparently direct voice of frank counsel, that is, becomes a highly oblique mode of satire. And this is part of the genesis of Geoffrey Hill's oblique, prophetic, and satirical way of offering political advice.

But Wyatt's poem to Bryan also points to a wider fact about the poetry of counsel. Poems can exhort, persuade, or offer moral or practical advice. But the poet who explicitly presents himself as offering counsel is generally less interested in the content of the advice which is offered than in *representing* the act of counsel. And such representations of the process of giving political advice tend to stress the forces which prevent the free flow of advice from counsellor to ruler. Poems about political counsel can implicitly invite their readers to read beneath or alongside the advice that is (apparently) being offered, and encourage them to think about the reasons why that advice might not be heard, or why it might fail of its intended effect. Counsellors might be crooked; monarchs might be tyrannical; acts of offering advice might be motivated by greed or driven by specific political interests; or, at the highest level, words might be so duplicitous that the high humanist ideal of virtuously and eloquently advising a monarch is in practice more or less impossible. Poets, that is, tend to represent political advice not as a smooth channel through which words of wisdom can flow freely from a counsellor to monarch, but as a ditch full of filth which is choked and blocked by obstacles.

However, the later 1530s were not a period of irreversible change in the ways in which counsel was practised or represented in English writing. The features I have highlighted in Wyatt's poem of counsel were the result of a particular set of accidents and agents: a group of men with a particular kind of rhetorical training travelled abroad as ambassadors. They read Castiglione and satires by Luigi Alamanni and Ludovico Ariosto.[12] They periodically fell out of favour. They wrote. And they also lived through the passage of the Treason Act of 1535, which brought words within the definition of treason, in an eery foreshadowing of the restriction of the right to silence which brought the wrath of Hill down on Parliament in 1994. It was these pressures, which arose from the tyrannical tendencies of later Henrician rule rather than Eltonian administrative reforms that made writers of the 1530s sound so new in the way in which they wrote about political advice.

## II

Literary history is not simply linear. A change can happen in one age that can be unpicked in the next – or indeed what appears to be a change can rather be a manifestation of a particular micro-climate of interests. If we return briefly to Sir Thomas Hoby's translation of Castiglione's *Il Cortegiano*, we can see how misleading it would be to regard Wyatt's poetry of bad counsel as marking a new age, rather than just a particular climate. Hoby's translation was published in 1561, early in the reign of Henry VIII's daughter Elizabeth. The preface to the translation was dated 1556, although Hoby had in fact begun it in 1551. The printer's address to the reader explains the delay in publication by saying it was 'misliked of some', and invites its reader to work out what these unnamed people thought was wrong with it.[13] That prefatory matter was intended to have a very clear illocutionary force: Castiglione's *Book of the Courtier*, with its elevated view of the efficacy of political counsel, was presented to its English readers as a good Protestant work completed during the reign of Elizabeth's Catholic sister Mary Tudor, which had been suppressed during that reign, and which should sustain the political life of a new age.[14]

That point was re-emphasized by the physical form in which this extraordinarily influential book was published. Its title page had an ornamental surround. Exactly the same ornamental surround was then used by Richard Jugge and John Cawood for the second volume of Elizabethan Homilies in 1562 (STC 13650). This made Hoby's translation appear to be a secular equivalent to the officially sponsored voice of the Elizabethan Church. In that context Castiglione's emphasis on the key function of the courtier – to master the arts of self-presentation so as to be able freely and frankly to advise a monarch – took on a new force. It became a statement about a new reign and a new religion. Hoby's *Courtier* ends with a digested summary of the book's contents which has two notable features. The first is that it gives particular emphasis to the 'FINAL END OF A COURTIER ... to beecome *An Instructer and Teacher of his Prince or Lorde* ... and to be francke and free with him' (sig. Zz2v). The second is that it ends by listing 'the chief conditions and qualities in a wayting gentlewoman'. It was such female intimate advisers to a monarch through whom, as Hoby well knew, political advice had to be filtered in order to have an influence during the reign of a female monarch.

Hence the physical presentation of Hoby's *Courtier* was itself a statement about a new culture of counsel which the translation sought to bring into existence. That culture of counsel was highly Protestant, feminized, and deeply committed to frankness, or free speech. Its implicit Protestantism was signalled by the fact that Hoby's translation included a dedicatory poem by Thomas Sackville and a final commendatory letter by Hoby's former tutor Sir John Cheke. Both of these men were strongly associated with a resurgence of active political advice in the early reign of Elizabeth. Cheke of course has been placed at the root of the 'Cambridge Connection' that played a significant part in fashioning the Elizabethan religious settlement.[15] Sackville was one of the authors of the neoclassical drama *Gorboduc* (performed before Elizabeth I in 1562), which implicitly counselled the queen about the dangers of division and the value of securing the succession. Sackville also composed the highly influential 'Induction' to the tragedy of Buckingham included in editions of the collection of complaints voiced by dead figures from the past called *The Mirror for Magistrates* from 1563. And *The Mirror for Magistrates*, as well as itself being an act of political counsel which advised monarchs and magnates on how not to decline into tyranny, was (like Hoby's Castiglione) a work which presented in its prefatory matter as having been suppressed during the reign of Mary.[16] These texts – *Gorboduc*, *The Mirror*, and Hoby's Castiglione – implicitly spoke to an early Elizabethan literary polity in which poets could freely counsel monarchs without fear that their works would be suppressed. Taken together these mid-century volumes were designed to imply that the 1560s provided an opportunity to open the lungs, and bellow counsel (perhaps channelled through a gentlewoman of the queen's privy chamber) to the receptive Protestant ears of the new queen.

This was of course more like a politically motivated fiction than a reflection of reality. Hoby's Castiglione, *The Mirror*, and indeed *Gorboduc* were themselves implicitly advising the new monarch and those who influenced her about the kind of queen she should be: Protestant, and receptive to counsel. In doing this these texts established what was to become in the Elizabethan period one of the main ways in which poets offered political advice: through a coercive form of implicit praise. They implicitly say 'Of course your Majesty is graciously willing to listen to frank counsel, unlike your Majesty's Catholic sister'; and implicitly too they ask the queen to choose the right counsellors and take their advice to heart.

The relation between political and literary history is multiplex. The historical reality of political advice in Elizabeth's reign was both more complex than, and semi-independent from, the poetic fictions which writers sought to impose upon it. Historians have for a number of years talked about the 'second reign' of Elizabeth I. From the later 1580s, according to John Guy, Elizabethan government experienced 'a sharp swing to the right', and the queen became less willing to take counsel.[17] This view has been questioned recently by Susan Doran among others, and indeed seeing a 'swing to the right' in the late reign may depend on taking the work of Hoby, Sackville and the literary generation of the 1560s as simple representations, rather than idealizations, of the reality of political counsel in the early reign.[18] But, whether or not it is historically accurate, Guy's picture of a 'second reign' tallies remarkably well with the literary record. That becomes apparent if we skip forward thirty or so years from the coercive praise of Elizabeth early in her reign to the very different literary world of the 1590s.

Edmund Spenser's epic romance called *Faerie Queene* appeared between 1590 and 1596. Spenser's work was deeply indebted to the ethos of Protestant counsellors or would-be advisers of the queen in the 1560s and 1570s. It frequently praises the queen for virtues which she manifestly did not possess, and it uses praise as a means of counsel. However its dominant rhetorical figure is not that of 'free speech' or *parrhesia*. Rather it operates in the realm of what Spenser's contemporary George Puttenham called in his *Arte of English Poesie* (1589) 'the Courtly figure Allegoria, which is when we speake one thing and thinke another, and that our wordes and our meanings meete not'.[19]

Allegorical counsel is a speech act only marginally more complicated than the supposedly 'frank' counsel offered earlier in the century by Thomas Wyatt to Francis Bryan. This is best illustrated by the moment in the tenth canto of the fifth book of Spenser's allegorical epic when the heroes Prince Arthur and Sir Arthegal stumble across the palace of a good queen called Mercilla. Mercilla is of course an implicitly panegyrical representation of Spenser's Queen Elizabeth, who carefully cultivated a reputation for mercifulness. The threshold of Mercilla's court, however, is marked by a terrifying image of what could happen to a failed poetical spad even in a court presided over by even the most merciful of monarchs. A poet who was formerly called Bonfont has had his old name erased and replaced by the new name Malfont. His tongue has been 'Nayld to a post, adiudged so by law: | For that therewith he falsely did reuyle, | And foule blaspheme that Queene for forged guyle' (5.9.25).

That is not a comfortable welcome to the 'court' of Mercilla. And that court itself, it turns out, is a kind of constitutional pun. It is more akin to the high court of parliament than to a court in the sense of the 'residence of the monarch', since when the princes arrive at Mercilla's court they interrupt a trial. The queen is being persuaded by her counsellors to condemn a wicked usurper called Duessa to death. And those counsellors really lay it on thick: 'Strongly did *Zele* her haynous fact enforce'. Zeal urges Mercilla to execute this usurper, as do counsellors called 'Authoritie', 'the Law of Nations' and 'Religion'.

Although Spenser's poem is presented to its readers as 'an allegory or dark conceit', when a character called Zeal urges a merciful queen to condemn a duplicitous figure called Duessa to death, the allegory is, if dark at all, then dark with exceeding brightness. This episode is a transparent representation of the trial and execution of Mary Queen of Scots in 1587. This particular historical moment has been seen as a watershed in the history of counsel. John Guy in particular regards it as one of the events that marked the end of the 'first reign' of Elizabeth. It was a moment when Elizabeth and her counsellors were at loggerheads. The queen did not wish to execute her cousin. Her male counsellors did. After elaborate displays of real or feigned reluctance the queen did eventually agree to the execution, and her unfortunate secretary William Davison (whose career is discussed by Jacqueline Rose in this volume) became in effect the fall guy who was burnt up by the friction between the queen and her counsellors.

Spenser's allegorical representation of these events is pitched exactly on the boundary between panegyric and persuasion. It is not itself an act of counsel which advises Queen Elizabeth to execute Mary Stuart. To have offered that advice in 1596, nine years after the execution had occurred, would have been, shall we say, both presumptuous and posthumous. What it does instead is *represent* the operations of conciliar government after the event. And it represents those processes from the perspective of the queen's counsellors rather than that of the queen herself, but it does so at several removes and with a great deal of anxiety. Perhaps the most visible marker of that anxiety is the complete absence from the episode of the words 'counsel' and 'advice'. The fiction Spenser presents to his queen about her actions in executing her cousin is that her judgement was not directed by the advice of partisan male counsellors, but that it was grounded entirely on evidence and the law.

Spenser was from a very different social class to Wyatt or Bryan or Sackville or Sir Thomas Hoby. That has a significant influence on how he represents political advice. He was not in any accepted sense 'a courtier', and was not, until he graduated as a sizar or poor scholar at Pembroke College, Cambridge, in the early modern sense even a 'gentleman', since his father is likely to have been a clothier of relatively modest means.[20] Spenser had periods of service to members of the clergy and the nobility as a secretary (a role which could be akin to that of an informal adviser in this period). He also had an early association with one of the queen's most influential courtiers, the Earl of Leicester. However, unlike Sir Thomas Wyatt or Thomas Hoby or Thomas Elyot he had no direct experience of being an ambassador, let alone of being an informal friend or counsellor to a monarch. In writing the Mercilla episode he worked largely from public propaganda about the execution of Mary.[21] And he was extremely coy about representing the thoughts and intentions of Mercilla herself. Instead he represents the itinerant princes (rather than Mercilla) as being successively swayed by each new argument. The male advisers speak. The male knights respond. And ultimately the queen follows their advice. But crucially Spenser *does not dare to represent her doing so.* Mercilla lets fall 'Few perling drops from her faire lampes of light' after the case for the prosecution has been presented. Then she ups and leaves in clouds of glory. And then Canto 10 is, like Mary Queen of Scots herself, simply sliced off abruptly. Very early in the next canto we learn that Duessa is dead. That gap, that expressive silence, was Spenser's way of representing Elizabeth's actual vacillation over the killing.

Spenser had absolutely no doubt that the Council was right and the queen was wrong about executing Mary, but he buries his sympathies. Indeed in the Mercilla episode he was attempting to reconcile two distinct conceptions of government, and he did so in a way that makes the ebb and flow of political advice go completely underground. The queen is granted her *imperium* by suddenly disrupting the trial and by her exaggerated display of clemency in those 'perling drops' of tears which she lets fall – and clemency is traditionally a central virtue of monarchs who enjoy imperial sovereignty.[22] But in the background her advisers (with whom she was publicly furious for having executed the warrant for Mary's death) get what they want. Elizabeth's earlier reign was influentially termed a 'monarchical republic' by Patrick Collinson.[23] But Spenser in the Mercilla episode created a representational mode more suitable for her second reign. He in effect represents in the Mercilla episode a constitutional oxymoron: this is what might be called an *imperial republic*. What you *see* is an apparently imperial ruler, overflowing with the tearful *clementia* of a Roman Emperor. But what *happens* between one canto's end and the start of the next implicitly shows that the queen's privy counsellors are in control. So although Spenser deliberately avoids the language of counsel, he nonetheless implies that counsel rules beneath an appearance of imperial sway.

This example reveals something else too. Changes in the ways political counsel is represented in literature may reflect changes in the ways in which political advice was actually offered. But changes in literary phenomena may reflect the distinctive position and social status of the person doing the representing rather than wider changes in the world. *The Faerie Queen* might be seen as registering some large changes in the wider history of counsel – that, say, in 'the second reign' of Elizabeth the courtier-counsellor can no longer afford to be Castiglione's frank speaker. The counsellor's traditional rhetorical figure of *parrhesia*, or plain, free speech, is more or less entirely overwritten by the darker figure of allegory, in which, as Puttenham put it, 'our words and our meanings meet not'. But this apparent change in the representation of political advice bears the marks of Spenser's individual history. He was reared on the conciliar literature of the mid-century, including Hoby's Castiglione, Sackville's *Induction* (which was among the most significant influences on his overall style), and *The Mirror for Magistrates*. But Spenser was also at several social removes from the actual practice of political counsel. Unlike Wyatt, he had no experience of the practice of political advice; and in the excruciatingly controversial case of the execution of Mary, Queen of Scots, he certainly did not wish to represent that practice directly in case he ended up in the same condition as the poet Malfont, with his tongue nailed to a post. He bites his own tongue lest a nail be put through it.

## III

Let us make a final and longer leap forward in time, and combine it with a leap into the very pit of hell. In Book 2 of *Paradise Lost* (1667) John Milton – that great spokesman for the English Republican cause – presents the best description anywhere in world literature of a meeting. This is the Great Consult of the Devils, which takes place inside the palace of Pandemonium in the darkness visible of Milton's hell. In this meeting a series of zealous speakers stand up before their defeated peers and advise the fallen angels on what they should do after their catastrophic defeat by the Almighty. Moloc – who displays his lack of strategic awareness by speaking first at the meeting, something a canny political operator would never do – wants to Make the Underworld Great Again by turning the Mother of All Bombs against the Almighty. He speaks with a counsellor's traditional frankness: he states 'My sentence is for open war: of wiles, | More unexpert, I boast not' (2.51–2).[24] The next speaker Belial, who 'could make the worse appear | The better reason, to perplex and dash | Maturest counsels' (2.113–15), argues for easy sloth. Mammon is in favour not of fighting but of spending eternity blinging up the nether world with gems and gold.

Each speaker at the hellish council offers his political advice with passionate intensity. But this is a meeting. So, as at all meetings, what people say is less important than what actually happens. The agenda and the minutes to this particular act of political consultation have all been written in advance by Satan. He sets off the council by asking for advice: 'who can advise, may speak' (2.42). But he has primed his crony Beelzebub to argue for Satan's own preferred outcome at the end of the debate. This is the proposal not to fight, nor retire from the fray, but for Satan himself to go out on an imperial voyage to earth in order to suborn humankind: 'Thus Beelzebub | Pleaded his devilish counsel, first devised | By Satan, and in part proposed' (2.378–80). So after a lengthy process of apparent political consultation a tyrant gets what he wants, and is allowed to be the hero of the poem.

Anyone who has ever served on a committee of any kind will appreciate the uncanny accuracy with which Milton represents the reality of political manoeuvrings. But a comparison between Milton's representation of the devils' quasi-parliamentary consultation and Spenser's Mercilla episode raises a rather more specific point. It suggests just how differently an Elizabethan poet and a republican writer in Restoration England might write about political advice. In *The Faerie Queene* the will of the queen's male counsellors is in effect sovereign, although Spenser tactfully retains the illusion that their monarch enjoys imperial sway over them. In *Paradise Lost* the vociferous republican rhetoricians display their frankness and masculine persuasive force through acts of counsel. But nonetheless the will of their ruler (who insists on appearing to be no more than first among equals) is what ultimately holds sway. Both of these representations of political advice in action imply that what actually happens in political life depends not on what is said, but on backstage manoeuvres – on what happens in the gap between cantos or in the backroom pre-meeting in hell. In the poetry of counsel it is, as it were, what Sir Humphrey murmurs in the right ear that determines the outcome, rather than overt acts of persuasion.

That point is reinforced by an extraordinarily consistent feature of Milton's language. Milton has often been thought of as the ultimate 'articulate citizen', or as the republican end product of a generations-long revival in the use of rhetoric to enable citizens to participate in civic life. But if he is thought of in this way then one tiny lexical detail of *Paradise Lost* becomes profoundly surprising. All of Milton's uses of the word 'counsel' in *Paradise Lost* are heavily burdened with a negative charge.[25] The word is used by or about every speaker in the Great Consult, which takes place in hell. It is also used when Milton describes the earlier council of the devils-to-be before they fall. The word 'counsel' is only otherwise used between Adam and Eve after their fall. Adam counsels Eve that wearing fig leaves is the antidote to shame, and Eve repeatedly says she needs Adam's 'counsel'. That relentless association of the word 'counsel' with fallen things and bad places is strikingly distinct from Milton's use of the words 'advice' and 'advise', which can occur in either good or bad contexts. We might say of the word 'counsel' after the Restoration what Satan says of Beelzebub when he first sees him in the flaming lake at the start of the poem: 'Alas, how fallen' (1.84). In *Paradise Lost* 'counsel' is a word irredeemably associated with deception or self-deception, and it is a natural denizen of the darkness visible of hell.

## IV

What wider observations emerge from examining this series of episodes? I have suggested that poems about counsel tend to focus on the mechanisms and processes by which political advice is delivered, or by which it fails to reach its targets, rather than simply offering counsel. They tend to explore, that is, *how* it is done, rather than simply doing it. And because many of these examples show counsel failing we might say that many poems about counsel show not how to do it, but how not to do it.

A wider narrative also emerges from this series of instances. Changes in the institutions of government – particularly in the relations between monarchs and their formal or informal agents of advice, be they members of the privy chamber, the privy council, or parliament itself – influence the ways in which poets both perform and write about counsel. But from a wider historical perspective the implication of these particular instances is both revisionist and counter-revisionist. It is revisionist in that I have suggested that each poet tackles counsel from a particular and identifiable perspective. Hence larger narratives about the history of political advice need to be very mindful of individual circumstances if they make use of poetic examples. But the overall picture presented here is counter-revisionist in that several of the literary instances I have considered endorse the claims of traditional historical narratives that at particular moments – the break with Rome, the later reign of Elizabeth, the Restoration – there were major changes in the ways in which political counsel was believed to be conducted.

This should give food for thought to radical revisionists, who find in the documentary evidence long-term continuities in the practices of counsel. It is possible that the institutions and methods by which political advice was offered did not change very much between the fourteenth and the late sixteenth centuries. But poets clearly *believed* things had changed. This must mean that something – whether general attitudes towards political advice or the narrower relationships between particular poets and particular political configurations – had indeed changed. Wyatt counselled another failed counsellor when neither of them could counsel their king. He did so in roughly the period in which, Elton argued, the Privy Council, and with it the nature of counsel, was changing its nature. Spenser allegorized the relation between Elizabeth and her parliament in the debate about whether or not to execute Mary Queen of Scots in a way that chimes very well with the established view that Elizabeth had a 'second reign', which rested on a narrower foundation of political authority than it did in the 1560s – although, as we have also seen, the receptiveness of the queen to political advice in her 'early reign' may be at least in part a fiction crafted by a group of Protestant writers who wanted it to be true. I would hesitate myself to counsel historians, but it is possible that poems can offer a clearer window onto how political advice is *perceived to be* practised in a given period than the narrow perspective on how it was actually practised which may be extracted from over-careful scrutiny of the bottom of a diplomatic bag.

But as I have also suggested, particularities matter. It is highly significant that in the 1530s it was people with ambassadorial experience and who had fallen from favour who meditated on what it might be to offer political advice. It also matters that Spenser was of a completely different social class from those earlier writers, and so had a view of counsel that derived principally from his reading rather than his experience. And Milton's distinctive personal history radically inflects the particular ways in which he used the word 'counsel' in his dark and sardonic representation of the practice of giving political advice. Milton had presented himself in the early 1640s as an orator for a nation when really he was nothing of the sort. He then took on a role within the council of state as secretary for foreign tongues, and then had to live through the return of monarchy. These distinctive experiences are why he wanted to suggest that the very word 'counsel' belongs to the fallen world of corrupted monarchs and failed advisers. The 'big story' about poets and counsel in early modern England is a synthesis of little stories, and syntheses can be synthetic in the negative sense of that word.

But, to voice a platitude, literary histories are best discovered through literary examples. Poets are usually the best readers of poets. And new poems can tease out patterns from earlier poems which can instruct us how to read them. This is why I began with Geoffrey Hill. Hill in his later and middle years could at times identify himself with the Milton of the Restoration, full of burning political righteousness but radically alienated from his times. The 'dark lantern' of Pugin and Barry above the 'unillumined | masters of servile counsel' in Hill's address to the High Court of Parliament with which this essay began is a late-twentieth-century response to the early-modern poetic representations of counsel on which this essay has focussed. Hill's 'dark lantern' is a twentieth-century version of the darkness visible of Milton's hell. Hill saw political advice as an activity doomed, if not to failure, then doomed to be transformed into the obscure voice of a prophet crying in the wilderness because he believed that in the present age the language of political persuasion was irredeemably corrupted. That is not an optimistic picture. But we live in an age in which Hill's pessimism seems more appropriate than any kind of optimism about the capacity of political counsel to do good. Stephen Bannon, one of the erstwhile advisers to Donald Trump (a man who has a passion for turning his advisers into erstwhile advisers if they do not simply do his bidding), has said 'darkness is good. Dick Cheney. Darth Vader. Satan. That's power'.[26] When political advisers are willing to rejoice in their associations with the prince of darkness we need to listen hard to what poets have told us about the diabolical distortions of political advice in our cultural tradition, even if what they tell us is that political advice is more likely to go wrong than it is to go right.

## Notes

1   Geoffrey Hill, *Broken Hierarchies: Poems 1952–2012*, ed. K. Haynes (Oxford: Oxford University Press, 2013), 664. Quotations reproduced by kind permission of the literary estate of Geoffrey Hill.

2   G. R. Elton, *The Tudor Revolution in Government: Administrative Changes in the Reign of Henry VIII* (Cambridge: Cambridge University Press, 1953).

3　　John Watts, 'Counsel and the King's Council in England, c. 1340–1540', in *The Politics of Counsel in England and Scotland 1286–1707*, ed. J. Rose (Oxford: Oxford University Press, 2016), 63–85.

4　　Richard Rex, 'Councils, Counsel and Consensus in Henry VIII's Reformation', in ibid., 135–50.

5　　Thomas Elyot, *Pasquil the Playne* (London: T. Berthelet, 1533), sig. 4v. See Greg Walker, *Writing under Tyranny: English Literature and the Henrician Reformation* (Oxford: Oxford University Press, 2005), and Colin Burrow, 'The Experience of Exclusion: Literature and Politics in the Reigns of Henry VII and Henry VIII', in *The Cambridge History of Medieval English Literature*, ed. D. Wallace (Cambridge: Cambridge University Press, 1999), 793–820. Cathy Shrank, 'Thomas Elyot and the Bonds of Community', in *The Oxford Handbook of Tudor Literature, 1485–1603*, ed. M. Pincombe and C. Shrank (Oxford: Oxford University Press, 2009), 154–69, resists Walker's interpretation of *Pasquil* as a satire *á clef*.

6　　Elyot, *Pasquil the Playne*, sig. 30r.

7　　Roger Bigelow Merriman, *Life and Letters of Thomas Cromwell* (2 vols, Oxford: Clarendon Press, 2000), 2.12. See Susan Brigden, *Thomas Wyatt: the Heart's Forest* (London: Faber and Faber, 2012), 221–4, 388–9.

8　　Thomas Wyatt, *Collected Poems of Sir Thomas Wyatt*, ed. K. Muir and P. Thomson (Liverpool: Liverpool University Press, 1969).

9　　*Letters and Papers Foreign and Domestic of the Reign of Henry VIII*, ed. James Gairdner, J. S. Brewer, and R. H. Brodie (22 vols, London: HMSO, 1864–1932), IV (3) 6346. Bonner asks Cromwell 'if you have it' for 'the *Cortigiano* in Italian'. See Peter Burke, *The Fortunes of the Courtier: The European Reception of Castiglione's Cortegiano* (Cambridge: Polity, 1995).

10　　Baldassarre Castiglione, *The Courtyer of Count Baldessar Castilio*, trans. T. Hoby (London: William Seres, 1561), sig. Mm4v. See David Starkey, 'The Court: Castiglione's Ideal and Tudor Reality, Being a Discussion of Sir Thomas Wyatt's 'Satire addressed to Sir Francis Bryan'', *Journal of the Warburg and Courtauld Institutes* 45 (1982): 232–38.

11　　David Colclough, *Freedom of Speech in Early Stuart England* (Cambridge: Cambridge University Press, 2005), 29.

12　　See Colin Burrow, 'Horace at Home and Abroad: Wyatt and Sixteenth-Century Horatianism', in *Horace Made New: Horatian Influences on British Writing from the Renaissance to the Twentieth Century*, ed. C. Martindale and D. Hopkins (Cambridge: Cambridge University Press, 1993), 27–49.

13　　Castiglione, *The Courtyer*, sig. A2r.

14　　Mary Partridge, 'Thomas Hoby's English Translation of Castiglione's *Book of the Courtier*', *The Historical Journal* 50 (2007): 769–86 suggests that the completion of the translation may have been part of an attempt by Hoby to ingratiate himself with Cardinal Pole. For the wider influence of Castiglione, see Mary Partridge, 'Lord Burghley and Il Cortegiano: Civil and Martial Models of Courtliness in Elizabethan England', *Transactions of the Royal Historical Society* 19 (2009): 95–116.

15　　Winthrop Still Hudson, *The Cambridge Connection and the Elizabethan Settlement of 1559* (Durham, NC: Duke University Press, 1980).

16　　The 1559 preface records that it was 'begun, & part of it printed.iiii. yeare agoe, but hyndred by the lord Chancellour that then was', William Baldwin, *The Mirror for Magistrates*, ed. L. B. Campbell (Cambridge: Cambridge University Press, 1938),

66. See further Scott Lucas, *A Mirror for Magistrates and the Politics of the English Reformation* (Amherst: University of Massachusetts Press, 2009).

17  John Guy, 'Introduction. The 1590s: The Second Reign of Elizabeth I', in *The Reign of Elizabeth I: Court and Culture in the Last Decade*, ed. John Guy (Cambridge: Cambridge University Press, 1995), 1–19. For a sceptical view of Guy's thesis, see Alexandra Gajda, 'Political Culture in the 1590s: The 'Second Reign of Elizabeth'', *History Compass* 8 (2010): 88–100.

18  Susan Doran, 'Elizabeth I and Counsel', in *Politics of Counsel*, ed. Rose, 151–69.

19  George Puttenham, *The Arte of English Poesie*, ed. G. D. Willcock and A. Walker (Cambridge: Cambridge University Press, 1970), 186.

20  See Andrew Hadfield, *Edmund Spenser: A Life* (Oxford: Oxford University Press, 2012).

21  See James Emerson Phillips, *Images of a Queen: Mary Stuart in Sixteenth-century Literature* (Berkeley: University of California Press, 1964).

22  See Colin Burrow, *Epic Romance: Homer to Milton* (Oxford: Clarendon Press, 1993), 132–9.

23  Patrick Collinson, 'The Monarchical Republic of Queen Elizabeth I', in *The Tudor Monarchy*, ed. J. Guy (London: Arnold, 1997), 110–34.

24  Quotations from John Milton, *Paradise Lost*, ed. A. Fowler (London and New York: Longman, 1998).

25  Milton, *Paradise Lost*, 1.88, 1.168, 1.636, 1.660, 2.20, 2.115, 2.125, 2.160, 2.227, 2.279, 2.304, 2.379, 2.506, 5.681, 5.785, 6.494, 9.1099, 10.920, 10.944, 10.1010. 7.610 is the one moment when the word 'counsel' is used by the heavenly hosts, but it refers to the 'counsels vain' of the devils. On 'the difficulty of applying republican virtues to a monarchical context' see Colclough, *Freedom of Speech*, 6.

26  https://www.hollywoodreporter.com/news/steve-bannon-trump-tower-interview-trumps-strategist-plots-new-political-movement-948747. Accessed June 2019.

# Chapter 5

## WILLIAM DAVISON AND THE PERILS OF ADVICE IN ELIZABETHAN ENGLAND

### Jacqueline Rose

William Davison played one of the most famous walk-on roles in Elizabethan history. It was William Davison who, in 1587, secured the queen's signature to the death warrant of Elizabeth's rival Mary Queen of Scots. Mary's execution ended nearly thirty years of arguments between Elizabeth and her leading councillors as to how to deal with the Scottish Catholic 'Jezebel'. It also prematurely terminated Davison's career, a mere five months after his appointment as secretary of state – a tenure even shorter than that of a modern special adviser. Fundamental to these events were disputes about the extent and role of political advice to the queen.

As Gloriana, Elizabeth I has had a fairly good popular press over the centuries, providing a model of leadership and a powerful woman in a male-dominated world. On the surface, her reign might look like a paradigm of leadership as a collaborative exercise in identifying and encouraging good advice. Defending the legitimacy of queenship in 1559, John Aylmer claimed that a female monarch was nothing to worry about because in reality power was shared with parliament and other councillors – a case that one historian compared to justifying Margaret Thatcher's premiership by saying that her cabinet could 'be trusted to keep her in order'.[1] Indeed, if we probe a little deeper, the picture of a happy partnership of monarch and adviser becomes more complicated.

In particular, since the 1980s historians have emphasized how frustrated Elizabeth's leading advisers like William Cecil, lord Burghley, and Francis Walsingham (sometimes anachronistically labelled her prime minister and her spymaster respectively) were with her.[2] She failed to implement a sufficiently zealous Protestant Reformation. She was reluctant to engage in military intervention to support fellow Protestants in the rest of Europe. Above all, she failed to marry or name a successor, leaving England a potential victim to Mary – a Francophile Scot who would, it was thought, return England to the tyranny of Romish popery. Mary's execution in 1587 can be seen as the final triumph of Elizabeth's advisers over the queen's own preferred policy. William Davison's experiences show just how perilous such aggressive advice was.

Today, political advisers, especially those operating outside formal institutions like parliament and cabinet, often get a bad press. In the sixteenth century advice was much more highly valued. This was, admittedly, the world of Machiavelli's *Prince*, but the cynical realism of that text was usually denounced – even as it caused some readers to agonize over how to incorporate its lessons into statecraft. Of course the political world of Elizabeth I was unlike that of Elizabeth II. Elizabeth I had the final say on policy. She was accountable to God, not to the people. But Gloriana's advisers were perfectly capable of telling her that she was wrong. Indeed, since there were few, if any, constitutional checks and balances, advice took on a greater significance. It was the only way to ensure that the monarch ruled for the good of the state, not for themselves. This did not exclude the idea of tyranny; indeed, most supporters of powerful monarchy had a finely honed concept of tyranny, by which they meant abuse of power for one's own private interests, and not simply someone having too much power. In pre-modern parlance, 'absolute monarchy' did not become 'arbitrary' or tyrannical as long as the monarch ruled for the common good. Hearing advice or counsel was a crucial element in directing royal wishes in the right direction.

This advice could come from a variety of sources. Some are still comprehensible, if less prominent, nowadays, such as the preachers and confessors who provided guidance on all sorts of matters ranging from the extent of religious toleration and the shape of the established Church to the morality of taxation and the justice of warfare. Others seem far more distant and alien: Henry VIII's concerns about the 'Holy Maid of Kent' Elizabeth Barton, a prophetess who warned him against discarding Katharine of Aragon and breaking with the pope; Oliver Cromwell and his fellow army leaders pausing in December 1648, on the brink of regicide, to hear the admonitions of another prophetess, Elizabeth Poole, against executing Charles I. (Prophecy, as these examples indicate, provided an avenue for women to make political statements in this period.) Navigating an international trade dispute in 1597, the government sought advice from a number of 'outside experts' including the polymath alchemist John Dee.[3]

Yet these monuments of a political landscape so different from our own occupied a territory with some apparently familiar features. Indeed, a few decades ago, sixteenth- and seventeenth-century England was thought to be the point where modern political institutions emerged – the privy council and cabinet, parliament and the supremacy of the House of Commons, limited constitutional monarchy. Such self-congratulatory 'whiggish' narratives were initially punctured by 'revisionist' scholars who challenged the idea that English history was one long march on the road to constitutional democracy. This scholarship sidelined or denigrated informal advice and became a story of institutional developments that engendered arguments about the exact chronology of changing patterns of administration, losing sight of advice (counsel) given outside institutional bodies (councils). Some readers may have encountered this approach at school, if brought up on a diet of Geoffrey Elton's *Tudor Revolution in Government*: the story of how Thomas Cromwell reorganized government on more efficient, formal, bureaucratic lines in the 1530s.[4] (At school in the late 1990s, I still wrote essays on Elton's *Tudor*

*Revolution.*) Reshaping Tudor administration might not make a great plotline for a novel or create the most captivating televisual screenplay – Cromwell the heroic bureaucrat does not really feature in *Wolf Hall*. But shadowy politicking resulting in the death of a queen, whether in Cromwell's time or in Davison's, took place in a world where crucial advice was given in chambers as well as councils, in privy galleries as well as in parliaments.

What follows therefore challenges both whiggish and Eltonian accounts of the emergence of 'modern' political institutions. It shows that advice often took place outside formal institutions and that Elizabethan secretaries of state like Davison held an office whose remit was still ill-defined. Yet it also suggests that the challenges these rather un-modern counsellors and secretaries faced echo those of political advisers now. With whom should they share knowledge in order to balance confidentiality with corporate responsibility? How accountable were they for collective conciliar decisions and could they create a paper trail to prove this? Could they cope with that paper trail, or were they faced with 'information overload'? And how, and how far, should they give unwelcome advice?

The first half of this chapter uses Davison's career as an ambassador to offer a positive account of the surprisingly large amount of scope for unsolicited and unwelcome advice in Elizabethan England. The second half looks at the crisis of 1587 to explore the problems surrounding secretarial secrecy and accountability and the greater sensitivity to these issues after Davison's disgrace. In this formative period for councillors and secretaries, we will see both a belief in formal institutional advice as the ideal, and a much more fluid, chaotic, reality – an ambiguity that, it seems, aptly reflects our own position now.

*I*

By the time of the great crisis of 1587, Davison was all too aware of the perils of advice. His career prior to the secretaryship included a stint as ambassador to what is now the Netherlands. In the 1570s and 1580s these territories were in the process of a rebellion against Spanish overlordship, a revolt in which they looked to Protestant England for aid. The issue raised large questions about how far to intervene to aid fellow-Protestants in a rebellion against their sovereign, something that Elizabeth was wary of doing. The core of the argument at this particular moment was over whether to give aid and, if so, whether to do so covertly by sending money, or overtly, by sending troops. Elizabeth favoured the more cautious approach. Many of her councillors supported greater aggression – as, too, did William Davison.

Davison's job was to provide information to the English government, and he often, naturally enough, offered his opinion on the likely outcome of negotiations. Davison was – entirely properly, in accordance with the unspoken rules of advice – quite deferential in most cases. 'In my poor judgement' he repeatedly writes. 'In my poor judgement ... under ... correction.' 'My rude [plain] opinion, under your Honour's [Walsingham's] correction.'[5] But Elizabeth's procrastination, combined with a sense that the chance to tie the Dutch rebels to English Protestant aid (as opposed to French Catholic support) was slipping away, increased the urgency of Davison's pleas. In two letters of March 1578 he again offered his 'rude advice' to Walsingham. The queen was in 'certain peril' if she did not act. One doesn't delay in treating the sick or repairing a house. 'Surety, honour, profit and necessity' required action.[6] This language of 'honour and profit' echoes the classical, especially Ciceronian, accounts of persuasive speech that Davison would have read at school. They were the terms that parliament employed when urging the queen to punish Mary Stewart in 1572.[7] This type of Ciceronian rhetoric squared the profitable (*utile*) course of action with the honourable one (*honestum*) – in contrast to the supposedly Machiavellian distinction between the two. While studying Cicero to improve their Latin, Elizabethan schoolboys would have engaged in a sort of vocational political training, with mock debates and practice speeches on political topics.[8] Service as a member of parliament or councillor was an opportunity to put this training into effect.

In framing urgent pleas in the deferential terms of his 'poor judgement', Davison engaged in typical advisory tactics, sharpening his letter with the invocation of 'peril' and 'necessity'. He might, he admitted, 'seem to go too far' in urging the queen to offer troops, not just money, 'yet shall it not be much amiss' that he do so.[9] His other letter, to an unnamed recipient, was blunter. Although Davison called himself 'a man in no way apt to give counsaill', he still complained that there was 'nothing more dangerous in matters of estate, than to fleet and waver in deliberation [decision]'.[10]

In one sense this advice failed. The queen gave money, not troops. Yet in another way Davison was surprisingly successful insofar as his letter was accepted as a legitimate piece of advice. Apparently someone read his discourse to the queen, which she heard, 'every word, and did very well allow'.[11] Adviser and monarch disagreed. The monarch decided. End of story.

Or so it should have been. The problem for Davison was thinking it was not the end. Reports circulated that he was complaining about (or at least not rejecting complaints about) Elizabeth's decision. Several friends, including Walsingham, warned him that, if he disliked the queen's policy, 'you must submit yourself to the same'. While one correspondent suggested that he might still 'with modesty ... interpose your judgement, under the correction and favour of your superiors',[12] Walsingham suggested that he would be better to:

> [F]orebear to set down your private opinion in the public letters you send us ... for that some give out that you are more curious [probing, invasive] in setting down your own discourses (a matter not incident to your charge) than in searching out the bottom of their proceedings there ...[13]

Davison took this advice. His letters afterwards express his opinion much less frequently and spend much longer apologizing for it when he does.[14] By the summer of 1578, it was Walsingham, not Davison, who was writing 'with a weary hand and a wounded mind' after Elizabeth rebuked him both for not keeping her informed and for disagreeing with her.[15]

These episodes capture the often unspoken rules of advice in the sixteenth century. The first was that one might speak freely when invited to do so. Such invitations are occasionally recorded. Elizabeth extended one to William Cecil, who would become her chief adviser, in the days after her accession. Davison received one in 1577: 'always ... lay the truth plainly open before Her Majesty and her Cownsel'.[16] The oaths taken by privy councillors might be considered as creating a duty (not just a right) of plain speaking. Yet, even were an invitation extended, and the second rule – speak humbly, and apologize for doing so – followed, there was one further crucial requirement. When the queen had decided, the time for advice was over. Further advice was not acceptable. Although these rules can be identified, their precise workings and boundaries were often left implicit. Are the 'rules' of advice any clearer now? Might there be some advantages in the boundary between acceptable and unacceptable advice being a bit fuzzy? Codes of conduct may provide some frameworks, but political dynamics are still affected by implicit or unspoken expectations.

Privy councillors like Walsingham and Burghley broke every one of the rules of their day, especially the last (put up and shut up) on the question of Mary Queen of Scots. Moving forward a decade, to the winter of 1586–7, takes us to the ultimate crisis over Mary. In September 1586, Davison reached the pinnacle of his career, appointed as secretary of state. He only lasted five months and his downfall was Mary Queen of Scots.

*II*

Since her deposition from the Scottish throne and flight to England in 1568, Mary had been accused of plotting to usurp Elizabeth. Calls to exclude her from the succession or to execute her had bubbled away ever since. They erupted in 1572, when Mary was accused of plotting with the Duke of Norfolk against Elizabeth. Elizabeth blocked parliament's demands to execute Mary, although she had to give in to the urging to sacrifice Norfolk. Such arguments emerged with renewed vigour with the discovery of the Babington plot to assassinate Elizabeth, Mary's trial and condemnation, and parliament's demand that Elizabeth enforce the death sentence in November 1586. Elizabeth – one of the great procrastinators of history – as usual, stalled. Burghley drew up the death warrant. Davison had to get Elizabeth to sign it. For six weeks the new secretary attended on the queen, waiting on events. On 1 February she signed. Before she could change her mind the warrant was dispatched, and Mary was finally executed at Fotheringhay on 9 February. When the news was brought to Elizabeth, she insisted she had not wanted the warrant sent. Davison got the blame: a spell in the Tower, a massive fine, sidelining for the rest of his life.[17]

Such are the agreed facts. Most historians looking at this episode are, naturally enough, interested in what Elizabeth's exact intentions were. The question of the sincerity of her grief at Mary's death, brilliantly encapsulated in the terse Latin of the first history of her reign, by William Camden, as 'conceperit aut praesetulerit' ('either conceived or pretended'), is impossible to assess.[18] Of course it was impossible to lay the blame for the execution on Elizabeth if she refused to accept it. But the circumstances in which Davison was trapped reveal much about what secrecy meant, especially in relation to the corporate responsibility of councillors, the greater sensitivity to secretarial accountability that resulted from the episode, and the extent to which advice was institutionalized and formalized.

Secrecy was the hinge on which Davison's trial turned. Elizabeth had told him to keep the fact of her signature 'as secretly as might be'. That he should 'not utter it to any body' made sense – if the news leaked out, the chance of a pre-emptive assassination of Elizabeth increased. But Davison insisted that secrecy meant: do not tell anyone except other privy councillors. He had to tell the Lord Chancellor to get the warrant sealed; on his way there, he bumped into Burghley and told him.[19] (Indeed, some accounts have him adding that Elizabeth jokingly told him to inform the then-ill Walsingham, as the joy would kill him.)[20] 'For the charge of secrecy, he conceived her meaning was, that it should be kept from the common and public knowledge only.' 'Privy counsellors and counsellors of estate', 'principal counsellors', were different.[21] Whether a specific command to keep secrecy or a particular order to tell others should have been expected was a question debated at Davison's trial.[22] Some of his judges were sympathetic. One said that the weightiest questions ought to be considered by the privy council.[23] But others, like the privy councillor Walter Mildmay, were not. Mildmay insisted that it was quite normal for one councillor to be told something secret from another.[24]

Was Mildmay correct? The oath of a privy councillor was rather ambiguous on this point. It swore a councillor to secrecy, but muddied the waters as to how this related to other councillors. '[You shall] keep secret the queen's counsail … without that you shall common it, publish it, or discover it … to any person out of the same counsail, or to any of the same counsail, if it touch him.'[25] Did this permit disclosure within the council if a matter did not concern a specific individual? A few centuries later, this ambiguity still remains in the current oath.[26]

The question of secrecy links to that of corporate conciliar responsibility. Davison well knew that he might be made a scapegoat, for Burghley had been blamed by Elizabeth for Norfolk's execution in 1572. On 3 February, the privy council met and agreed to dispatch the warrant without further reference to Elizabeth.[27] This collective responsibility eventually mutated into scapegoating Davison, who came off worst in the end, though Burghley was banned from court for several months.

In the aftermath of Davison's disgrace, we can detect an increasing sensitivity to secretarial accountability. What had Elizabeth said? What had she implied? What was the difference? Davison had reassured the queen that Mary's execution was honourable, just, and lawful – Ciceronian rhetoric again – but according to his account it was the Lord Admiral (Howard of Effingham) whose speech had 'moved' the queen to act.[28] Yet it was Davison's actions rather than his advice that attracted attention. It is no coincidence that there was a flurry of writing on secretarial duties in England in the years after Davison's fall.[29] The longest was penned by Robert Beale, who, as clerk to the council, had carried the death warrant to Fotheringhay. Beale's acute awareness of the secretary's position is shown in his advice to get instructions from the queen written down. Beale explicitly links this to Davison's fall:

> If you be commanded to write any matter of importance, do what you can to procure that the same may be done by a special letter from her Majesty herself, or if that may not be, set it down in writing. Make as though you doubted whether you had conceived her highness' mind or not and read it before her and alter it as she will have it. Keep that Minute and a note of the day, lest afterwards you be charged with it, as was the case of Mr. Davison …[30]

Other secretaries showed a similar awareness of their 'care and peril', given their trusted, but precarious, status.[31]

These tensions were not unique to English secretaries. The rise of the secretary across early modern Europe stimulated a wave of writing about the position, precariously combining personal service, representation of one's master or mistress, and an increasing role as an officeholder of an impersonal state.[32] And it was not only secretaries who were vulnerable. Intriguingly, Mary's conviction had turned on the evidence that her secretaries Claude Nau and Gabriel Curll provided. Her correspondence to Babington was drafted by Nau (according to him, from minutes of her instructions) and translated and ciphered by Curll.[33] Their testimony incriminated Mary, although the postscript enquiring about Elizabeth's prospective assassins, forged by Walsingham's decipherer, was not shown to them and not used at Mary's trial.[34] Mary's fury at being convicted on such evidence was patent: the majesty and safety of all monarchs could not, she said, depend on the word of their secretaries, who might make additions to royal correspondence, claim that monarchs saw letters that they never had had sight of, be bribed or intimidated or fearful, and who had sworn an oath of fidelity.[35] Both Nau and Curll said they had warned Mary of the dangers of conspiring with Babington, but such advice would hardly have been written down – and the minutes of Mary's instructions to Nau could not be found.[36] As with Davison, it was the secretary's word against the queen's.

Of course this formal paper trail – so important to Beale and Davison and Nau and Curll to have, so crucial for Elizabeth and Mary to avoid – would have been easy to create if the privy council's meetings had been the exclusive forum for the exchange of advice and major decisions or if, as in sixteenth century Spain, advice was often written down. The accounts of the duties of secretaries point to this – but as an aspiration, not a reality. The privy council certainly had formal meetings and a record of its decisions exists. It had set days and times and places to meet, rules for who spoke and the order in which business was to be conducted; it had its own archive.[37] Likewise, secretarial accounts emit a false air of bureaucratic efficiency: lists of books in which to note information, instructions to lock confidential papers in a cabinet, the notebooks in which Walsingham recorded his tasks. But this impression of control could not be further from reality. Every secretary from the late-sixteenth to late-seventeenth century complained that they could not find information in the council records, that they were surrounded by stacks of paper, that they really must get round to tidying up their office. In 1673 notes mention the office containing a miscellaneous-sounding 'mixtae' stuffed, with the council papers, papers of state, and documents about the army and navy, in the chimney.[38] No wonder, when one looks at the list of things that Beale wanted a secretary to know about: letters, nobles, maps, arms, ports, ships, musters, corporations, coins, revenue, taxes, religious groups, religious controversies and (just in case) Mary Queen of Scots.[39] Secretaries worried that secrets might leak out to people who shouldn't know them (people like MPs). But keeping something secret was actually less of a problem than retrieving a piece of information when it was needed. Does this sound like a familiar problem?

This bureaucratic confusion reflected the wider practice of chaotic counsel, thinly veiled by the fiction of formal rule-bound organization. Secretaries scurried round the court getting signatures to documents: Beale's account is redolent of Harold Wilson's comment on the US president being 'badgered' to sign papers 'in the lift'.[40] The privy councillors at court assembled on 3 February 1587 in Burghley's rooms, but the record for the day in the *Acts of the Privy Council* says not one word about Mary Queen of Scots.[41] Davison kept the warrant for Mary's execution in his own chamber, he met Elizabeth in the privy chamber and one of the women of the privy chamber, Mistress Brooke, was sent to announce his arrival. This bleeding into one another of 'public' and 'private' spaces may sound uncannily like the spatial crossovers inherent in more recent government practices held to be too informal. They may seem like attributes connected to 'court politics' or 'sofa government', or as necessary digressions from political norms in an emergency. Yet nothing in Davison's account of the settings for advice-giving should be interpreted as abnormal. His reassurance to Elizabeth that executing Mary was the honourable and just thing to do was a chance piece of counsel given in a conversation that included, it seems, a chat about a walk in the park and bad jokes about Walsingham's illness.[42] This was not an unusual feature of the crisis of 1587; it was the normal milieu in which advice was given in this period – oral and unrecorded; fluid, and disorganized; haphazard, contingent, and often successful.

## III

Historians of course find institutions with paper trails useful because such bodies provide a record that lasts down the centuries. As citizens of a democracy, we like the idea of accountability, the sense that there is a solemn due formality when the government is making 'big decisions', and the idea that advisory institutions – privy council, parliament, and cabinet – are being respected as the 'proper' and 'traditional' ways of providing advice. Davison's experiences give us cause to rethink some of these instinctive assumptions. Perhaps we should think about the apparent breakdown of those traditions, which political commentators have spent so much time fretting about in the late twentieth and early twenty-first centuries, with an awareness that they have always been more mythical than real. A political system that combines the aspiration to institutional formality in order to observe the constitutional proprieties while also surviving – and thriving – on chaos and grey areas may be the real Tudor legacy to modern-day politics.

## Notes

1  John Aylmer, *An Harborowe for Faithfull and Trewe Subiectes* ('Strasborowe' [act. London], 1559), sigs. H2v-[H4]r; Patrick Collinson, 'The Monarchical Republic of Queen Elizabeth I', *Bulletin of the John Rylands University Library of Manchester* 69, no. 2 (1987): 394–424, at 399.

2  There is now a vast literature on this, stemming from Collinson's 'Monarchical Republic' article. See, in particular, Stephen Alford, *The Early Elizabethan Polity: William Cecil and the British Succession Crisis, 1558–1569* (Cambridge: Cambridge University Press, 1998); *The Monarchical Republic of Early Modern England*, ed. J. F. McDiarmid (Aldershot: Ashgate, 2007).

3  William Sherman, *John Dee: The Politics of Reading and Writing in the English Renaissance* (Amhurst, MA: University of Massachusetts Press, 1995), 198–9. 'Outside experts' is Sherman's description.

4  First edn, Cambridge: Cambridge University Press, 1953.

5  J. M. B. C. Kervyn, Baron de Lettenhove, *Relations politiques des pays-bas et de l'Angleterre, sous les regne de Philippe II* (11 vols, Brussels: F. Hayez, 1882–1900), x. 4–5, 48, 50. Spelling in quotations from early modern sources has been modernized except where there are ambiguities (mainly over spellings of counsel/council).

6  Lettenhove, *Relations*, x. 313–17.

7  'Arguments against Mary Queen of Scots ... by some of both Houses', in *Proceedings in the Parliaments of Elizabeth I*, ed. T. E. Hartley (3 vols, Leicester: Leicester University Press, 1992–5), i. 274–90.

8  Markku Peltonen, *Rhetoric, Politics, and Popularity in Pre-Revolutionary England* (Cambridge: Cambridge University Press, 2013).

9  Lettenhove, *Relations*, x. 315.

10  Lettenhove, *Relations*, x. 304. Davison addresses the recipient/s as 'my lord' and 'Your Honours', suggesting Walsingham and other privy councillors were the addressees. 'Estate' and 'state' were used interchangeably.

11  Lettenhove, *Relations*, x. 337.

12  Lettenhove, *Relations*, x. 450.

13  Lettenhove, *Relations*, x. 439.

14  For an example of his caution, see Lettenhove, *Relations*, x. 607.

15  Lettenhove, *Relations*, x. 664. Again Walsingham invoked his desire to serve the Queen's honour and safety; as he had done the previous month: ibid., x. 535.

16  The National Archives (henceforth, TNA), State Papers (henceforth, SP), 12/1, no. 7; Lettenhove, *Relations*, x. 27. The letter implies that Davison gives information and that advice will then be taken on it but, as the above shows, the distinction between these processes was blurred.

17  On the ambiguities of his treatment see R. B. Wernham, 'The Disgrace of William Davison', *English Historical Review* 46 (1931): 632–6.

18 This is the translation by Robert Naunton in the third edition of 1635: *Annales*, 349; the phrase was a concoction by Camden and Robert Cotton: Patrick Collinson, 'William Camden and the anti-myth of Elizabeth: Setting the mould?', in Collinson, *This England* (Manchester: Manchester University Press, 2011), 281.

19 The various accounts of these events are brought together by Nicholas Harris Nicholas, *The Life of William Davison* (London, 1823). While varying in their individual renderings of words and occasionally in points of detail, there is a degree of common ground over the problems Davison encountered. On secrecy, see Nicholas, *Davison*, 235 (qu.), 272, 292 (qu.), 293–4, 296, 235, 237, 250.

20 Nicholas, *Davison*, 235 (Davison's account to Walsingham), 298 (his interrogation on 16 March).

21 Nicholas, *Davison*, 336–7, 251; another account has Davison invoking the law and his duty to inform others: ibid., 282.

22 Nicholas, *Davison*, 310–16.

23 Camden, *Annales*, 348.

24 Nicholas, *Davison*, 339–40.

25 Walter Mildmay's oath, taken 7 July 1567, Bodleian Library, Oxford, Tanner MS 88, fo. 4r.

26 https://privycouncil.independent.gov.uk/wp-content/uploads/2016/11/privy-counsellors-oath.pdf. Accessed 28 August 2017.

27 Nicholas, *Davison*, 238–42; Camden, *Annales*, 340, describes how Davison 'easily persuaded them being apt to believe what they desired'. See Collinson, 'Camden', 280.

28 Nicholas, *Davison*, 232 (Davison's letter to Walsingham, confirmed in another account, p. 258). Camden (*Annales*, 338) vaguely blames those who hated Mary, which hardly narrows it down.

29 Although Angela Andreani links this to the vacant secretaryship: *The Elizabethan Secretariat and the Signet Office: The Production of State Papers, 1590–1596* (New York: Routledge, 2017), 41–2.

30 Robert Beale, 'A Treatise of the Office of a Councellor and Principall Secretarie to Her Majestie', printed in Conyers Read, *Mr Secretary Walsingham and the Policy of Queen Elizabeth* (3 vols, Oxford: Clarendon Press, 1925), i. 438–9.

31 Note the full title given to Robert Cecil's account: *The State and Dignitie of a Secretarie of Estates Place, with the Care and Perill Thereof* (London, 1642).

32 There is a growing literature on this including *Secretaries and Statecraft in the Early Modern World*, ed. Paul M. Dover (Edinburgh: Edinburgh University Press, 2016); Douglas Biow, 'From Machiavelli to Torquato Accetto: The Secretarial Art of Dissimulation', in *Educare il corpo, educare la parola nella trattatistica del Rinascimento*, ed. Georgio Patrizi and Amedeo Quondam (Rome: Bulzoni, 1998); Alan Stewart, 'The Early Modern Closet discovered', *Representations* 50 (1995): 76–100; Jonathan Goldberg, *Writing Matter* (Stanford: Stanford University Press, 1990), ch. 5; for an older-style approach, see Florence M. Greir Evans Higham, *The Principal Secretary of State: A Survey of the Office from 1558* (Manchester: Manchester University Press, 1923).

33 Stephen Alford, *The Watchers* (London: Allen Lane, 2012), 214, 233; *Mary Queen of Scots and the Babington Plot*, ed. John Hungerford Pollen, Scottish History Society, 3rd series, 3 (Edinburgh: T. and A. Constable for the Scottish History Society, 1922), cxlvi–vii, 139–48; for the letters, see Pollen, *Mary*, 18–23, 26–46. On Nau, see the *Oxford Dictionary of National Biography* and Claude Nau, *The History of Mary Stewart*, ed. Joseph Stephenson (Edinburgh: William Paterson, 1883), ch. 1.

34  Alford, *Watchers*, 217–18, 233, 237, 239.

35  Jayne E. Lewis, *The Trial of Mary Queen of Scots* (Boston: Bedford/St Martin's Press, 1999), 103–7; Camden, *Annales*, 319, 322, 323; Pollen, *Mary*, cxci-ii.

36  Alford, *Watchers*, 233–4, 237, 239; Pollen, *Mary*, cxlvi, n. 1, cxli.

37  For example, see the account by Sir Julius Caesar in TNA, SP 16/8, no. 77.

38  TNA, SP 29/339A, inside back cover.

39  Beale, 'Treatise'.

40  Beale, 'Treatise', 425; Wilson, qu. in Jack Brown, *No. 10: The Geography of Power at Downing Street* (London: Haus Publishing, 2019), 201.

41  Nicholas, *Davison*, 240, see, similarly, 265, 268; *Acts of the Privy Council of England*, ed. John Roche Dasent (46 vols, London: Her Majesty's Stationery Office, 1890–1964), xiv. 317. As Collinson points out ('Camden', 281) Camden's Latin always refers to individual councillors/counsellors (consiliarii), not a council (consilium).

42  Nicholas, *Davison*, 233, 270–1; see likewise accounts of such conversations at pp. 242–4, 262–3. Mistress Brooke is probably Frances, Lady Cobham, one of the typically well-connected Elizabethan court women whose political influence has probably been underestimated.

## Chapter 6

## THE PARLIAMENTARY WAY OF COUNSEL

## Paul Seaward

Parliament and counsel are closely related ideas, for both concern the processes of deliberation, decision-making, and legitimation in a state.[1] The association has attracted particular scholarly attention in the context of the politics of the sixteenth and early seventeenth centuries, especially over a series of proposals for a much closer, more formalized, link between parliament and the king's closest advisers;[2] and on a period in the early years of the reign of Elizabeth I when, it is argued, some of the queen's most senior advisers may have conscripted parliament's help to try to persuade her to take actions – in particular securing the succession and the disposal by execution of Mary Queen of Scots – that they deemed essential for the stability and survival of a Protestant state.[3]

It is no doubt true that the conception of parliament as giving counsel had particular resonance in the 1560s.[4] The association, though, is much older than that, fostered by a reference to 'common counsel' in the writs sent out to summon members of both Houses to each parliament, and by the enacting clauses included in statutes ('by advice and assent of the lords spiritual and temporal and of the commons').[5] In the sixteenth century, it was commonplace to talk about parliaments as giving 'counsel'. Thomas Starkey, writing in 1529 to 1532, referred to the 'common counsel of parliament'.[6] John Hooker, writing in the 1570s, described the king summoning parliament in order to 'seek and ask the advice, counsel and assistance of his whole realm'.[7] Those who sat in the Commons as knights of the shire, he wrote, were expected to be knowledgeable about military affairs, in order to give the 'king and realm good advice and counsel'.[8] Members of parliament (both Lords and Commons) he called 'councillors, because they are assembled and called to the parliament, for their advice and good counsel in making and devising of such orders and laws as may be for the commonwealth'.[9] Elizabethan ministers were not shy, either, of using the word to apply to parliament. Sir Christopher Hatton in 1586 said that the queen 'hath thought meet to use you as a council (for so you be) to be made acquainted with such things as touch merely [nearly?] both her and yourselves'.[10] Parliaments were routinely asked for counsel or advice by ministers like Burghley, who suggested in 1589, for example, that the queen should tell parliament that she had 'no doubt, but to receive from you representing the whole realm whose cause this is, both good advice, and aid convenient to enable her Majesty to continue the just and honourable defence of her realm against any power what so ever of the enemy'.[11]

But there is something odd about parliamentary proceedings being referred to as a process of giving counsel, and the application of the word to parliament seems in some senses an anachronism, left over from a time when parliaments were much more closely related to the royal council than they had become by the time of Elizabeth I. What was involved in councillors advising a prince, either individually or within a small and select group, was very different to what was involved in attempting to secure a common position within an assembly whose numbers were never less than 300. Unlike the council, or individual councillors, parliament was not able to engage in direct dialogue with the prince, but had to speak through an intermediary, usually the Speaker or a councillor. Counsel provided by councillors either individually or in a session of council was provided under conditions of secrecy, sealed with the oath of a councillor; by contrast, although the proceedings of the House of Commons were supposed to be secret and privileged, the circulation of information about the doings of the House of Commons is well-attested.[12] Councillors were supposed to be sophisticated and experienced advisers; the main virtue of those sitting in the House of Commons was their status as representatives of their constituents, a qualification that carried with it no necessary connotations of expertise.

Above all, by the early sixteenth century, parliament did rather more than simply offering advice. It could and did offer advice through addresses or petitions to the crown – the petitions of 1563 requesting that the queen sort out the issue of the succession are a good example – but its characteristic process was to legislate, and it did so on the basis that it was the national representative assembly. It is true that legislation could in some ways be described as counsel too: the Commons would draw up some proposal that was intended to address a problem and the Lords and the Crown would agree to it. But a bill was much more than advice: it was the expressed will of the kingdom, which the monarch could only accept or reject – not amend or adjust to suit him or herself. Parliament's great virtue and point was, as Sir Thomas Smith wrote in *De republica Anglorum*, as a body whose role was to express the unity of the kingdom by making authoritative law: 'What is done by this consent is called firm, stable, and *sanctum*, and is taken for law'; parliament 'representeth and hath the power of the whole realm both the head and the body'. Parliament was there, he wrote, to 'advertise, consult and shew what is good and necessary for the common wealth, and to consult together'; its bills became law 'upon mature deliberation', and after 'the Prince himself in presence of both the parties doeth consent unto and alloweth', the bills would become the deed of the prince and the whole realm.[13] As such, it had come to do something very different from, and ultimately much more powerful than, any other organ of counsel. For a government this was the point of parliament: to endorse its wishes in a way that could commit the entire community to give the most effective form of communal assent to what it wished to do.

*I*

Parliament's own distinctive style as a council is reflected in the works of Hooker and Smith, the two earliest accounts of parliamentary procedure, both written in the first half of the reign of Elizabeth I, which give a remarkably sanguine picture of the parliamentary process.[14] Hooker, who had trained in civil law and theology and studied with some of the foremost continental Protestant scholars, served as a member of the Irish parliament in 1568 and of the English parliament in 1571 and 1586; his *Order and Usage of the Keeping of a Parliament in England* was written after his first experience of the Commons at Westminster. The *Order and Usage* insists on the need for members of the highest quality. Each one

> [O]ught to be a grave, wise, learned, skilful [man] and of great experience in causes of policies, and of such audacity as both can and will boldly utter and speak his mind according to duty, and as occasion shall serve, for no man ought to be silent or dumb in the house, but according to his talent he must and ought to speak in the furtherance of the king and commonwealth.[15]

Hooker compared Members of Parliament to senators of Rome, 'ancient, grave, wise, learned and expert men of the land' who were called '*Patres conscripti* for the wisdom and care that was in them in governing of the commonwealth'.[16] Smith, whose glittering credentials as a humanist and civil lawyer were widely known, had also served in parliament in 1547 and 1559 and had been closely involved with preparations for parliament as secretary to Protector Somerset, before he wrote *De republica Anglorum* in the early 1560s. Smith writes of 'marvellous good order' in the Commons, of 'perpetual oration not with altercation', and conveys his wonder that 'in such a multitude, and in such diversity of minds, and opinions, there is the greatest modesty and temperance of speech that can be used. Nevertheless with most doulce and gentle terms, they make their reasons as violent and as vehement the one against the other as they may'.[17]

These texts suggest a civilized process of deliberation and discussion mediated by rules that ensure the freedom and good temper of debate. At the centre of it is the idea of extended and discursive speech creating a rational debate between opposing opinions, and a basic assumption of freedom of speech. One prominent member of the Commons, Thomas Norton, told the House in 1571 that 'where many men be, there must be many minds, and in consultations convenient it is to have contrary opinions, contrary reasonings and contradictions, thereby the rather to wrest out the best; but this by the rule of reason, and reasoning must be *sine iurgiis* [without quarrelling]'.[18] Historians of rhetoric have made much of how the principle of arguing in turn for and against a question, 'in utramque partem', became embedded in parliamentary rules through a decision of the House in 1593, suggested by Sir Edward Coke, that when a number of people stood up to speak the Speaker should seek to ensure that there was an alternation of speeches on either side of a question. But it was probably older than that, for, as Markku Peltonen has remarked, diaries of Elizabethan parliamentary proceedings frequently refer to speeches made 'pro et contra'.[19] (Norton commented on an alternative way of arranging debate in order of seniority offered in a self-deprecating speech by one member in 1572, but the remark seems to have been jocular.)[20]

Debate was also governed by some basic rules, which both Hooker and Smith outline: each speaker could make only one contribution on any individual question, in order to prevent a few voices becoming dominant; they were required to address the subject under debate, rather than digress into other topics; speakers should refer to each other by circumlocution, rather than directly, and should avoid personal abuse. There were procedures about the progress of bills (three readings and the committee process), and about the process of voting; but neither Hooker nor Smith referred to any rules about what could be proposed, when, and how debates were to be brought to an end.

Such principles sketch an image of an assembly dedicated to a discursive process, and the Finnish political theorist Kari Palonen uses these passages from Hooker and Smith to illustrate the origins of what he terms 'the parliamentary way of politics', or a 'debating parliament' (as opposed to a 'representative parliament', or a 'legislative parliament'). 'Historically indebted to the rhetorical culture of the English Renaissance', the principle of the parliamentary way of politics is the alternation in debate of opposing points of view, debate 'pro et contra', or 'in utramque partem', supported by the development of a set of procedures whose 'underlying regulative idea' was 'fair play'. Parliamentary rhetoric, he argues, has to be distinguished from oratory: its end is to engage in 'pro et contra' debate, rather than to set out a single point of view.[21]

## II

As Palonen explains, the parliamentary way of politics is an ideal type, although he has argued that the Westminster parliament is a sort of paradigm for it, both in principle and operation. The picture of parliamentary counsel provided by both Hooker and Smith is also, no doubt, an idealized one, though how idealized is hard to say. Hooker's comment on proceedings in the Irish parliament in 1568 (at which he was present), that members 'rose up in very disordered manner, far differing from their duties in that place, and as contrary to that gravity and wisdom, which was or should be in them', suggests that he was capable of drawing a distinction between the ideal and the practical reality.[22] But there is plenty of evidence of noise and disorder during debates at Westminster, at least for the early seventeenth century, when commentators were routinely censorious about behaviour in the Commons chamber.[23] The tendency of members to speak tediously and at length was a source of constant frustration to all concerned. There is much evidence of anger, too.[24] Frequent complaints and comments about the inexperience and incompetence of a large number of youthful members suggested that Hooker's stress on the 'ancient, grave, wise, learned and expert' was far from an accurate picture of the Commons.[25]

Moreover, while a high rhetorical value was placed on the way in which parliamentary statute expressed the unity of the kingdom, it could be easily jeopardized by the divisive process of getting there through parliamentary debate. In a famous passage in *Gorboduc*, the 1562 play that dramatizes questions of the succession and good counsel, Thomas Norton and Thomas Sackville recognized that in a world that was divided already, parliaments might just make the situation worse.

> Alas, in parliament what hope can be,
> When is of parliament no hope at all?
> Which, though it be assembled by consent,
> Yet is not likely with consent to end,
> While each one for himself, or for his friend,
> Against his foe, shall travail what he may …[26]

How well an assembly behaved and to what extent it became divided, though, may be of smaller significance than its ability to come to a clear and decisive conclusion. When seeking counsel from a small group of advisers, a monarch could identify the question to be discussed, listen to counsel, orchestrate the different voices, decide when the question had been sufficiently discussed, and, crucially, bring debate to a conclusion. In an assembly whose members all have an equal voice, and an equal right to speak, there is no formally authoritative voice: the assembly's chair (the Speaker) is not determinative. The House was the collective judge of its own rules, and would come to most decisions on its procedures by consensus.

This leaderless, atomized, potentially anarchic and certainly divisive quality was something that worried monarchs and their parliamentary managers. As far as they were concerned, there was not only little point in an assembly that was incapable of reaching a decision, but it could be positively pernicious, wrecking their international reputation as well as failing to solve their domestic problems. Parliament, particularly the Commons, had a habit of infuriating Elizabeth I and, exercising her talent for colourful language, she complained in 1567 that the prince's 'opinion and good will ought in good order [to] have been felt in other sort than in so public a place', and complained about 'lip-laboured orations' and 'wrangling subjects'.[27] The queen was graciously tolerant of accepting information from members of the House of Commons about problems affecting the commonwealth; she could become incandescent about their interventions in those matters of state that she regarded as the province of the prince alone.[28] No doubt as a result, Thomas Norton, writing a paper on strategy and the choice of a Speaker in advance of the session of 1572, offered his thoughts on how 'to have a Parliament least offensive'.[29] As James I is reported to have complained to the ambassador from Spain in 1614, the House of Commons was composed of little fewer than 500, and 'of these men there was no head, and they voted without order, nothing being heard but cries, shouts and confusion. He was astonished that the kings his predecessors had consented to such a thing'.[30]

*III*

In such circumstances, how could it be possible to achieve coherence and clarity in a debate, or for the House of Commons ever to come to any decision? It is now just about impossible to reconstruct how debates worked in practice in the sixteenth century, to come to a firm view about how business was scheduled, how it was moved on, how it was possible to bring it to an end. But scholarship of the last thirty years or so has been able to show how the early Elizabethan council built up a network of members to manage business on the floor of the House of Commons to support their own efforts.[31] Their credibility was based on an understanding of the sensitivities of its members to interference. Norton's note, giving his advice on parliamentary management, explained how it was helpful for the government or the Speaker to avoid delivering instructions or even a steer about which bills should be accepted or rejected, as it would 'by and by be raised by some humorous [i.e., angry] body some question of the liberty of the house, and of restraining their free consultation perhaps offensive to her Majesty, and assuredly with long speeches to the troublesome prolonging of the session'.[32]

Most of Norton's note is occupied with the critical question for government of the choice of a new Speaker. In Bishop Russell's opening sermon for the parliament of 1483, he remarked that 'all is directed by the Speaker', and in the sixteenth century it seems likely that the Speaker had an enormous influence on the timing and organization of business, working closely with the small group of government managers and their allies.[33] The Speaker would be instrumental too in shaping the nature of the decision put before the House. Frequently, a debate would begin with many different proposals from many quarters, often contradictory, often containing detail which it would be difficult to fit into a coherent single motion, and it would be the role of the Speaker to define a specific question for decision. A later-seventeenth-century procedural manual explained that following a debate started off by a motion, 'the Speaker, collecting the sense of the House upon the debate, is to reduce the same into a question, which he is to propound, to the end that the House in their debate afterwards may be kept to the matter of that question'. Amendments might be proposed to it, but essentially it would become the text on which a vote would be taken.[34] The Speaker could define the shape and course of a debate, just as the councillor William Cecil and his ally, Thomas Norton, could prepare texts which would become the advice of the House.

The parliamentary way of politics depended on a subtle and fragile balance between outward respect for parliamentary autonomy and the right to speak, and an informal, though broadly effective, respect for the leadership of government elites. The reasons why that balance came to be upset towards the end of the reign of Elizabeth I and particularly in the reigns of her two Stuart successors is much argued over, and the extent to which policy or process was to blame is still unclear; but it is evident that it was upset, and that the capacity of the government to exercise informal influence within the Commons was radically diminished.[35] One result was to foster the development – still imperfectly understood – of increasingly sophisticated and elaborate procedural mechanisms which were used by both the court and their opponents to seize a tactical advantage.[36] Another was to push further the tendency within the court – always present, as Elizabeth clearly demonstrated – to regard parliamentary counsel as an enormous waste of time, if not positively dangerous, and best avoided. As Jacqueline Rose has suggested, the idea that parliament merely provided 'counsel' could be used in the 1620s and 1630s to disparage it, emphasizing its lack of real determinative power.[37] The failure of that balance culminated in the remarkable achievement of a relatively small group of leading politicians in the early years of the Long Parliament in 1640 to 1642 in wrecking the court's ability to manage parliament entirely. Their success would end in an extraordinary, though brief, period in which parliament took control of executive, as well as legislative, power, a development which created for a short time an entirely different dynamic of parliamentary counsel.

## *IV*

The reinstallation of royal government in 1660 revived the language and methods of pre-Civil War politics. But over the course of the century and a half after the 1689 Revolution, British politics found ways of reconciling an untrammelled right to speak with the need to conclude essential business: one of these was a systematic and cynical use of the expansion in government offices to secure the attendance, support, and tactical silence of many members. But in the last analysis the system continued to depend, as it did during the sixteenth century, on the basic acceptance by the vast majority of members of the leading role of government ministers. The Austrian political scientist Josef Redlich, reviewing in the early twentieth century the parliamentary procedure of the eighteenth, assumed that it could only have worked on the basis of a 'feeling of political responsibility which has so strikingly distinguished' the 'ruling classes of England'; a feeling without which 'no self-government, whether aristocratic or democratic in type, is possible'.[38]

The language of 'counsel' survived the revolution of 1640 to 1660 and was routinely, if probably insincerely, used, for some time thereafter. But political discourse eventually dropped 'counsel' in favour of 'deliberation', signalling the fact that parliament was seen more clearly as a sovereign legislator, and emphasizing that while it was still a body for debate, it was one that was required to take the weightiest decisions.[39] Burke's famous 1774 characterization of the House of Commons as a 'deliberative Assembly of one Nation, with one Interest, that of the whole; where, not local Purposes, not local Prejudices ought to guide, but the general Good, resulting from the general Reason of the whole', was designed to underline an insistence that members were elected to exercise their own judgments on the basis of the debate they heard, rather than to accept an imperative mandate, but in doing so it indicated that parliament would be guided by deliberation and the pursuit of collective reason. 'What sort of reason is that in which the determination precedes the discussion, in which one set of men deliberate and another decide, and where those who form the conclusion are perhaps three hundred miles distant from those who hear the arguments?'[40]

Always contested, the claim of individual Members of Parliament to take part in a high-minded policy discussion independent of the opinion of their constituents came under greater pressure both as their activities came under greater scrutiny from a metropolitan and provincial press, and as an extended electorate demanded more visibility from its representatives. The increasing number of members wishing to contribute to debate was a common subject of comment from early in the nineteenth century, if not before, a development that coincided with a growing expectation that governments should regulate society, industry and the economy through legislation. It meant that a culture of parliamentary discussion could easily be seen as in conflict with the progress of legislation (and, indeed, the legislation of progress).[41]

The two great statements of parliament as a forum for debate and the exchange of ideas both came in the context of discussions of the effect of introducing new, and working class, voters into the political system. The first of them comes in J. S. Mill's *Considerations on Representative Government*, published in 1861. Mill dismissed those who complained about representative assemblies 'being places of mere talk and *bavardage*':

> I know not how a representative assembly can more usefully employ itself than in talk, when the subject of talk is the great public interests of the country, and every sentence of it represents the opinion either of some important body of persons in the nation, or of an individual in whom some such body have reposed their confidence. A place where every interest and shade of opinion in the country can have its cause even passionately pleaded, in the face of the government and of all other interests and opinions, can compel them to listen, and either comply, or state clearly why they do not, is in itself, if it answered no other purpose, one of the most important political institutions that can exist anywhere, and one of the foremost benefits of free government.[42]

Mill's argument depended on distancing parliament from executive responsibility, and even legislative initiative. His insistence that a parliament should be properly and democratically representative of the nation as a whole brought with it an assumption that it would not be made up of 'the greatest political minds in the country', the 'experienced and exercised minds', minds 'trained to the task through long and laborious study' who would be the appropriate people to govern and legislate. Instead it would be 'a fair sample of every grade of intellect among the people which is at all entitled to a voice in public affairs', whose role would be 'an organ for popular demands', and as 'a place of adverse [i.e., antagonistic] discussion for all opinions relating to public matters, both great and small'.[43]

If in Mill's view parliaments needed to be a place of discussion rather than action because a properly democratic parliament was quite unsuited to exercising power, in the mind of his contemporary, the journalist Walter Bagehot, the great virtue of discussion was that it would prevent governments from exercising power altogether, or at least exercising power quickly and thoughtlessly. Bagehot invented the phrase 'government by discussion' in his 1872 essay, 'The Age of Discussion', later republished in *Physics and Politics*. 'If you want to stop instant and immediate action', he wrote, 'always make it a condition that the action shall not begin till a considerable number of persons have talked over it, and have agreed on it. If those persons be people of different temperaments, different ideas, and different educations, you have an almost infallible security that nothing, or almost nothing, will be done with excessive rapidity'. The British habit of government by discussion, he argued, 'has fostered a general intellectual tone, a diffused disposition to weigh evidence, a conviction that much may be said on every side of everything which the elder and more fanatic ages of the world wanted'.[44]

Bagehot's slightly flippant formulation laid bare to others the problem with parliament's obsession with debate. The idea of parliament as a centre for discussion, rather than an engine of progress, was already regarded by some modernizers as absurdly outdated and inefficient: the campaigns of obstruction mounted from the late 1870s by the Irish party and (to a lesser extent) by a faction of the Conservative party started to bring the already acute and much-discussed problem of concluding debate to a critical point. 'Obstruction' made crystal clear that the existing mechanisms for ensuring that debate produced a decision were hopelessly inadequate, resting on Redlich's 'feeling of political responsibility' – a feeling that the Irish party did not share – rather than on enforceable procedural rules. At the same time, the rapid growth of national party structures before and after the third Reform Act of 1884 stimulated an increased expectation that when parties developed programmes for government the consequent legislation should be authorized quickly and effectively. The foundation of the National Liberal Federation in 1877 under the dynamic leadership of the Birmingham businessman Joseph Chamberlain was a significant moment in shifting the focus of politics from debate in the Commons to sentiment in the constituencies, and for years the impact of an American-style 'caucus' system on the structure of parliamentary life was a subject of acute anxiety for many Conservatives as well as Liberals. When a member of the Gladstone cabinet in 1882, Chamberlain was already articulating a view that 'the primary object of a parliamentary assembly is … to carry out the decisions at which the nation has arrived … The House of Commons is the people's House, and public opinion can make it what it will'.[45]

The remedy was the introduction of closure and guillotine procedures in the 1880s, a set of tools designed to bring an end to overextended debate. It was followed by the concession to the government in 1896 and 1902 of control over all but a small proportion of the time of the House. During the debates on the new rules of 1902 the Liberal leader Campbell-Bannerman and the Unionist minister Chamberlain sparred over the nature and purpose of parliamentary debate:

> This [said Campbell-Bannerman] is not a mere factory of statutes; not a mere counting-house, in which demands on the public purse are being checked, approved, and provided for … it would be better that the House should be less efficient in its transactions of business, and retain the full faculty of exercising the functions to which I refer, rather than that it should be diminished, and the House should become the most perfect legislative machine in the world.[46]

When Chamberlain came to respond, he directly confronted Campbell-Bannerman's arguments:

> [W]hen you talk about curtailing the powers of the Government, what you mean, and it is better to say so at once, is curtailing the powers of the majority, and increasing the powers of the minority ... I believe that the people who elect the majority of the House have a right to see that that majority has power to carry out what is ex hypothesi the will of the majority of the nation; and our elections and our representative system are a perfect and absolute farce if with one hand you pretend that the majority elects a Government, and then with the other hand prevent that Government from doing its proper work.[47]

The contrast between a vision of parliament as a forum for debating and finding solutions to the nation's difficulties, as Campbell-Bannerman put it, and Chamberlain's vision of it as the efficient processor of the will of the people could scarcely have been put more starkly. With political parties, using their own (non-parliamentary) networks, now determining their own solutions to the nation's problems and seeking to enact them as quickly as possible, the idea of parliament offering ruminated 'counsel' could seem quite redundant.

## V

The new rules developed between 1882 and 1902 have ensured that the great majority of debate in the House of Commons now takes place on motions determined by the government, and (with subsequent modifications) that they are strictly timetabled to ensure that the business is concluded and determined as required. It seems rather different from the idea of parliament as a body for the open discussion and testing of ideas. But that conception has always been complicated by the fact that parliament is also a body designed to provide binding law that addresses the current preoccupations of a people and, whether or not on their behalf, of its government. The rhetorical notions of *pro et contra* debate perfectly suited academic disputations, legal argument, and even discussion before a monarch about policy options, in which there is a clear question to decide and an external judge – an audience, a jury, the king, or queen – decides the result. But its application to an assembly which has to come itself to a decision is more problematic. To avoid a wide-ranging, inconclusive discussion, some management and moderation of debate has always been essential. In the sixteenth century it was largely informal, the result of deference to the Crown and broadly accepted leadership and guidance within the assembly. Since the nineteenth century it has become a much more formalized process mediated by party, with time limits and specific roles for leading speakers.

Does this mean that the 'parliamentary way of politics' through discussion is a sham – a species of cant as Chamberlain implied – masking the fact that the real decisions are taken by an electorate on the basis of proposals put by party elites? Parliamentary debate has often disappointed observers. Sixteenth- and seventeenth-century observers suggested that the reality was very different to the pictures drawn by Hooker and Smith. Even in the eighteenth century, there was little expectation that a debate would actually change anyone's mind on an issue of importance. In the nineteenth century, Mill complained of 'inexperience sitting in judgment on experience, ignorance on knowledge'.[48] But the quality of discussion, he observed, was not necessarily the point, and commentators from Sir Thomas Smith to Bernard Manin have suggested that parliamentary debate is important more because of what is being represented, than because of what is being said. 'It is the collective and diverse character of the representative organ', Manin has written, 'and not any prior or independently established belief in the virtues of debate, that explains the role conferred on discussion'.[49] Parliaments are ultimately about taking decisions in a way that is supposed to deliver the assent of the entire community, and not debate for the sake of it. But there's more to it than that, for the legitimacy of an outcome depends not just on the credentials of the process, but on how well that process has tested it on its way: on whether the right questions have been asked and satisfactory answers secured before consent is given. At a time when the impatience of an electorate has become the touchstone of policy, there is more need than ever for 'grave, wise, learned [and] skilful' parliamentarians, and for them to think like Elizabethan counsellors.

## Notes

1   See, for example, the discussion in J. R. Maddicott, *The Origins of the English Parliament, 924–1327* (Oxford: Oxford University Press, 2010), 74–96.

2   John Guy, 'The Rhetoric of Counsel in Early Modern England', in *Tudor Political Culture*, ed. Dale Hoak (Cambridge: Cambridge University Press, 1995), 293.

3   For parliament as a council before the reign of Elizabeth I, see Paul Cavill, *The English Parliaments of Henry VII, 1485–1504* (Cambridge: Cambridge University Press, 2009), 221, 228–9; for discussion of parliament as council during the reign of Elizabeth, see Anne McLaren, *Political Culture in the Reign of Elizabeth I: Queen and Commonwealth, 1558–1585* (Cambridge: Cambridge University Press, 2009).

4   See Stephen Alford's discussion of Alexander Nowell's sermon of January 1563, in *The Early Elizabethan Polity: William Cecil and the British Succession Crisis, 1558–1569* (Cambridge: Cambridge University Press, 1998), 105.

5   For the origins and variations in the phrase in statutes, see S. B. Chrimes, *English Constitutional Ideas in the Late Fifteenth Century* (Cambridge: Cambridge University Press, 1936), 101–4; for the 'duty of counsel' as a function of medieval representative bodies, see now Michel Hébert, *Parlementer: Assemblées représentatives et échange politique en Europe Occidentale a la fin du moyen âge* (Paris: Editions de Boccard, 2018), 100–103.

6   Thomas Starkey, *A Dialogue between Pole and Lupset*, ed. T. F. Mayer, Camden Society, 4th series, 37 (1989), 70, cf. 112, 113.

7   Vernon F. Snow, *Parliament in Elizabethan England: John Hooker's Order and Usage* (New Haven and London: Yale University Press, 1977), 145.

8   Snow, *Parliament in Elizabethan England*, 152.

9   Snow, *Parliament in Elizabethan England*, 183.

10  *The Bardon Papers: Documents relating to the Imprisonment and Trial of Mary Queen of Scots*, Camden Society, 3rd series, 17 (1909), p. 90.

11  *Proceedings in the Parliaments of Elizabeth I*, ed. T. E. Hartley (3 vols, London: Leicester University Press, 1981–95), II, 412–13.

12  See, for example, Alasdair Hawkyard, *The House of Commons 1509–1558: Personnel, Procedure, Precedent and Change*, Parliamentary History Texts and Studies Series, 12 (Chichester: Wiley, 2016), 247–51.

13  Thomas Smith, *De republica Anglorum*, ed. Mary Dewar (Cambridge: Cambridge University Press 1982), 78–9.

14  The earliest description of the functioning of parliament is the model for Hooker's text, the *Modus tenendi parliamentum*, written in the first half of the fourteenth century; but this provides almost no information about how decisions were arrived at.

15  Snow, *Parliament in Elizabethan England*, 151.

16  Snow, *Parliament in Elizabethan England*, 183.

17  Smith, *De republica Anglorum*, 82–3.

18  *Proceedings in the Parliaments of Elizabeth I*, I, 241.

19  Markku Peltonen, *Rhetoric, Politics and Popularity in Pre-Revolutionary England* (Cambridge: Cambridge University Press, 2013), 138–9.

20  *Proceedings in the Parliaments of Elizabeth I*, I, 351 (cf. Galleise, i.e. Richard Gallys, at 349).

21  Kari Palonen, 'A Comparison between Three Ideal Types of Parliamentary Politics: Representation, Legislation and Deliberation', *Parliaments, Estates and Representation*, 38 (2018), 6–20, quotation at 10. For Palonen's ideas concerning the parliamentary way of politics, see also his *The Politics of Parliamentary Procedure: The Formation of the Westminster Procedure as a Parliamentary Ideal Type* (Opladen, Berlin and Toronto: Barbara Budrich, 2019), and *Parliamentary Thinking: Procedure, Rhetoric and Time* (London: Palgrave Macmillan, 2019).

22  *The Second Volume of Chronicles: Conteining the Description, Conquest, Inhabitation and Troublesome Estate of Ireland; First Collected by Raphael Holinshed; and Now Newlie Recognised, Augmented and Continued … by John Hooker alias Vowell, Gent.* (no place of publication, 1586), 'The supplie of this Irish Chronicle', 121.

23  See Chris R. Kyle, *Theater of State: Parliament and Political Culture in Early Stuart England* (Stanford, CA: Stanford University Press, 2012); Jason Peacey, 'Disorderly Debates: Noise and Gesture in the Seventeenth Century House of Commons', *Parliamentary History*, 32 (2013), 60–78.

24  E.g. *Proceedings in the Parliaments of Elizabeth I*, I, 214, reactions to Goodyear's speech.

25  See M. A. R. Graves, *Elizabethan Parliaments, 1559–1601*, 2nd edn (Harlow: Longman, 1996), 79–80.

26  V, 2.1770–75, in *Two Tudor Tragedies*, ed. William Tydeman (Penguin Books, Harmondsworth, 1992).

27  Quoted in Stephen Alford, *Burghley: William Cecil at the Court of Elizabeth I* (London: Yale University Press, 2008), 135.

28   See the discussion by Susan Doran in 'Elizabeth I and Counsel', in *The Politics of Counsel in England and Scotland*, ed. Jacqueline Rose, *Proceedings of the British Academy*, 204 (2016), 156–7.

29   British Library, London, MS Harley 253, discussed in G. R. Elton, *The Parliament of England, 1558–1581* (Cambridge, Cambridge University Press, 1986), 322–9. Elton wrote that he and Graves were agreed on the date and the recipient, but not the author; by the time he published *Thomas Norton the Parliament Man* in 1994, Graves seems to have decided that it was by Norton, but to have become less certain on the recipient (343, 346–51).

30   Quoted in Kyle, *Theater of State*, 37.

31   See M.A. R. Graves, 'The Management of the Elizabethan House of Commons: the Council's "Men-of-Business"', *Parliamentary History*, 2 (1983), 11–32, and *Thomas Norton, the Parliament Man* (Oxford: Blackwell, 1994).

32   British Library, London, MS Harley 253, fo. 34.

33   J. S. Roskell, *The Commons and their Speakers in English Parliaments, 1376–1523* (Manchester: Manchester University Press, 1965), 96–7.

34   *Observations, Rules and Orders of the House of Commons*, ed. W. R. McKay (London: H.M.S.O., 1989), 57; See also Catherine Strateman, 'Policies in Parliaments: An Early Seventeenth-Century Tractate on House of Commons Procedure', *Huntington Library Quarterly*, 15 (1951), 48.

35   For a recent discussion, see Andrew Thrush, *The House of Commons, 1604–1629* (6 vols, Cambridge: Cambridge University Press for the History of Parliament, 2010), I, 436–9.

36   See Thrush, *House of Commons, 1604–1629* as above; and Sheila Lambert, 'Committees, Religion, and Parliamentary Encroachment on Royal Authority in Early Stuart England', *English Historical Review*, 105 (1990), 60–95.

37   See on this point Jacqueline Rose, 'Sir Edward Hyde and the Problem of Counsel in Mid-Seventeenth Century Royalist Thought', in *Politics of Counsel*, ed. Rose, 253–5.

38   Josef Redlich, *The Procedure of the House of Commons: A Study of Its History and Present Form*, trs. A. E. Steinthal (3 vols, London: Archibald Constable & Co., 1908), I, 69.

39   See Paul Seaward and Pasi Ihalainen, 'Key Concepts for Parliament in Britain (1640–1800)', in *Parliament and Parliamentarism: A Comparative History of a European Concept*, ed. Pasi Ihalainen, Cornelia Ilie and Kari Palonen (New York: Bergahn, 2012), 41–2.

40   Edmund Burke, Speech at the Conclusion of the Poll 3 November 1774, in *The Writings and Speeches of Edmund Burke, Vol. 3: Party, Parliament, and the American War: 1774–1780*, ed. Warren M. Elofson, John A. Woods and William B. Todd (Oxford: Oxford University Press, 1996), 69.

41   For these themes, see Ryan A. Vieira, *Time and Politics: Parliament and the Culture of Modernity in Britain and the British World* (Oxford: Oxford University Press, 2015); Gary Cox, *The Efficient Secret: The Cabinet and the Development of Political Parties in Victorian England* (Cambridge: Cambridge University Press, 1987).

42   *Considerations on Representative Government*, chapter V (J. S. Mill, *Utilitarianism, On Liberty and Considerations on Representative Government*, ed. H. B. Acton (London: Everyman, 1972), 240).

43   Mill, *Utilitarianism, On Liberty and Considerations on Representative Government*, 241.

44  *The Collected Works of Walter Bagehot*, ed. Norman St John-Stevas (8 vols, London: The Economist, 1974), VII, 126, 127.

45  Speech in Birmingham, 5 January 1882 Garvin, *The Life of Joseph Chamberlain, I, 1836–1885: Chamberlain and Democracy* (London: Macmillan, 1932), 377.

46  House of Commons Debates (Hansard) 6 February 1902, col. 550–1.

47  House of Commons Debates (Hansard) 6 February 1902, col. 568.

48  Mill, *Utilitarianism, On Liberty and Considerations on Representative Government*, 232–3.

49  Bernard Manin, *The Principles of Representative Government* (Cambridge, Cambridge University Press, 1997), 187.

# Chapter 7

## SMITH AS SPAD? ADAM SMITH AND ADVICE TO POLITICIANS

## Jesse Norman

Over a period of two decades or so, Adam Smith gave a good deal of advice to politicians. In 1766–7, he supplied information about French taxes to, and corrected the calculations of, Charles Townshend, then Chancellor of the Exchequer, in relation to the Sinking Fund designed to repay debt incurred during the Seven Years War; the fund was topped up in Townshend's 1767 budget. He also advised Lord Shelburne on colonial policy at this time.[1] Lord North thanked Smith for his advice on his 1777 Budget, when he took ideas from the *Wealth of Nations* for two new taxes, on manservants and on property sold by auction. He took two more ideas in 1778: the malt tax and a very Smithian duty on the rentable value of buildings.[2] Also in 1778, Smith wrote 'Thoughts on the State of the Contest with America', a long and considered memorandum setting out different options for British policy towards the American colonies, then in revolt, at the request of his friend Alexander Wedderburn, the Solicitor General.

In 1779, Smith gave advice to Henry Dundas, Lord Advocate of Scotland, on the idea of a consolidating union between Britain and Ireland, which would free up trade and relieve the Irish of the burden imposed by the Navigation Acts. He was invited to give evidence on how to limit smuggling to a House of Commons committee in 1783. And in the mid-1780s, there is the famous story of the younger Pitt, then prime minister, and many of his cabinet acknowledging Smith as their teacher. Apocryphal or not, it underlines Smith's intellectual influence, and may hint at specific advice as well. Still more influenced perhaps by the writings of Josiah Tucker, Pitt made serious efforts to liberalize trade with Ireland and France, including through his support for the short-lived Eden Treaty of 1786.[3]

A fair amount has been written by Smith's biographers and others about these individual occasions for advice. But there has been no overall treatment.[4] One reason for this is a dearth of specific evidence. There are a large number of public issues or political events – ranging from the slave trade to the Union of 1707 – on which we know Smith's views, and his advice was regularly sought by public figures, especially after publication of the *Wealth of Nations* in 1776. Smith also wrote more than a few letters offering specific advice to others, including notably to William Cullen in 1774 on the proposal in Scotland to restrict medical practice to those with two years of certified medical study. But these various episodes of advice are glimpses; the written record is generally thin, and we know little from other sources about any oral advice Smith may have given, or of any other work or working practices he may have had as adviser.

Still, we can say a few things up front. Smith's advice was sporadic, delivered largely informally and outside official channels to politicians working at the highest level, at their request, including two serving prime ministers and one future one. Smith himself was a professor at the University of Glasgow between 1751 and 1764, and a tutor and independent scholar from 1764 to 1778. But he was far from naïve about politics, or indeed life.[5] He was well connected through his friendships with officials such as Sir Grey Cooper, Secretary of the Treasury after 1765, and with political 'men of business' such as Townshend, Dundas and Burke. And he was drawn closer to politics after publication of the *Wealth of Nations*, and especially during his own service as a Commissioner of Customs for Scotland from 1778 until his death in 1790.

In a world starting to be defined by political groupings if not recognizable political parties, Smith was eclectic, maintaining good relations with politicians in different parts of the Commons. His work as adviser began on a purely personal basis for Townshend, who had earlier arranged for Smith to accompany his stepson the Duke of Buccleuch on a European tour; and except for his customs work it remained so. Overall, his various pieces of advice covered the provision of information, mathematical calculation, contextual analysis, presentation of policy options, and specific recommendations alongside supporting argument and evidence. It ranged from technical aspects of taxation to specific matters of political economy to political issues of the widest contemporary importance. Finally, it covered what we might think of as a subcategory of advice, recommendations of specific individuals to others for support or advancement.

Outside a few set pieces, Smith gave incidental advice to senior politicians, such as to William Eden in 1780 on new potential sources of public revenue; this practice followed the same expanding pathway after 1776. Smith was very active as a Commissioner of Customs after 1778, notably in the regulation and suppression of smuggling, and the Board of Commissioners was expected to give advice on a corporate basis to the Lords of the Treasury in London on revenue and trade matters, and to help in the preparation of bills for parliament. Smith himself as Commissioner appears to have made specific proposals for the automatic warehousing of imports, and for higher remuneration of customs officials, both foreshadowed in the *Wealth of Nations*.[6] Finally, Smith gave the young Duke of Buccleuch, an important public figure if not a politician, a considerable amount of advice, both as mentor in their tour of France in 1764 to 1766, and later in helping the Duke to reconstruct his estates and his fortune after his disastrous losses from the collapse of the Ayr Bank in 1772.

My focus, however, is not on these pieces of advice as such. It is to ask more fundamental questions. What was the intellectual context for Smith's work as adviser? How did Smith himself think of advice, and the role of an adviser? How far does reflection on these issues have implications for advisers and politicians working today? I will try to address these questions not only from an academic perspective, but also in the light of my own personal experience as a government minister and former director of a UK think tank.

*I*

The first question, on the intellectual context for Smith's work as adviser, requires a much longer treatment than can be given here, not least because of the very wide range of his intellectual interests. But we can usefully distinguish some key themes. As several scholars have highlighted, questions of advice and counsel to rulers, and of the relation between the counselled and the counsellor, or councillor, have been relatively little explored in the academic literature.[7] Attention has mainly focused on three areas: on the emergence of conciliar traditions in England and Scotland, especially through the privy council and parliament; on counsel to monarchs during the constitutional and ecclesiastical crises of the sixteenth and seventeenth centuries; and on the Renaissance mirror of princes tradition. So far at least, little specific work has been done on counsel in the later eighteenth century.

Of these areas, the most explored is perhaps the mirror of princes tradition: the body of Renaissance writings, originating with formal letters and speeches in the Italian city states, which laid out forms of address and communication, and in due course substantive principles, for the guidance of virtuous rulers.[8] In the early sixteenth century many of these themes were taken up or contested in different ways, notably by Machiavelli in *The Prince*, Erasmus in *The Education of a Christian Prince*, Castiglione in *The Courtier* and Thomas More in *Utopia*.[9]

With one important exception, there is not much to suggest that Smith engaged in any deep way with this literature. This most resolute of anti-utopians must surely have read *Utopia*, which contains a very important dialogue on counsel. Otherwise, however, there is little evidence that More, or indeed Erasmus or Castiglione, positively influenced Smith's thought, and none of their works is listed in Mizuta's index to Smith's library.[10] The exception is Machiavelli, whose collected works were in the library, and to whom Smith refers regularly.

Matters are very different, however, in relation to ancient Greek and Roman literature. In the famous 'ship of state' analogy of Book 6 of Plato's *Republic*, Socrates argues that the state is like a ship, which can only be steered or governed by those with the requisite skill or *technê*. For Socrates, that implies a specially reared and trained class of guardians able to unite the intelligence and dispassion of the philosopher with a king's capacity for leadership. Ruling cannot simply be a matter of contingent character and circumstance; there must be *technê* involved as well. If the captain of the ship is not himself a pilot, according to Plato's Socrates, he may need a pilot with the requisite *technê* to advise him.

We can identify three strands of distinct but interlocking response or development to these ideas within classical literature: philosophical, exemplary and prescriptive. Where does the *technê* required for excellent or virtuous rule (the ideas overlap heavily in Greek) come from? For Aristotle in the *Nichomachean Ethics*, it comes from habituation through practical experience, after a period of education. Processes of education and practical learning are given canonical expression within a single famous life in the *Education of Cyrus* by Xenophon, and for multiple pairs of notable figures in Plutarch's *Lives*. Both works are studded with moralizing episodes designed to distinguish effective from ineffective rule, virtuous from vicious conduct; and Plutarch is explicit about drawing out specific lessons. Finally, there are works which actively seek to give advice to actual or would-be rulers: in particular, Seneca's *De Clementia*, addressed to the young emperor Nero, recommending mercy as part of virtuous rule, and Cicero's *De officiis*, setting out a general approach to virtuous conduct as part of a preparation for public life.

These ideas retained their currency into the eighteenth century. The *Nichomachean Ethics* remained a central part of the Scottish university curriculum at that time. The exemplary strand of counsel was given new life in Fénelon's *Les Aventures de Télémaque* (1699): the fictional education of Odysseus's son Telemachus and his tutor, Mentor, which was a huge success across Europe. And Seneca's works had earlier been critically edited by Justus Lipsius in 1605, as the culmination of Lipsius's well-known defence of Senecan stoicism in a Christianized form. All these works were in Smith's library at his death.

In England, traditions of conciliar statecraft are rooted in the Germanic patterns of assembly and advice recorded by Tacitus. These assemblies could be small groups of wise men, but by the time of Æthelstan in the tenth century there also appear assemblies with a more regularized and national character. Three hundred years before the establishment of parliament in the second half of the thirteenth century, a distinction was already being drawn between decisions on public questions made by the monarch in council, that is on advice, and decisions made by the monarch in a personal capacity, without advice; and it was increasingly accepted that the former possessed a degree of legitimacy which the latter did not. This was still more the case when an assembly was charged with gathering or spreading information from others; and when a larger assembly took on a representative character, as parliament started to do in the thirteenth century.[11]

Over time it became an expectation, indeed a duty on the monarch, to take counsel on great public matters, a trend which was gradually reinforced through parliament. And both in its deliberative and legislative functions, parliament was itself a hotbed of talkers whose debates and business required increasingly expert management, and hence advice, from those around the monarch, when management was possible at all. Overall, then, a ruler might consult or take advice from friends or *familiares*, from courtiers or officials, from a smaller assembly or privy council, and from a large assembly or parliament. All of these overlapping circles had their uses.

In his own time, Smith had a direct opportunity to observe these different circles of advice in operation, albeit in very different contexts. But he also had insights into the early historical record, through his friend David Hume's best-selling *History of England*. Among much else, this traced with great care the origins of parliament from its Germanic origins to the English Civil War, and it also explored issues directly relating to advice, including legal formulas such as 'advice and consent', the relationships of intimacy and status conferred through advice, and the risks associated with advice given in writing rather than orally.

Smith's library also included Robert Brady's *Introduction to the Old English History* (1684), which digested and reproduced early charters and other legal source material, in addition to a range of English legal texts by Coke, Blackstone, Hale, Hawkins, Selden, Spelman and others, attesting to and informing his interest in jurisprudence. And it is worth noting that Edmund Burke, to whom Smith grew increasingly close in the 1770s, had himself written a short history of England and a separate history of the laws of England, both unfinished. So there is good reason to think Smith had, not merely a sophisticated understanding of law – his *Lectures on Jurisprudence* make that clear – but access to nuanced explanations of the historical development of legal–constitutional counsel.

Finally, there are the advisory claims to be derived from the emerging subject of political economy itself. Smith was famously tight-lipped in his acknowledgement or praise for other writers in that broad area, and this may encourage the idea that he was not widely read in their works. But the suggestion seems unlikely. According to Rae, Smith once professed himself 'a beau in nothing but my books'.[12] At one point in his letters he pesters his publisher Cadell for four boxes of books he has ordered, and thanks him for sending works on trade by Adam Anderson and Malachi Postlethwayt;[13] in another he outlines to Lord Hailes the extreme care he has taken to amass books and pamphlets on corn prices.[14] These examples underline the attention he paid to gaining comprehensive and accurate information. Smith had regular access to libraries in London and Scotland, so the books in his own library are likely to be working volumes. Books were expensive, and in an age of reviews but before dust jackets or Wikipedia articles, there were limited opportunities to glean their contents indirectly. Scholars bought books because they wanted to read them and draw on their ideas.

Alongside his collections on history and jurisprudence, at his death Smith had a very substantial library of books on political economy, which included works by Bentham, Hume, Jenyns, Price, Steuart, Tucker, and Young, as well as earlier works by Josiah Child, John Law, and Thomas Mun. Among French writers, he owned works by Cantillon, Mirabeau, Necker, Quesnay, Turgot, and d'Holbach, as well as specific studies of agriculture, customs and excise, taxation and finance, the latter including annuities, banking, coinage, credit, money, weights and measures, and analyses of commodities such as corn, herring, potash, salt, wheat, and wool. As regards specific individuals who had served as advisers, Smith had access to information about men such as John Law, who had advised the Duke of Orléans, regent to Louis XV, ultimately ruinously; and he had the specific example to hand of the French physiocrats, led by Francois Quesnay, whom he knew personally, and for whom he developed both a great affection and, in the *Wealth of Nations*, a blistering intellectual critique.

*II*

What, then, did Smith take to be the content of advice on matters of political economy? In the first place, we can see that he appears to share certain wider assumptions and expectations about the activity of advising itself: that the provision of coherent advice was actually possible, and could be effective. More specifically, these assumptions included: that the world was an imperfect place, in which evils could exist and persist; that there was nevertheless such a thing as a common good, a good (since the mid-seventeenth century at least) not necessarily to be identified with the interests of the monarch; that this good, and likewise certain specific evils, could be improved or damaged by actions taken by a ruler or government; that wise advice could be helpful, and bad advice hurtful, in formulating and taking such action; and that the state could be a more or less effective instrument by which to act. These views stand in stark contrast to later *laissez-faire* caricatures of Smith.

That said, it is important to be clear that the status, value and nature of commerce, let alone its specifics, were contested topics in late eighteenth century Britain. 'Political economy' was not a recognized body of knowledge as such; it had no sanctified texts, no authorizing institutions and no recognized experimental basis to give it external credibility. And it appeared of limited applicability, since it related to commerce in peacetime, in a time of recurrent and energy-sapping warfare. Even the phrase itself had a feeling of novelty – James Steuart's *Inquiry into the Principles of Political Economy* (1767) was the first English-language work to feature it in its title – combining as it did the latent paradox of two hitherto contrasted Greek ideas, *polis* and *oikos*, city(state) and household.

But this is far from the end of the story. Smith brings other assumptions, indeed a specific orientation, to his own work. From Hume he derives the idea of a 'science of man': a unified and general account of human life in all its major aspects, based on facts and human experience. In Newtonian spirit, Hume had written in the Introduction to the *Treatise* that 'There is no question of importance whose decision is not comprised in the science of man'. It followed from this that 'Even mathematics, natural philosophy and natural religion are in some measure dependent on the science of man'.[15] And Smith himself had tracked his preferred conception of science back to Newton in his essay on *The Principles which Lead and Direct Philosophical Enquiries; Illustrated by the History of Astronomy*. There Smith argues that scientific discovery is reliant on the imagination, and the history of astronomy illustrates this through a progression of imaginative attempts to find such order in chaos: first among the ancients, then in the Ptolemaic system, and more recently in the work of thinkers such as Copernicus, Brahe, Kepler, Galileo, Descartes and Newton himself.

Bringing political economy under the heading of science thus meant the imaginative elucidation of leading principles which reduced the epicycles of other thinkers to a small set of basic principles, in the manner of Newton's laws. It was the evident ambition of both Steuart and Smith – underlined in the latter's case by the full title of *An Inquiry into the Nature and Causes of the Wealth of Nations* – to give this emerging subject a systematic and comprehensive theoretical treatment. Thus when Smith remarked of Steuart's own *Inquiry* in a letter to his friend Pulteney in 1772 that 'I flatter myself, that every false principle in it, will meet with a clear and distinct confutation in mine', he was not merely point-scoring; he was making the deepest intellectual criticism he could of Steuart's work, and asserting the Newtonian primacy of what would become the *Wealth of Nations*.[16]

However, Smith also gives this theoretical viewpoint what might be termed a Baconian-Scottish-Montesquieuian practical twist. His science of man is not simply a 'remedy against superstition'. The *Wealth of Nations* is clearly intended to be more even than a pathbreaking analysis of the principles and workings of political economy; it is also an argument for Smithian political economy itself as an *improving* science or source of good policy, and still more prescriptively, as a polemic against the evil policy effects of what he refers to as the agricultural and mercantile systems.

Smith thus brings a sophisticated theoretical and practical viewpoint to the idea of advice on political economy, so that the picture sketched earlier becomes itself the subject of sustained examination and qualification. He does not merely accept the idea of a common good; he has a theory of it. This focuses on the historical development of a commercial society, in which he saw personal dependency as replaced by presumptive relations of equality between individuals. He argues that commerce in such a society should generally take place through markets, in which people can trade as they see fit subject to law. That in turn reflects a policy governed by his 'system of natural liberty', not by agricultural or mercantile preference.

The state can be effective or ineffective, the ruler venal or statesmanlike. But, crucially, for Smith the broad test for policy in political economy is one of utility, and that utility is to be assessed not in relation to the position of the ruler, the state or its producers (which may have interests of their own) but by reference to the interests, wealth and wellbeing of consumers, or more widely, of those affected by the policy. As Smith says, 'The law ought always to trust people with the care of their own interest, as in their local situations they must generally be able to judge better of it than the legislator can do'.[17]

The effect of this striking intellectual *démarche* is to cut through prior debates as to the aims of economic policy – be they the acquisition of foreign exchange or bullion, maintenance of employment, leadership in strategic industries, domestic value addition, support for manufacturing or the expansion of state or royal power – in favour of a focus on consumers and the common interest. Smith is not a classical utilitarian in the Benthamite sense; he is much more qualified, and more focused on the overall usefulness of rules and institutions than on the utility-maximizing effects of actions. He makes no appeal to religious principles, but he does not seek to prescind questions of ethical value from political economy; so, for example, his four maxims of taxation reflect a concern for fairness, and so legitimacy and justice, as well as for efficiency. But his viewpoint remains broadly utilitarian, and this brings with it a commitment to analysing policy in terms of outcomes, of ordering or ranking those outcomes so as to be able to choose the best, and so in many cases to forms of what would now be called cost–benefit analysis.

How far Smith is original or not in all this remains much debated. But what is so striking to a modern eye is not just the depth and quality of his thought, but the sheer scale and persistence of the intellectual reorientation it represents.

Commerce, utility, interests, consumers, wellbeing, competition, markets, improvement, a science of political economy, emphasis on the exchange of ideas, a certain presumed intellectual equality with and among the audience ... we are recognizably in the modern world of policy creation and development.

Remarkably, the same is true for language itself. Smith's early *Lectures on Rhetoric and Belles Lettres* – the closest he comes to the mirror of princes tradition, but inspired by his reading of the classical rhetoricians – make clear his preference for directness and simplicity in language, and his rejection of the ornate tropes of the classical rhetoricians. The lectures were in part designed to assist young Scotsmen making their way in polite society, while at the same time assisting the creation in Scotland of an effective common language encouraging to professional work, commercial exchange and scientific progress. As Smith put it, 'when the sentiment of the speaker is expressed in a neat, clear, plain and clever manner, and the passion or affection he is possessed of and intends, by sympathy, to communicate to his hearer, is plainly and cleverly hit off, then and then only the expression has all the force and beauty that language can give it'.[18]

Language is thus a crucial part of Smith's developing vision of commercial society. As with all human exchange, commercial transactions rely on imagination. It is imagination that enables buyers and sellers to anticipate each others' needs; but this in turn relies on sympathy, for Smith an immediate human capacity to detect and reflect the psychological states of others; and the operation of sympathy relies on proper and perspicuous language.

Following John Guy, historians have identified distinct languages or modes of advice or counsel in the early modern period, including 'feudal-baronial', 'humanist-classical' and 'prophetic-providential' modes in the sixteenth century.[19] We can read Smith two hundred years later as both arguing for and theorizing the claims of another linguistic mode, a descriptive-pragmatic commercial mode. It is a mode he uses to great effect in the *Wealth of Nations*, but it is especially evident in his memorandum to Wedderburn of 1778 on the American war, which in enumerating and examining four specific options is cool, exhaustive and analytic in tone.[20] One reason why that memorandum retains a modern feel to it even today is that this Smithian mode of expression has remained the preferred language of policymaking into the twenty-first century.

### III

Smith described his political–economic thought on occasion as 'the system of natural liberty'. But in relation to rulers, governors and states, he also describes it as 'the science of a legislator'. What is this science? We can get a more precise feel for it by considering what Smith says in one specific context of advice: on trade policy. As is now well understood, Smith's views on trade are far from the *laissez-faire* caricature. Indeed, in the *Wealth of Nations* he advocates a wide range of what would now be termed interventions. These include: the Navigation Acts; taxing spirits more than beer to reduce consumption of alcohol; the granting of temporary monopolies to stimulate overseas trade in remote or hostile regions; a duty in law to pay workers in cash rather than in kind, as protection against fraud; higher taxes on rents in kind than on money rents; the compulsory registration of mortgages; enforcement of building standards; sterling marks on silver plate and stamps on textiles, to show quality; special regulation of the banks, and of currency; and even a five per cent limit on the maximum rate of interest.

Overall, we can very crudely summarize the core of Smith's view of trade as follows: trade permitted both sides to realize mutual benefit and, by increasing market size, to increase productivity. From this flows his general preference for free exchange ('All systems, either of preference or of restraint, therefore, being thus completely taken away, the obvious and simple system of natural liberty establishes itself of its own accord'); and so for the abolition of import restraint and export promotion via duties, subsidies, tariffs and bounties. Markets required government in the first instance to secure property rights, but government interventions were inevitably shaped by partial information, shortsightedness, and conflicting interests. As Smith put it,

> The sovereign is completely discharged from a duty, in the attempting to perform which he must always be exposed to innumerable delusions, and for the proper performance of which no human wisdom or knowledge could ever be sufficient; the duty of superintending the industry of private people, and of directing it towards the employments most suitable to the interest of the society.[21]

This, however, is not by any means the end of the matter. Zoom in a little, and we see that Smith's detailed approach to free trade – his view in context, as it were – is a qualified one. National security trumps political economy, for one thing; hence his support for the (highly restrictive) Navigation Acts. For another, he is prepared to contemplate deviations from free exchange in general where there is a clear public policy case based on other priorities; such as the need to shield workers from exploitation, or the restraint of usury and speculation. Moreover, although Smith holds that a nation's interest is best served by maintaining its own openness to trade even where other nations do not – since on balance their duties, subsidies etc. tend to raise domestic prices, reduce activity and limit competition – this view too is qualified. Sometimes retaliation may be worthwhile, in order to keep the other side honest and encourage them to reopen their markets. But even where import duties are to be lowered, that should be done gradually to prevent the dislocation and damage of a flood of imports.

## IV

But the idea of a 'science of a legislator' carries a further implication in relation to our topic of advice. This is that Smith is in effect seeking to reorient the whole field away from its traditional preoccupations. Instead of advice being the province of one or more senior individuals chosen for their wisdom and loyalty, he is trying to depersonalize the provision of advice altogether, for the Smithian legislator is one 'whose deliberations ought to be governed by general principles which are always the same'. The focus is on the content of advice rather than on the identity or status of the adviser. And there appears to be a latent contrast here with the figure of the Lycurgan patriotic statesman presented by James Steuart, whose powers and knowledge are such that he is almost above advice.

Part of the systematizing effect of a science, according to Smith, is to render explicit what had previously been hidden or confused: to exhibit the assumptions and logical workings of a body of thought so that they can be publicly scrutinized and challenged. In principle, then, the Smithian picture seems to be that anyone can offer useful opinions to a political leader, provided that they have thoroughly absorbed and understood, and can reason in accordance with, the blend of political economy, jurisprudence and normative moral psychology that constitutes Smith's science of a legislator.

Yet this cannot be quite right, for two related reasons. The first is that Smith was far too much of a realist to think that any human activity could ever be theorized in any complete or final sense, and the picture he paints of dynamic and concatenating human economic and moral activity is quite at odds with this. For similar reasons, he is not well understood as a proto-general equilibrium theorist, as I have argued elsewhere.[22]

But this in turn leads on to a crucial distinction, which is sometimes elided in the literature of and on advice. Policy is not the same thing as advice. Policy is usually defined as the plan or approach of government, or another agent, to a given public issue. It may relate to a new issue or to a standing or recurrent area of activity, as in monetary or fiscal or health policy. But it is silent on two central matters: as to exactly how, and how far, its rules are to be applied in a specific context; and as to the character and capacity of the decision maker. Advice, by contrast, is the recommendation of a specific course of action to a client. The adviser's task is to identify or craft the best course of action in the (potentially changing) circumstances, all things considered. The task of the client – the prince, the government, the agency – is to sift rapidly through often conflicting advice until he or she can establish the preferred option, while remaining alert to bias and adverse interest among their advisers, and (ideally) sensitive to their own personal or institutional limitations and resource constraints. Amid much else.

Smith observes, if he does not quite explicitly frame, this important distinction. The *Wealth of Nations* constantly moves, in its immense heterogeneity and breadth, between more general and more specific contexts of policy. It was mined from first publication for policy ideas, as we have noted. It approaches very closely to advice, especially on tax matters, where client and context are already understood. But ultimately it is a work of policy, not of advice. It is interesting to note that there is no epistle dedicatory; the work is not addressed to any individual. That is part of its point.

Arguably the book's central achievement is to orient political economy for the first time firmly around markets and competition, and its treatment of markets makes the point well. On the one hand, we have Smith's broad theory of market exchange; on the other, his detailed discussions of numerous different markets, ranging from those for capital, land and labour to wool, herring and bills of exchange. Just as Smith qualifies his overall views of trade policy in specific contexts, so he qualifies his overall view of markets in relation to specific markets.

It follows from Smith's analysis that different markets operate in different contexts, which may demand very different advice to be given to legislators if those markets are to work effectively. Thus, for example, Smith argues that the market for corn should be deregulated, but that for bills of exchange should be regulated to deter speculation. The market for labour is an intermediate case: 'Whenever the legislature attempts to regulate the differences between masters and their workmen, its counsellors are always the masters. When the regulation, therefore, is in favour of the workmen, it is always just and equitable; but it is sometimes otherwise when in favour of the masters'.[23] The same differentiated approach can in principle operate at any level of specificity: the market for land in Bristol may be very different to that for land in London, and so on. But it would be a further step, one not taken in the book, to set out tailored and dated advice to a government as client on whether and how to regulate or deregulate these markets in context to best effect.

## V

We can be more explicit about the contrast between policy and advice – and the nature of *technê* – by drawing on the Aristotelian idea of the practical syllogism, which describes a piece of reasoning ending in an action.[24] In relation to general policy creation, this might yield the following:

[Political principle P]: Increase the value of consumable goods annually produced by Great Britain[25]

| 1 | Adopt the policy which best achieves P |
|---|---|
| 2 | Policy A best achieves P |
| | — — |
| 3 | Adopt policy A |

In relation to advice, it might look more like this:

[Political principle P]: Increase the value of consumable goods annually produced by Great Britain

| 1* | In relevant circumstances X, Y, Z, to achieve P, adopt policy B |
|---|---|
| 2* | The relevant circumstances here and now are X, Y, Z |
| | — — |
| 3* | Adopt policy B |

where 'relevant circumstances X, Y, Z' might cover such things as a named client, a specific market, a location, a stipulated time period, a political context (parliament, media reaction, public opinion), a regulatory environment, current or anticipated governmental tax, spend or regulatory powers laid down in law, the capacity and energy of the implementing agency or minister, and the potential effect of feedback loops liable to undermine or negate the effect of the policy. All these against a context of irreducible uncertainty about the future.

This analysis allows us to draw a rough-and-ready distinction between the political level (debate about the ends of policy, here P), the technical or expert level (here, 1*), and the specific advisory level (here, 2*). Of course it is crude: among other things, there will be political debate at every 'level', and debate about whether the concluding policy action is on balance more worthwhile than the status quo. But it has other merits. First, it gives a fairly clear separation between the policy and advisory levels. Secondly, it brings out the crucial importance of context, since circumstances X, Y, Z may pragmatically encourage policy B, while circumstances X', Y', Z' – singly or collectively – may encourage policy C. And thirdly, it highlights the value of Smith's political economy, indeed his 'science of man': as a specific but non-idiosyncratic inspiration for political principle P, as a tool for means–end policy reasoning (1* vs possible alternative 1', 1", etc.) and as a utility-based intellectual framework within which to debate and advise on policy (P, 1*-3*). All in all, it underlines how much 'art' is involved in the provision of good, effective advice, however putatively 'scientific' it may also be.

But this analysis also allows us to be more precise about one of Smith's most famous remarks. In the final edition of *The Theory of Moral Sentiments*, he denounced the 'Man of System … who seems to imagine that he can arrange the different members of a great society with as much ease as the hand arranges the different pieces upon a chessboard'.[26] For Smith, the man of system has made an intellectual mistake: 'He does not consider that the pieces upon the chessboard have no other principle of motion besides that which the hand impresses upon them; but that, in the great chessboard of human society, every single piece has a principle of motion of its own, altogether different from that which the legislature might choose to impress upon it'. We might characterize the error thus: the man of system is acting according to an abstract theoretical principle, rather than one relativized to circumstance and context. His commitment to theory has blinded him. He cannot be advised.

However, the man of system also makes a pragmatic mistake, in attempting to enforce his narrow vision on others. This is oppressive and unjust; but it is also imprudent, for it fails to consider all the dynamic factors X', Y', Z' that may cause the policy to fail. As the examples of free trade and domestic market regulation make clear, this is a fate Smith's pragmatic, qualified approach to policy is designed to avoid. It is no accident, then, that for a work of 'science' the *Wealth of Nations* contains a great deal of history. History and experience help to create the sensitivity to context on which effective advice relies. Far from creating epicycular embarrassment, Smith's qualifications are a central part of the overall picture.

This Montesquieuian preoccupation with context in turn implies a deep critique of utopian, memoryless, one-size-fits-all solutions or swingeing attempts at policymaking divorced from circumstance, a critique Smith did not shrink from making in relation to Quesnay and the physiocrats. But as often with Smith, there is also a deeper latent contrast here between Britain and France. By the late-eighteenth-century Britain's system of government required much domestic policy in particular to be debated by MPs in parliament before it could be authorized, legislated for or funded. It contained mechanisms of feedback and review for policies once launched, and it exhibited a healthy distrust of personal authority. Parliamentary debates were increasingly reported after 1771, as punishment for breaches of privilege fell away. These facts encouraged the emergence of a more 'constitutional' approach to advice. And they continue to underwrite the remarkably sanguine popular acceptance of huge centralized power in Britain even today.

France was different. The structures of absolute monarchy around the French court permitted political appointees to exercise personal power as *intendants des finances* and ministers, and the country's dire financial situation pushed would-be reformers to act quickly. That was what Turgot, and then Necker, sought to do. And that was why outside experts, even philosophers, could be brought to the centre of executive decision-making. The same was not true in Britain. The wider lack of consent, and the inevitably limited duration of personal power by appointment, placed extreme difficulties in the face of French reformers. Their British advisory counterparts had to settle for influence at the fringes of politics, if at all.

## VI

It is likely that Dr Richard Price was one of those whom Smith had in mind in discussing his Man of System. Certainly Price was a principal target for Burke's parallel attack in his *Reflections* on the pernicious effects of abstract reasoning in politics. And Smith was privately scathing about Price: 'Price's speculations cannot fail to sink into the neglect that they always deserved. I have always considered him as a factious citizen, a most superficial Philosopher and by no means an able calculator'.[27]

The same dismissal was true in relation to Lord Shelburne. Smith was polite but reserved in his dealings with politicians, and maintained a cordial working relationship with this notoriously difficult man over twenty-five years. But as John Rae records, he was privately contemptuous of Shelburne's behaviour in spreading false information against Fox in 1763, and full of praise for Burke's decision in 1782 not to stay in post when Shelburne became prime minister.

This illustrates a wider point. Great political leaders might be 'men of system' and 'projectors'. But for Smith the mass of politicians conformed to a very different type: what he called 'that insidious and crafty animal, vulgarly called a statesman or politician, whose councils are directed by the momentary fluctuations of affairs'.[28]

There is a contrast here with Smith's positive and inclusive view of ordinary citizens; he does not appear to share Hume's commitment to the 'just political maxim [that] every man must be supposed a knave'.[29] Outside politics, that is.

But within politics there is another archetype: that of the man of public spirit, who configures 'his public arrangements to the confirmed habits and prejudices of the people ... When he cannot establish the right, he will not disdain to ameliorate the wrong; but like Solon, when he cannot establish the best system of laws, he will endeavour to establish the best that the people can bear'.[30] Similarly, for Smith the adviser should also aspire to the wisdom of Solon, and of the realistic 'second best'. They should be engaged but independent, non-aligned and cautious, aware of the uncertainties and risks of deliberate but mistaken action. They should speak *in propria persona*, and not on behalf of an institution or interest; and there is little suggestion with him of the idea, prevalent in British politics until at least the middle of the twentieth century, that those close to positions of power should be wealthy and landed, that is 'interested' in a more general sense.

In his own case Smith must have benefitted as an adviser from having all these characteristics. He evidently had no interest in becoming a principal himself. He was of the intelligentsia, possessed of an income but uninterested in further accumulation, without great wealth or property, an academic not a courtier or merchant or financier, a Fellow of the Royal Society, Scottish and so not readily classifiable, but of perhaps reassuringly lower social status to senior politicians. His tone is cool, appraising; and as we would say today, professional.

Over more than two decades Smith himself built a serious record as an adviser. Indeed, more than anyone before him perhaps even including Locke, he anticipates the modern idea of the academically credentialed expert (credentials in his case greatly enhanced by his published works) giving advice from outside politics – however fragile and imperfectly realized that idea has proven to be of late. But his contribution went far wider than that. He set out a canonical and recognizably modern statement of political economy as a means to describe and analyse human behaviour; he reshaped the tools of policy analysis; he characterized the baleful effects of specific interests on politics; and he massively reoriented both the context and the very language of private and public economic decision-making. His qualified, realistic and pragmatic approach to policy again belies the twentieth-century caricatures of him as a *laissez-faire* theorist, or early advocate of the efficient market hypothesis or rational economic man. And in his own time, it belied the caricature of him by Thomas Paine and the French revolutionaries as a revolutionary radical – as any of them could readily have discovered.

In our own time, as I have argued elsewhere, there are many aspects of Smith's thought that policymakers still fail to grasp, to their cost.[31] These include: the emptiness of political rhetoric about free markets; the central importance of effective market competition; the individuality of different markets and the policy responses that market failure or inadequacy in each case demands; the escalating dangers of rent extraction, especially as enabled by new technology; and more generally the dynamic and ever-evolving nature of economic life. But Smith has much to teach us outside modern economics too: about the central importance of legitimacy and norms of justice and fairness to effective policymaking; the importance of human dignity; and the need to nudge policy back from a focus on firm profits and towards wages. These lessons appear more relevant than ever today.

In relation to advice, Smith's practice exemplifies his recognition of the value and the limits of expertise, the centrality of context and history, the importance of the state, and the need to tailor advice to political circumstance and to the ability and capacity of the client. These ideas remain at the heart of the effective provision of advice to political leaders today. But when advisers become public figures, when they aspire to a more Napoleonic system of government, when they call for drastic upheavals in policy or practice, we may hear echoes of physiocracy unsuited to 'the confirmed habits and prejudices' of the British people.[32] Those in and around British politics have never been free from inflated political self-presentation, paper-thin claims to expertise, ideology, and interests masquerading as the public good, or a yearning for personal control. To all of these, Smith's work and his example stand as something of a corrective.

## Notes

I am extremely grateful to Richard Bourke, Stephen Furlong, Colin Kidd, and Richard Whatmore for their comments and suggestions.

1    Cf. W. R. Scott, 'Adam Smith at Downing Street, 1766–7', *Economic History Review* 6 (1935): 79–89.

2    John Rae, *Life of Adam Smith* (London: Macmillan, 1895), ch. 18.

3    On the Pitt-Tucker link see Istvan Hont, 'The "Rich Country-Poor Country" Debate Revisited: The Irish Origins and French Reception of the Hume Paradox', in *David Hume's Political Economy*, ed. Margaret Schabas and Carl Wennerlind (London: Routledge, 2007), 243–321.

4    Though the subject recurs throughout the work of Donald Winch, notably in *Adam Smith's Politics* (Cambridge: Cambridge University Press, 1978); in 'Science and the Legislator: Adam Smith and After', *Economic Journal* 93 (1983): 501–20; and in *Riches and Poverty* (Cambridge: Cambridge University Press, 2008).

5    The range of Smith's experience is sometimes forgotten. He lived in six important cities – Glasgow, Oxford, Edinburgh, London, Paris and Toulouse – as well as staying in Geneva, Bordeaux and Montpellier; and he had a very broad professional, business, scholarly and political acquaintance. See R. H. Hartwell's 'Comment', in Thomas Wilson and Andrew S. Skinner (eds.), *The Market and the State: Essays in Honour of Adam Smith* (Oxford: Oxford University Press, 1976).

6    Cf. Gary M. Anderson, William F. Shughart III and Robert D. Tollison, 'Adam Smith in the Custom House', *Journal of Political Economy* 93 (1985): 740–59.

7    See e.g. John Guy, *Politics, Law and Counsel in Tudor and Early Stuart England* (London: Routledge 2000); and J. E. Rose (ed.), *The Politics of Counsel in England and Scotland, 1286–1707* (Oxford: Oxford University Press, 2016).

8    Quentin Skinner, *The Foundations of Modern Political Thought* (2 vols, Cambridge: Cambridge University Press, 1998), vol. I.

9　　And by More also in *A Dialogue of Comfort Against Tribulation*, ed. Louis L. Martz and Frank Manley (New Haven and London: Yale University Press, 1976), III.10 (pp. 212–19).

10　Hiroshi Mizuta, *Adam Smith's Library: A Supplement to Bonar's Catalogue with a Checklist of the whole Library*, rev. 2nd edn (Cambridge: Cambridge University Press, 2009).

11　See J. R. Maddicott, *The Origins of the English Parliament* (Oxford: Oxford University Press, 2010), chs 1–3.

12　Rae, *Life of Smith*, ch. 21.

13　Letter to Thomas Cadell, 15 March 1767: *The Correspondence of Adam Smith*, ed. Ernest Campbell Mossner and Ian Simpson Ross (hereafter *CAS*; Glasgow Edition of the Works and Correspondence of Adam Smith, Oxford: Clarendon Press, 1977; repr. Indianapolis, Liberty Fund, 1987), 124.

14　15 January 1769: *CAS*, 139.

15　David Hume, *A Treatise of Human Nature*, ed. L. A. Selby-Bigge, 2nd edn, rev. P. H. Nidditch (Oxford: Clarendon Press, 1978), xvi, xv.

16　Letter to William Pulteney, 3 September 1772, *CAS*, 164.

17　Adam Smith, *An Enquiry into the Nature and Causes of the Wealth of Nations*, ed. R. H. Campbell, A. S. Skinner and W. B. Todd (hereafter *WN*, Glasgow Edition of the Works and Correspondence of Adam Smith, 2 vols (cont. pag.), Oxford: Clarendon Press, 1976; Indianapolis, Liberty Fund, 1981), IV.v.b.16, p. 531.

18　Adam Smith, *Lectures on Rhetoric and Belles Lettres*, ed. J. C. Bryce (Glasgow Edition of the Works and Correspondence of Adam Smith, Oxford: Clarendon Press, 1983; Indianapolis, Liberty Fund, 1985), i.iv.56, p. 25.

19　Cf. John Guy, 'The Rhetoric of Counsel in Early Modern England', in *Tudor Political Culture*, ed. Dale Hoak (Cambridge: Cambridge University Press 1997); A. N. McLaren, *Political Culture in the Reign of Elizabeth I* (Cambridge: Cambridge University Press, 1999).

20　The editors to the Glasgow Edition note that, as befits a mainly political document, Smith is not above making two suggestions in the Wedderburn memorandum which are pragmatic to the point of cynicism. These are that, to secure the newly independent Americans as allies, Britain should restore Canada to the French and the Floridas to Spain; and that while ostensibly reverting to the 1763 colonial relationship, Britain and the American colonies might secretly plan to separate. Tellingly, these ideas do not jar with the tone of the rest of the memorandum. Indeed, they reflect Smith's wider concerns about empires as mercantile systems.

21　*WN*, IV.ix.51, p. 687.

22　Jesse Norman, *Adam Smith: What He Thought and Why It Matters* (London: Allen Lane, 2018), ch. 8.

23　*WN*, I.x, Part 2, para 61, pp. 157–8. Again, we can see here Smith's concern for equity and justice at work.

24　I have also explored this analytical approach in 'Burke, Oakeshott and the Intellectual Roots of Modern Conservatism', Michael Oakeshott Memorial Lecture 2013, LSE, available on www.jessenorman.com.

25　Taken from *WN*, IV.ix.38, p. 677.

26　Adam Smith, *The Theory of Moral Sentiments*, ed. D. D. Raphael and A. L. Macfie (hereafter, *TMS*, Glasgow Edition of the Works and Correspondence of Adam Smith, Oxford: Clarendon Press, 1976; Indianapolis, Liberty Fund, 1982), VI.2.ii.17, pp. 233–4.

27   Letter to [George Chalmers], 22 December 1785, *CAS*, p. 290.

28   *WN*, IV.ii.39, p. 468.

29   David Hume, 'Of the Independency of Parliament', in *Essays Moral, Political and Literary*, ed. Eugene Miller, rev. edn (Indianapolis: Liberty Fund, 1987), 42.

30   *TMS*, VI.2.ii.16, p. 233. See also Smith's very similar remarks on the wisdom of Solon at the end of the 'Digression on the Corn Trade' in *WN*, Bk IV, p. 543. The wisdom of Solon and related ideas are discussed at length in Winch, *Riches and Poverty*, ch. 4.

31   Norman, *Adam Smith*, conclusion.

32   Cf. Peter Oborne, *Alastair Campbell* (London: Aurum Press, 2004). Also: 'You may see a change from a feudal system of barons to a more Napoleonic system'; Tony Blair's adviser and later Chief of Staff Jonathan Powell, quoted in Christopher Foster, *British Government in Crisis* (Oxford: Hart Publishing, 2005), 159.

## Chapter 8

# A MIRROR FOR PRINCES? BRITISH ORIENTALISTS AND THE PERSIAN QUESTION

## Ali M. Ansari

*If you wish my countrymen to understand you, speak to their eyes not their ears.*[1]

This chapter will explore a form of political advice generally overlooked within the field, namely literary precursors of what might now be called area studies. Politicians and diplomats need to be able to pursue their own countries' interests without trespassing clumsily by way of misstep or mistranslation on the cultural sensitivities of other nations. In the modern academy area studies has emerged as a means of inculcating this sort of sensitivity. Nevertheless, there is much to be learnt from less formalized approaches to this kind of understanding, not least from an earlier era when a sedate pace of life enabled travellers to acquire a more intimate knowledge of other cultures than is possible even in the jet and internet age. This case study focuses on a neglected form of advice literature found in discussions by British orientalists of Persian manners and political etiquette in the nineteenth century.

Britain's relations with Iran – or Persia as it was generally known in the vernacular[2] – enjoy an almost unrivalled historical pedigree. The earliest regular contacts, largely trade-based, though by no means omitting politics, began in the seventeenth century. With the establishment of British power in India from the eighteenth century, relations with Persia became a matter of immediate concern, initially on its own account but as the nineteenth century wore on, as a vital buffer against Russian expansion. Iran was more than a neighbour: Britain in a very real sense became part of the wider Persianate world, so much so that British aspirants for the Indian Civil Service had to pass exams at the East India Company College at Haileybury that included Persian language and literature. Indeed, Britain may have been the first country where Persian was systematically taught via a curriculum for the purposes of an examination. The acquisition, production, and dissemination of knowledge about Iran was undoubtedly enhanced by a developed facility in the Persian language and its cultural frame of reference.

This proximity was reflected in the ease with which British officials absorbed their cultural surroundings. Prejudice was ever-present, but their prejudices were not the same as ours, and they had little difficulty in recognizing the importance of history, mythology and folklore when embellishing and further refining their linguistic proficiency. Nor were they averse to acquiring knowledge (as opposed to gathering information) from the 'natives', of which there were many in late Mughal India, along with a few in Britain itself. One cultural phenomenon they confronted was a noted Persian genre of political advice, the many and varied mirrors of princes popular throughout the Persianate world, which sought through historical example, analogy and parable to educate rulers with the wisdom of statecraft. In time such texts would be appreciated more for their literary than their political value, but the early British orientalists who visited Iran at the turn of the nineteenth century were voracious readers (and translators) of such material. Translating one such text in 1832, David Shea was keen to point out to his readers that a passage contained within it would be of high interest to 'those who cultivate the science of political economy', since it contained 'a summary of the Oriental doctrines on that subject'.[3] Significantly, Shea acknowledged the help of Mirza Ibrahim, a native of Shiraz, and the Persian scholar in residence at Haileybury for two decades, whose 'intimate knowledge of the customs and languages of Western Asia unites an extensive acquaintance with English and European literature'.[4] Mirrors for princes constituted, of course, a well-established genre of advice, though perhaps better known to students of political advice in its western than its middle-eastern mode.[5] This chapter will show that political advice could be contained in a genre of works by diplomats and travellers less frequently mined by scholars of advice. It will reflect on some examples of this, showing that advice in this format sometimes took the form of advice on tactics – including matters of protocol and behaviour – and sometimes on a higher strategic plane. Moreover, it will also show how the formulation and expression of this advice – at least in published form – was constrained by whether the advice-giver was simply an observer or, more problematically, a practitioner implicated in the political process.

A good example of the cultural proximity attained by nineteenth-century orientalists can be seen in the writings of Sir John Malcolm, an officer and administrator in the East India Company (EIC). Malcolm became famous for his prudent administration and development of the principles of good governance in the Company's burgeoning Indian possessions, but also developed a productive sideline on political advice with regard to relations with Iran.[6] As an 'Indian' power it was natural that the EIC would have to consider relations with Iran; and, as a Company with an eye on its finances, it was anxious to find the most economical way of achieving constructive relations. While the exercise of force was always available to the Company, it was far better if it could achieve its aims by diplomatic and political means. In many ways the EIC was simply following a strategy honed over decades by the British government itself; but the situation was more acute in the subcontinent because of the distances involved and the fact that for all the growing size of the EIC army (and its successor), Britain was at heart a maritime power that eschewed long-term military commitments. In this sense it was quite different from Russia whose manpower appeared unlimited and which obviously shared an immediate border with Iran and was clearly pushing south.

Indeed, between Malcolm's first and second embassies, at the beginning and end of the first decade of the 1800s, the geopolitical situation had changed quite dramatically, with a focus on containing Iran changing to that of obstructing Russia. The key was to seek influence in Iran and to establish Iran as a friend and ally. With the luxury of time and experience in India,[7] Malcolm was well placed to develop an appreciation of the Iranian state and its Persian culture, becoming so enamoured and interested that he authored the first comprehensive history of the country in the English language.[8] This was a monumental two-volume study drawing on extensive Persian sources including the many and varied sources of Iran's mythical history which have largely been discarded by later historians who, armed with the tools of the new and emerging discipline, dismissed these 'myths' as fairy tales of little political relevance. Malcolm on the other hand regarded these myths and tales as important windows onto the cultural world in which he sought to operate. When one of his Persian companions was unable to disguise his contempt for Malcolm's interest in various parables, Malcolm responded that

> I quite understand, my good friend, the contempt you bestow upon the nursery tales with which the Hajee and I have been entertaining each other; but, believe me, he who desires to be well acquainted with a people will not reject their popular stories or local superstitions. Depend upon it, that man is far too advanced into an artificial state of society who is a stranger to the effects which tales and stories like these have upon the feelings of a nation; and his opinion of its character are never likely to be more erroneous than when, in the pride of reason, he despises such means of forming his judgement.[9]

Another advantage enjoyed by Malcolm, as we can see here, was his willingness to engage and learn from Iranian interlocutors. Thus armed and culturally prepared, Malcolm entered the fray with his first diplomatic mission in 1800, which was the basis for his *Sketches of Persia* which was published in 1827. While Malcolm's two volume history had been framed as a serious piece of scholarship – and he was indeed praised for it by Sir Walter Scott[10] – his *Sketches* were much more explicitly a political manual situated within a travelogue-cum-memoir, though one replete with political insight: a diplomatic guide for the perplexed. Among the important pieces of advice he picked up from an Iranian diplomat in India was the suggestion that, 'If you wish my countrymen to understand you, speak to their eyes not their ears'.[11] In other words the visual was paramount and how one presented oneself was crucial, especially in early encounters where the parameters of engagement would be laid out and established.

Malcolm therefore took great pains to ensure that his mission behaved according to strict rules and regulations and presented an ordered and disciplined front to all those observers he knew would be dispatched to report on his progress. Iran was not a law-bound society in the way in which he would have understood it, but it was rules-based, with strict codes of etiquette to regulate behaviour and distinguish insiders from outsiders. Malcolm wanted to ensure that his hosts took him seriously and spoke their language (metaphorically as well as literally) and consequently would welcome him as an equal 'inside' their culture. Only in achieving this could he hope to effect influence. It was important therefore to be alert to slights, however small, to ensure that gifts were never interpreted as tribute and to be aware of the importance of micro-level rules that might otherwise be regarded as trivial. As Malcolm noted, 'These matters may appear light to those with whom observances of this character are habits, not rules; but in this country they are of primary consideration, a man's importance with himself and with others depending on them'. Moreover, 'The regulations of our risings and standings, and movings and reseatings (*sic*), were, however, of comparatively less importance than the time and manner of smoking our kelliâns and taking our coffee. It is quite astonishing how much depends upon coffee and tobacco in Persia ... '

> Men are gratified or offended according to the mode in which these favourite refreshments are offered. You welcome a visitor, or send him off, by the way in which you call for a pipe or a cup of coffee. Then you mark in the most minute manner, every shade of attention and consideration, by the mode in which he is treated. If he be above you, you present these refreshments yourself, and do not partake until commanded: if equal, you exchange pipes, and present him with coffee, taking the next cup yourself: if a little below you, and you wish to pay him attention, you leave him to smoke his own pipe, but the servant gives him, according to your condescending nod, the first cup of coffee: if much inferior, you keep your distance and maintain your rank, by taking the first cup of coffee yourself, and then directing the servant, by a wave of the hand, to help the guest. When a visitor arrives, the coffee and pipe are called for to welcome him; a second call for these articles announces that he may depart; but this part of the ceremony varies according to [the] relative rank or intimacy of the parties.[12]

Such attention to detail was to serve Malcolm well in an encounter he labelled the 'battle of ceremonies'. En route to the court in Tehran, Malcolm and his entourage were to pay their respects at the regional court in Shiraz overseen by one of the Shah's many sons, who was at that stage still in his minority. Having read the 'programme' for the ceremony, Malcolm was acutely aware of the respect that was due to him according to the stated seating plan which had him situated next to the Prince with his 'right thigh' to 'rest of the Prince's Nemmed' (the felt on which the Prince himself sat). On approaching the audience, Malcolm noticed that this had been denied him but that instead the master of ceremonies had appointed him to a lower place in the room, physically obstructing Malcolm from making his way to his allotted place. Malcolm made a point of not protesting at this slight, sat down when requested and proceeded to take his coffee and pipe. However, when the second round of refreshments were about to be offered Malcolm abruptly got up and proceeded to leave the audience, much – as he had anticipated – to the consternation of his hosts. The important point here was that Malcolm had not made a vocal protest when the offence had taken place but instead waited for a suitable time to withdraw with his dignity, and that of the ceremony itself, intact. When officials were dispatched to bring Malcolm back and to query his displeasure, Malcolm retorted, 'That the British representative would not wait in Shiraz to receive a second insult', and

[T]hat regard for the King, who is absent from his dominions, prevented my showing disrespect to his son, who is a mere child; I therefore seated myself for a moment but I have no such consideration for his minister, who has shown himself alike ignorant of what is due to the honour of his sovereign and his country, by breaking his agreement with a foreign envoy.[13]

Mounting his horse, Malcolm proceeded to give the impression that he was about to withdraw the embassy altogether, a move that he correctly calculated would increase the anxiety among his hosts, especially if the Shah himself were to discover what had happened. It was done with the minimum of drama but the greatest apparent determination and indeed the lack of any overt theatrics – the whole episode was a calculated performance – appears to have disorientated his hosts such that they dispatched successive emissaries to plead with him, and furthermore his deputies – since Malcolm himself was keen to display a disdain born of distress. Officials urged him not to take the slight so seriously and, realizing that nothing appeared to work, proceeded to plead with him to return, promising to take all sorts of punishment by way of repentance.

[W]ould his disgrace – his punishment – the bastinado – putting his eyes out – cutting off his head, satisfy or gratify the offended Elchee? To all such evasions and propositions the Envoy returned but one answer: – "Let Cheragh Ali Khan [the offending official] write an acknowledgement that he has broken his agreement, and that he entreats my forgiveness: if such a paper is brought me, I remain; if not, I march from Shiraz".[14]

Malcolm's Iranian hosts quickly agreed to this request, adding that it was their earnest desire that the Shah did not hear of this misunderstanding. Malcolm expressed himself satisfied at the outcome and was persuaded by his own Persian companion to add the following line to the response, 'That everything disagreeable was erased from the tablet of the Elchee's memory, on which nothing was now written but the golden letters of amity and accord'.[15] In essence the slate had been wiped clean and Malcolm's hosts could rest assured that nothing would be raised with the Shah. Malcolm's triumph was complete, not only had he won the battle but he had won the peace ensuring these officials would henceforth be indebted to him and supportive of his mission. Quite apart from the importance of detail and etiquette, aspects of Iranian behaviour which continue in importance to this day but which are largely neglected – either through ignorance or contempt –

by modern diplomats, Malcolm had provided a test case of how to manage such situations. The key was to be prepared to establish the template for future relations by reinforcing *mutual* respect: to show such knowledge of the cultural hinterland that one felt comfortable enough navigating through it without causing further offence. Thus, Malcolm did not protest loudly at the indignity imposed upon him and neither did he show emotion (which would have been taken as a sign of weakness). His Iranian hosts had needled him to find his weaknesses. He had not initially reacted, thus lulling them into a false sense of security, while his abrupt – if dignified – departure had startled them. It was a cool and calculated move, part of the reason that Iranians have admired Britons for being 'cold blooded' (*khunsard*), in other words rational and level-headed. Finally Malcolm resolved the affair by securing an apology in writing, and, on the advice of his Persian companion, embellishing his own note with the sort of reset in relations that would reassure everyone and effectively seal a diplomatic triumph.

This was not the last time that Malcolm would be tested, but in establishing a frame of reference in which each other's dignity would be respected, Malcolm ensured that his mission, and the perception of the British as a whole, was placed on a sound footing. That he was able to do this reflected both his linguistic and cultural fluency. His hosts knew he knew and understood, and they respected him both for the effort he had made to cross the cultural divide and, more importantly, for his ability to act as an insider. He was in effect able to get under the skin of the Persians and to practise their politics arguably better than they could. Malcolm's *Sketches* functioned as a manual of 'tactical' advice, dealing with particulars rather more than strategic generalities. Yet here too in Malcom's text we can trace, perhaps, the origins of the longstanding Iranian anxiety about British political expertise and cunning. It was a text that sought to understand the Persians on their own terms and is distinctive in giving the Persians themselves a voice. If Malcolm's *Sketches* were a form of early ethnography, observing the idiosyncrasies of a people, his record of discussions from the importance of fables, the role of Islam and that of women within Iranian society, provided acute insights into the mentality of the Persians. He appreciated their pride as both a strength and a weakness, and while he never doubted the superiority of his own political system, he developed an affection for the Iranians he encountered. Indeed what was striking about the account in comparison with some that were to appear later in the century was the absence of racial stereotyping. Ethnicity, insofar as it was characterized, was as dependent on education and 'manners' as it was on birth. Malcolm's confidence was born of a sense of *political* not *racial* superiority.

This proved an important part of his success in engaging with the Iranians and in eliciting a mutual respect and affection. Indeed his decision to put down his reflections was in part a reaction to the runaway success of James Morier's satire on Iranian society, *The Adventures of Haji Baba of Isfahan*, a work of fiction that in his eyes, as well as those of other British orientalists of the period, had the unfortunate effect of embedding a dangerous caricature of Iranian attitudes among Britons. One of the members of the British embassy to Tehran, who had accompanied Morier (who was not elsewhere unappreciative of the virtues of the Persians),[16] opened his own memoirs with a protest against the pervasive influence of Morier's satire and the erroneous way it represented the Persians.[17] Buried in the body of the memoir was the following withering assessment of Morier's 'expertise': 'Mr Morier was at that time very young in Persia, and what between a barbarous foreign accent, and scant knowledge of the language, could scarcely make himself understood in the very commonest colloquy'.[18] The impact of Morier's satire on public perceptions in Britain should nonetheless not be underestimated even if the adoption of such a 'fable' might ironically tell us more about emerging attitudes in Britain than about the Iranians themselves.[19]

Charles James Wills published his memoirs in 1893, a year after George Nathaniel Curzon published his magnum opus on *Persia and the Persian Question*. Curzon was an ambitious young politician impatient to make a name for himself in the realm of foreign policy and had determined to do this by making himself an expert on 'Persia', to which end he had spent some months touring the country in 1889–90 (following an earlier trip in 1888 throughout Central Asia).[20] His detailed study of the country was avowedly policy-orientated and if Malcom provided advice on the tactical aspects of diplomatic engagement, Curzon's ambitions were altogether of a strategic nature. Indeed the bulk of the text can be read as an extended preamble – a vital supporting act – to the main event, which was an assessment of British policy towards Iran and a plea for a more proactive, consistent and strategic perspective. The introduction famously set the scene. In a much quoted, if somewhat romantic, call to arms Curzon laid out the importance of his subject: 'Turkestan, Afghanistan, Transcaspia, Persia – to many these names breathe only a sense of utter remoteness or a memory of strange vicissitudes and of moribund romance. To me, I confess, they are the pieces on a chessboard upon which is being played out a game for the dominion of the world'.[21]

As befitted a strategic survey, Curzon's treatment of Persia depicted it as part of a wider struggle against Russia in defence of India. If in the earlier period the defence of India had loomed large with a view to potential Persian and French transgressions, the focus now was quite specifically Russia and her ambitions to move south and threaten British India. Gazing at a map, such anxieties can appear exaggerated, the distances were enormous and the logistical feat involved in moving troops southwards would have been immense. But the anxiety was not wholly misplaced when the comparative strengths and weaknesses of each power were assessed, along with the possibility of Persia becoming a Russian client and, in a single bound, allowing Russian forces to circumvent the Afghan mountains and appear on the Indian border. Not only had Russia been absorbing much of Central Asia with alarming efficiency in the decades after the Crimean War, but the vulnerabilities of British power in India were made acutely visible during the Indian Mutiny. The idea therefore that Russian progress and political interference could spark further uprisings was never far from the mind of British statesmen who were similarly aware that continued British rule in India, as with much of her empire, relied more on the projection of prestige, and on soft rather than hard power.

Curzon's enthusiasm for an anti-Russian strategy was in many ways a continuation of the policy articulated by Sir Henry Rawlinson, whose collection of essays published as *England and Russia in the East* was, in his words, 'intended as a sort of manual for students of the Eastern question'.[22] Curzon's study was more comprehensive but he fully endorsed Rawlinson's argument that Persia 'is a country, which for good or ill, may powerfully affect the fortunes of Great Britain's empire in the East, and which requires, therefore, to be studied by our statesmen with care, with patience, and above all, with indulgent consideration'.[23] This required strategic foresight, consistency and the skilful exercise of soft power to draw Iran into the British orbit by encouraging a political economy that would be more aligned with and sympathetic to Britain. Consequently, economic and political development which drew the country away from autocracy and towards constitutionalism and the rule of law were to be supported. Fundamental to this strategy of course was the conviction that Persia was capable of reform and that contrary to the then Prime Minister Salisbury's view, Persia was capable of resuscitation. In this key respect Curzon's sentiments lay with Malcolm and the early orientalists who had argued that Persia's problems lay with her politics not her people.

The key figure in this regard was Nasir al Din Shah, the Qajar potentate who had been on the throne since 1848 and who had alternatively waxed and – more recently – waned in the estimation of British statesmen. The then Prime Minister Lord Salisbury appeared to have taken a personal interest in the fortune of Iran, and in his capacity as both prime minister and foreign secretary he had dispatched a close confidante and erstwhile diplomat Henry Drummond Wolff to Iran to assess the possibilities of reform. Drummond Wolff's initial assessments were cautiously optimistic, noting as other British diplomats had done before (and were to do again) that the Persians themselves were possessed of great potential but were hampered by an unsympathetic political system, at the centre of which was an indolent and capricious Shah. It was vital to unlock this political obstacle to progress. Following consultations within the country Drummond Wolff concluded that, 'I have been told by more than one authority ... that the one thing necessary for the development of Persia is a decree securing to everyone his life, liberty, and property so long as he conforms to the law and leads the life of a peaceable citizen'.[24]

Nasir al Din had issued just such a decree, with the assistance it would seem of the British embassy prior to his departure for a visit to Britain where he was hosted by Lord Salisbury at Hatfield House. It is not clear what sort of impression Nasir al Din Shah made but on his return to Iran, the decree was quietly ignored and the British, much to the chagrin of Iranian reformers, had likewise lost interest in trying to persuade the Shah, becoming embroiled instead in a series of negotiations over economic concessions which did little to enhance British prestige, and drove the otherwise cheerful Drummond Wolff to a nervous breakdown. British policy had fallen victim to an excess of enthusiasm rudely awakened by Russian obstructionism and lack of royal interest.

There was much anger among Iranian political reformers at the British failure to take action to encourage Nasir al Din Shah to apply his Decree and one in particular, Jamal al Din al Afghani, was scathing in his criticism of British inaction: ' … All Persians believed that a firman [decree] thus issued and communicated to the European powers gave the Powers, England first and foremost, the diplomatic right to insist upon its due observance, or at least to demand the explanation for any gross violation of it … But no not a word'.[25] Indeed Britain appeared to have resigned itself not only to the realities of Nasir al Din Shah's inadequacies, to which policy would have to adapt, but also, in stark contrast to Curzon's overall thesis, to an accommodation with Russia. Indeed one of the anomalies of Curzon's text was his chapter on the royal family and the character of the Shah in particular which was unusually laudatory. The discussion was not bereft of criticism and indeed the astute reader would realize Curzon was couching his text carefully and diplomatically but he was keen to conclude his prognostication with the remarkable statement that 'There is a consensus of opinion in Persia that he is the most competent man in the country, and the best ruler he can produce. Nor will any deny him the possession of patriotism and of genuine interest in the welfare of the nation'.[26]

Such a conclusion contrasted starkly with other opinions voiced in the period, perhaps most notably by the British orientalist (and founder of Persian studies in Britain) Edward Browne in his *A Year amongst the Persians*. Browne was not only a contemporary of Curzon, but he had also visited the country at about the same time, was certainly more culturally attuned (his Persian was certainly of a much higher standard) and he enjoyed good contacts with a number of Iranian political reformers most notably al Afghani.[27] Consequently his views of Nasir al Din Shah chimed with those of the increasingly frustrated political reformers within Iran. Objecting to the laudatory way in which the British press had described the Shah, Browne stressed that, 'in reality he is a selfish despot, devoid of public spirit, careful only of his own personal comfort and advantage, and most averse to the introduction of liberal ideas amongst a people whose natural quickness, intelligence, and aptitude to learn cause him nothing but anxiety'.[28]

The truth is of course that Browne's bluntness also reflected many of the private views held by British diplomats and one cannot but conclude that Browne had a degree of latitude not afforded to Curzon whose policy advice was constrained by the realities of power and ambition. Indeed, correspondence between Lord Salisbury and Curzon reveals that the first draft of the chapter on the royal family had more in common with Browne's assessment than the final published text suggested. In short, Salisbury had warned Curzon to change the text if he wanted to remain in government.[29] The correspondence is worth reviewing in some detail for the light it sheds on the political and diplomatic limits on political advice. Curzon clearly did not believe what he was ultimately convinced to publish, but policy now dictated that his political assessment should be amended in order to serve the policy being pursued. Salisbury did not pull his punches. Having taken Curzon to task for describing the Shah as mean and petty, and in a line reminiscent of Browne, suggesting that the Shah enjoyed a military 'parade as a child enjoys a punch and Judy show', Salisbury continued:

Consider the supposed publication further stating that his reign had been "disfigured by one or two acts of great barbarity of which the black and ineffaceable stain could never be washed out" & then describing in detail the tortures he had inflicted. Further imagine it to describe the manner in which the 'miserly sovereign" practised systematic extortion of various kinds upon his subjects; and then to finish with a personal delineation of the Empress of Germany, describing her as resembling a melon in her outline, and usually spending her time when at home in a ballet girl's dress with naked legs, & petticoats only reaching half way to her knees ...[30]

Salisbury concluded his review by noting that Curzon could not expect to remain in government with the chapter as it was written, and that, 'The whole of the thirteenth chapter would have to come out – or to be entirely rewritten'. Curzon responded the next day suitably humbled by the critique while attempting something of a rear-guard defence of his text, 'After your severe but no doubt just strictures I should be singularly wanting in both loyalty and respect if I did not conform at once and in all respects to your judgement ... ', before digressing on several options available to him, from a suppression of the entire text, which he swiftly discounted on the basis that he had devoted three years of his life to it; to the elimination of the troublesome chapters which related to the government, which he also considered unpalatable because it would remove any value from the text 'and would reduce interest if not its value by quite fifty per cent. I think I would rather burn the whole thing than do that'. The final option would be to remodel and amend the offending chapters – as requested by Salisbury – though he felt the urge to point out that, 'the difficulty of performing this task satisfactorily – at this stage of [the] printers progress is considerable'. Nonetheless he would submit himself to the task and allow the required government oversight and final read through of the text. Despite this acquiescence (and obvious determination to stay in government) Curzon was keen to point out that many of his critical passages had already appeared in print and that 'the murders and tortures alluded to are indisputable acts of history'.[31]

As the published text shows, Salisbury was unmoved by such pleading, however obsequiously framed it might have been, and in print at least Curzon's criticism of the Shah was understated and framed in the sort of language that would allow for a degree of diplomatic latitude. But the main thrust of Curzon's thesis was clear. Persia remained important for the defence of India and as a barrier against Russian expansion, and British policy had to be strategic, consistent, and proactive. Underpinning these arguments was the conviction that the country was not only capable of reform and progress but worthy of it, and in this respect for all the differences in approach and temperament, Curzon was following a path beaten by Malcolm and his associates, as well as more critical observers like Edward Browne. Indeed, while Curzon is often caricatured as an 'imperialist' and juxtaposed unfavourably with Browne, their political positions were remarkably similar, the real difference being that Curzon was a practitioner and Browne merely an observer.

Curzon was constrained by the realities of high office but when out of office he could be just as critical of the ineptitude (as he saw it) of government policy as Browne was. Indeed both were highly critical of the Liberal government's abandonment of the Constitutionalists in 1907, when the then Foreign Secretary Edward Grey decided, against the advice of his diplomats, to sign the Anglo-Russian Convention and leave the constitutionalists to the mercy of a vengeful Russia. But even when Curzon did enjoy the reins of power, he was undone by his own enthusiasm for a project that others did not share and the shortsightedness of an imperial administration that was anxious to cut costs. Keen to realize Rawlinson's ambition in the aftermath of the Great War, with Russia absent in the throes of revolution and the Persians looking for help, Curzon misread the situation on the ground, in both Iran and Whitehall, to find his policy in tatters and bitterly lamenting the attitude of the chief of the General Staff – '... the sooner you are out of these places altogether the better ... ' – to which Curzon had retorted, 'You are destroying the work of a century'.[32]

One might conclude that the other characteristic Curzon shared with Malcolm (as representatives of the early and later orientalist traditions) was that of failure. Malcolm discovered to his consternation that Morier's satire had a more profound impact on British attitudes towards and perceptions of Iran than a work of fiction should justifiably enjoy.[33] Even if Morier's intention had been to educate through entertainment, the effect of 'Haji Baba' was to inculcate a sense of 'allergic' complacency among British officials who opted for a policy of passive containment as opposed to the proactive engagement preferred by Curzon. They were encouraged in this view by the apparent fact that a policy of engagement had rarely yielded positive results – quite the contrary. But as Curzon would have pointed out it was not the policy of engagement that was the problem but the inconsistency of application; the lack of strategic patience and the failure of diverse, often competing, policy imperatives (and institutions) to appreciate what was at stake.[34]

In policy terms the consequence has arguably been more severe insofar as a 'diplomatic tradition' born of the Persianate world has largely been dismissed as the echoes of a somewhat embarrassing imperial age. But these bygone British orientalists still have much to teach today's policymakers. Cultural literacy was an essential supplement to linguistic fluency. Historical awareness mattered along with strategic patience. Above all, ideas mattered, not in the sense of crudely transposing one set of ideas onto another context, but in terms of a subtle dialectic which a cultural literacy born of experience in India afforded several generations of British diplomats. British officials absorbed ideas, digested and then reapplied them with a keen sense of the locality within which they needed to operate. In particular, they learnt from their Persian colleagues that power depended on prestige, and prestige on presentation – to speak to their eyes not their ears. 'Soft' power is often underpinned by its own distinctive forms of advice, the details of which are perhaps inadequately captured – and frequently neglected – in the advice which derives from contemporary area studies.

## Notes

1   The Persian Ambassador to India, Mohammad Nubbee Khan to Sir John Malcolm, quoted in Malcolm's *Sketches of Persia* (London: John Murray, 1827), 26.

2   In this essay the terms 'Persia' and Iran will be used interchangeably. British observers were well aware that 'Iran' and 'Iranian' were the name used locally but Persia was the term in widespread use in English for much of the period under review and will largely be used here.

3   Mirkhond, *History of the Early Kings of Persia: From Kaiomars, the First of the Pishdadian Dynasty to the Conquest of Iran by Alexander the Great*, trans. David Shea (London: Oriental Translation Fund, 1832), ii.

4   Mirkhond, *History of the Early Kings of Persia*, i–ii. On Mirza Ibrahim see Michael H. Fisher, 'Persian Professor in Britain: Mirza Muhammad Ibrahim at the East India Company's College, 1826–44', *Comparative Studies of South Asia, Africa and the Middle East* 21 (2001): 24–32.

5   The most obvious example of this is Machiavelli's *Prince*, though Xenophon's *Cyropaedia* also became popular among early modern rulers and thinkers. In the eighteenth century Voltaire was to produce a series of royal biographies that would serve as historical examples for the education of the prince. Nevertheless the mirror of princes was also an established genre in Islamic political thought. See e.g. Louise Marlow, 'Surveying Recent Literature in the Arabic and Persian Mirror for Princes Genre', *History Compass* 7 (2009): 523–38; Mehrzad Boroujerdi (ed.), *Mirror for the Muslim Prince: Islam and the Theory of Statecraft* (Syracuse NY: Syracuse University Press, 2013); Lisa Blaydes, Justin Grimmer and Alison McQueen, 'Mirrors for Princes and Sultans: Advice on the Art of Governance in the Medieval Christian and Islamic worlds', *Journal of Politics* 80 (2018): 1150–66.

6   For a short biography of Malcolm see R. Pasley, *Send Malcolm! The Life of Major General Sir John Malcolm, 1769–1833* (London: British Association of Cemeteries in South Asia, 1982).

7   Malcolm for example used the extensive sea voyages to practice his literary Persian by translating poetry, see Pasley, *Send Malcolm*, 31.

8   Sir John Malcolm, *History of Persia* (2 vols, London: Longman, 1815).

9   Malcolm, *Sketches*, 190–1. Malcolm wrote the text in the third person referring to himself as the Elchee (ambassador or envoy).

10   Pasley, *Send Malcolm*, 86.

11   The Persian Ambassador to India, Mohammad Nubbee Khan to Sir John Malcolm, quoted in Malcolm's *Sketches*, 26.

12   Malcolm, *Sketches*, 63.

13   Malcolm, *Sketches*, 65.

14   Malcolm, *Sketches*, 65.

15   Malcolm, *Sketches*, 66.

16   See, for example, J. Morier, *A Journey Through Persia, Armenia, and Asia Minor to Constantinople, in the Years 1808 and 1809* (Elibron Classics, 2008; first published London: Longman, Hurst, Rees, Orme and Brown, 1812), 364–6.

17   Harford Jones Brydges, *An Account of the Transactions of His Majesty's Mission to the Court of Persia in the Years 1807–11* (London: James Bohn, 1834), viii. On Malcolm's own protestation see *Sketches*, xiii.

18   Brydges, *Account*, 412.

19   C. J. Wills, *In the Land of the Lion and Sun or Modern Persia: Being Experiences of Life in Persia from 1866–81*, 2nd edn (London: Ward Lock & Bowden, 1893 (new edn published by Mage Publishers, 2004)), 3.

20   For a comprehensive treatment of Curzon and Iran, see C. Ross, *Lord Curzon, the 'Persian Question', and Geopolitics, 1888–1921* (Ph.D. diss., University of Cambridge, 2010).

21   George N. Curzon, *Persia and the Persian Question* (London: Longman, 1892), vol. I, 3.

22   H. Rawlinson, *England and Russia in the East* (London: John Murray, 1875), xi.

23   Curzon, *Persia*, vol. II, 588.

24   Drummond Wolff to Salisbury, Tehran, 21 April 1888, reprinted in *Iran: Political Diaries 1888–1966*, Cambridge, Archive Editions, vol. I, 45.

25   Jamal al Din al Afghani, 'The Reign of Terror in Persia', *The Contemporary Review* 61 (1892): 238–48, reprinted in L. Ridgeon (ed.), 'Religion and Politics in Modern Iran' (London: I.B. Tauris, 2005), qu. 12.

26   Curzon, *Persia*, vol. II, 401.

27   On the parallels between E. G. Browne and Curzon, see C. Ross, 'A Tale of Two Experts: Lord Curzon and E. G. Browne Confront the "Persian Question"', *The Historical Journal* 52 (2009): 385–411.

28   Edward G. Browne, *A Year amongst the Persians* (London: Century Publishing, 1984) first published in 1893, 99. For all his reputation as a liberal, Browne's characterization of Iran being divided between quick witted Persians and dull Turks is among the most explicitly racist texts on Iran in this period, and certainly more blunt than anything provided by Curzon, see in particular pp. 108–9.

29   On this correspondence and the subsequent revision to the text, see K. Rose, *Superior Persian* (London: Phoenix Press, 1969), 237–9. Note that my reading of the correspondence differs in some ways from that which appears in Rose. In the section on the Shah's meanness Rose notes £30,000,000, whereas I read the document as referring to £3,000,000. This latter sum would be equivalent to around £390m in current values.

30   Salisbury to Curzon, 27 November 1891, Hatfield House Archives

31   Curzon to Salisbury, 28 November 1891, Hatfield House Archives

32   G. Waterfield, *Professional Diplomat: Sir Percy Lorraine* (London: John Murray, 1973), 62.

33   See, for example, the striking note to the British ambassador in Iran in 1978, FCO 8/3191, 'Annual Review for 1977', Weir to Parsons. '… whatever happened to Hajji Baba? Having been accustomed to regard your average Persian as the epitome of idleness, deceitfulness, corruption, charm and conceit, are we now witnessing a change in the national character?'

34   Curzon, *Persia*, vol. II, 605–6.

## Chapter 9

## REFLECTIONS ON THE CENTRAL POLICY REVIEW STAFF

## William Waldegrave

The Central Policy Review Staff (CPRS), of which I was a member from 1971 until the autumn of 1973, was a multidisciplinary unit of the British civil service established as a result of the White Paper, *The Reorganisation of Central Government,* published in October 1970, after the victory of the Conservative Party under Edward Heath in June of that year.[1] The CPRS existed until 1983, when it was abolished by Margaret Thatcher after her election victory of that year.

The CPRS remains of interest, I believe, partly because the Conservative Party in opposition under Heath before 1970 had done an unusual amount of analytical work for an incoming administration on the reform of the machinery of Whitehall government, including the relationship between departments and the centre, and the nature of what there should be at the centre. There had been various different streams of work undertaken, partly by former civil servants consulted by Heath, and partly by party researchers. The CPRS is therefore quite rich in parentage, and among those parents were a number of very distinguished former public servants who had thought carefully about such matters, and some unusually thoughtful political advisers. Both groups produced work which remains of value today.

Second, the late 1960s had seen much discussion of whether Britain's institutions had sufficiently modernized themselves: the civil service was amongst those subject to criticism, including self-criticism. This had led in 1966 to the establishment, after a select committee of the House of Commons had levelled the accusation of amateurism at the modern service, of the Fulton Committee. The Committee's terms of reference (to its own frustration) precluded it from making representations about the machinery of government – the structure of departments and their relation to the centre – but it made trenchant criticisms of what it saw as the cult of the generalist, the lack of influence by scientists, poor training and recruitment practices and other matters. It reported in 1968 and the Labour government accepted its recommendation to separate management of the civil service from the Treasury, and establish a Civil Service Department (CSD), as well as a Civil Service Training College.

Third, a number of those who served in the CPRS were themselves academically well equipped to write about it, and did so, foremost among them William Plowden and Tessa Blackstone, whose *Inside the Think Tank* (1988) remains a good account not just of the CPRS but of the general issues which lay behind its invention, many of which continued to be matters of debate up to the date of publication of their book, and indeed remain so to this day.[2] Equally useful, particularly in relation to the style and culture of the CPRS, is Peter Hennessy's Strathclyde Paper of 1985, *Routine Punctuated by Orgies*.[3] Hennessy was of course an academic and a journalist rather than an insider, although even then so well connected was he that it was sometimes difficult to remember the fact. There are also many references and partial accounts of the unit in the memoirs of the day, including of all four prime ministers whom it served, and also of political advisers such as Bernard Donoughue and Ferdinand Mount, and in papers presented to conferences by many of the participants such as Kenneth Berrill and John Ashworth. Thus the CPRS happened to provide the locus for some high-quality discussion around what should be the arrangements for the central capability of Whitehall.

The CPRS was located in the Cabinet Office, in 70 Whitehall, mostly on the fourth floor, where I shared an office with Robin Butler, with the office of Lord Rothschild, its first head, on the second floor. It was accountable for 'pay and rations' as the old civil service jargon had it, to Sir Burke Trend, the Cabinet Secretary although Rothschild also had permanent secretary rank. In practice, Trend did not involve himself in its management, though as a new recruit I had a formal interview with him (it consisted of a discussion of the funeral speech of Pericles) to represent the fact that he was in terms of the civil service hierarchy my ultimate boss, but this was only after I had already been offered the job by Rothschild following an interview which characteristically took place in his flat at 23 St James's Place.

The members of the original CPRS were drawn roughly half and half from inside the civil service and from outside, though all those who came from outside became temporarily established civil servants and were subject to normal civil service discipline, for example in relation to talking to the press or attending party conferences or other party political occasions. I remember it being made clear to me that my rank, as an Assistant Principal, which for example allowed me to eat in the Cabinet Office mess rather than the canteen, was temporary: if I tried to become an established civil servant I would go down several rungs on the ladder and gain no accumulated pension rights – that is, if I succeeded in gaining proper admission to the service at all, which should not, Mr Moss the establishments officer told me, be taken as a foregone conclusion. The other members when I arrived, and as they subsequently gathered, were people of very high ability. Rothschild's formal number two was Professor Dick Ross, an academic economist who had at one time been considered for the top job. In fact the deputy in reality was Peter Carey, an exceptionally able civil servant whose heroic war in the Balkans as a Serbo-Croat-speaking intelligence officer, endeared him particularly to Rothschild, but also made him an ally of Rothschild's in showing no great respect for normal bureaucratic procedures. He was an energetic and entrepreneurial public servant, and became Permanent Secretary in the Department of Trade and Industry before a successful career in the private sector. The Treasury and the Foreign Service provided others of its very brightest and best: Robert Wade-Gery, Fellow of All Souls and skilled diplomat who later became High Commissioner in New Delhi; Robin Butler, later Cabinet Secretary and head of the civil service, and other officials of distinction.

Half insider and half outsider was William Plowden, who had established himself as one of the country's leading transport economists as well as serving on the Board of Trade. From outside came Brian Reading, another economist of high ability, sympathetic to the revived economic liberalism of the early Heath years, and a series of scientifically trained experts on energy, initially from Shell, where Rothschild, himself a distinguished biological scientist and FRS, had been head of research. Plus me – when I started a good deal the youngest, just back from a Kennedy Scholarship at Harvard, often to be used, I discovered, as an irregular dogsbody for Rothschild, who enjoyed upsetting the hierarchical Whitehall of the day by inserting me, with rather too much hair and flared trousers, into meetings far above my grade, at which you could almost literally see grand officials holding their noses as I arrived.

It was a small unit, never more than twenty, and at the beginning much less. Some discipline was provided by John Mayne, a distinguished Ministry of Defence official, and Chris Saunders from the same department, who had the unenviable task of attempting to establish normal civil service procedures in Rothschild's office. Madeleine Aston, Susanne Reeve, Kate Mortimer and later Tessa Blackstone provided some gender balance in the junior ranks of the unit, but more nearly achieved that balance than their small number might suggest by sheer ability and force of personality.

Although as I have mentioned we were all subject to civil service rules in relation to political activity, it was known that I had political ambitions (I had been Chair of the Oxford University Conservative Association, though I had never worked in the Conservative Research Department, as Plowden and Blackstone wrongly claim)[4] and I was sometimes deployed as a liaison officer in relation to the Conservative Party, but infrequently. Rothschild, by means of both the prestige of his name and the range of his connections, could open any door, political or not, without any help, across the political or any other spectrum. In the brief period after the War when he took his seat in the Lords he had favoured the Labour Party, while sitting in so far as he did sit on the cross benches, allowing his friend Churchill to comment, 'Sitting on your dividends, I suppose?'

That is what the unit was when it was established. But it had many fathers and mothers, who were variably loyal to their offspring, depending on how well we were perceived to be doing. Amongst these were Lord Fulton, and his report, as I have said, which was published not long before Mr Heath's election, and which had proposed the establishment of a Civil Service Department charged with modernizing and reforming the civil service to make it fit for the twentieth century. One item on Fulton's modernizing agenda was that this new department should include a strategic planning unit. This, and the general background provided by Fulton's attack on the allegedly amateurish nature of the still largely surviving Northcote-Trevelyan civil service which his committee had studied, meant that Heath, whose pitch to the electorate had been that of a hard headed practical modernizer, found fertile ground for his own inclination to be a reformer of government structures. He also found a good deal of support from among progressive civil servants. Indeed, Heath had established in opposition an informal group of outstanding former civil servants who retained close connections inside Whitehall. They were led by Lady Sharp, recently retired Permanent Secretary at the Ministry of Housing and Local Government, Sir Freddie Bishop, Sir Eric Roll and Sir Henry Hardman, all former Permanent Secretaries, with William Plowden as secretary. Many of these former officials had been close to Heath when, under Macmillan, he had led the UK's first attempt to join the then European Economic Community. Separately, Edwin Plowden, William's father, and Lord Roberthall, former government chief economic advisers, had recommended a 'small but high quality' Office of the Prime Minister and Cabinet Co-ordination which would advise the prime minister and non-departmental ministers. They correctly warned that the establishment of such a unit would be bitterly opposed by Whitehall departments.

The other background weather of the time was the application of business school management theory, along with academic cybernetics, to the theory and practice of government, above all in the United States. This was the time of Robert McNamara from Ford in the Department of Defense in the United States, bringing with him doctrines of bottom-up programme budgeting, objective-based departmental strategies and the aura of highly successful free market businesses as well as the mystique of the new management consultancy profession. The concept of British muddling through under the guidance of generalists was not the flavour of the day. The British equivalents of Ford were Marks and Spencer and Shell; advice from these sources would, it was proposed, revitalize Britain: the blueprint for the action part of the *Action Not Words* of Mr Heath's 1966 Election Manifesto would be found not in the pages of Michael Oakeshott nor in Rab Butler's ambiguous aphorisms, but in the corporate planning departments of the best private sector businesses. Managerialism of this kind was in the air, and in the books of major political scientists like Daniel Bell, whose *The End of Ideology* (1960) was a fashionable text.[5] It was also in the minds of the party political researchers Heath had set to work between his defeat in 1966 and his somewhat unexpected (to most people but not to him) victory in 1970. These Conservative Party preparations had been led, in relation to the reform of Whitehall, by two exceptionally able younger Conservatives, David Howell (now Lord Howell) and Mark Schreiber (now Lord Marlesford). Before 1970 they had travelled widely, and met all the main players in the United States in particular, from Lyndon Johnson downwards, and brought back what were then revolutionary new doctrines. In fact, in the coherence of their ideas, they went a good deal further than most of their American interlocutors. They linked management theory to political doctrine in a more interesting way than is found in most of the American work of the time, which tended to present itself as 'apolitical' or 'post-political'.

In the minds of Howell and his colleagues, managerial efficiency was related to the development of modern liberal free-market doctrines which would help to define a more limited but more effective role for the state. Many years later, when in John Major's government I was responsible for civil service reform after 1992, I found that the Americans had caught up: the then fashionable text I discussed with Vice-President Al Gore, *Reinventing Government: How the Entrepreneurial Spirit Is Transforming the Public Sector* (1992) by David Osborne and Ted Gaebler could have been written by Howell and Schreiber twenty five years earlier.[6]

Howell and Schreiber started with the question of 'what government is for', and sketched policies which would steadily gain traction until they reached fulfilment in the Thatcher, Major and Blair years. Howell's pamphlet *A New Style of Government* of May 1970 saw for example the first deployment in the UK of the word 'privatization' – borrowed, according to Howell, from the then management guru Peter Drucker.[7] At the centre of the Howell-Schreiber proposals was the concept of programme budgeting for all activities of government steered by a central strategic capability. This would be led by a new and powerful department at the centre containing the expenditure side of the Treasury as well as the functions of Fulton's proposed Civil Service Department (in charge of personnel matters such as recruitment and training of civil servants). It would take up the idea mooted by Fulton but not embodied in the CSD, of a central strategic capability. It would contain a McKinsey type 'Crown Consultancy'. This new department, which was partly inspired by the Office of Management and Budget in Washington, would take over an expanded Cabinet Office. The strategic coherence of the new Programme Analysis and Review system would be ensured by a Central Policy Review Staff – in the Prime Minister's Office in 10 Downing Street.

As will be obvious from my description earlier of the unit I joined, this was not quite what was established. We were not in 10 Downing Street but in 70 Whitehall and had to ask a Private Secretary in Burke Trend's office for the key to the then blue baize door which separated the two. We were not leading businessmen and women from Marks and Spencer's – though there were some others from that and some other stables deployed around Whitehall, most notably Derek Raynor (later Lord Raynor) in the new Procurement Executive of the Ministry of Defence. Rothschild did indeed come most immediately from Shell – but he had run their research and was not a manager. The Programme Analysis and Review system was set up, and CPRS had initially some role in coordinating it, but Whitehall soon buried it, and the Treasury easily saw off any serious attempt to interfere with its iron control of resource allocation. We were not, as Fulton had recommended, part of the CSD; although we were in the Cabinet Office.

Let us examine what lay behind the partial dashing of the pre-election hopes for radicalism proposed both by reform minded former and current civil servants, and by the young party political thinkers, which Howell laments in his book *Look Where We're Going*.[8] What were the origins of the resistance to the 'big bang' version of reform in 1970, well founded though the support for such radicalism seemed to be, not only politically, but in management theory and among many reform-minded present and former distinguished and influential public servants, validated, moreover, in spite of his restricted terms of reference by Lord Fulton's Committee?

First, of course, there were the universal laws of bureaucratic inertia. No extremely busy bureaucracy, staffed by high-quality people conscientiously carrying out clearly important and urgent work, will welcome upending itself at the behest of new doctrines, perhaps particularly if these doctrines derive a good deal from foreign academic sources. What is more, naïve parallels from business can easily be resisted by the public service. Ford, after all, could walk away from production of its disastrous 1958 Edsel model (with the shareholders taking a hit but otherwise few consequences); the public sector cannot simply retreat from a democratically mandated task which it finds difficult to undertake. A new government with a very strong and united ideology can overcome such inertia, of course, but there were plenty of traditional politicians among the Conservative leadership who did not, to put it mildly, put reform of the machinery of government very high among their priorities. Lord Howell reports Douglas Hurd as having overheard the following conversation in February 1970 before a dinner at the Carlton Club where ideas for the reform of government were to be discussed:

> Reggie Maudling (Shadow Home Secretary): "What's all this balls we're having a dinner about at the Carlton tonight?"
>     Lord Carrington (Shadow Leader of the Lords): "Well, Reggie, I am sorry you feel like that. I regard it as very important."
>     Maudling: "Well, I can't say I understand what it's all about. Still, hope it's a good dinner."[9]

Then there is, for any new government, the pressure of events. As these pressures mount, and ministers come to rely on the machinery to hand, rebuilding that machinery, on which you have already come to rely, seems of lower priority. How do you redesign the aeroplane when you are already airborne?

So such reform, if radical rather than incremental, is always difficult to undertake. Easier bits are completed: more difficult and perhaps important change is postponed. Thus Mr Heath amalgamated smaller departments into large strategic entities, most spectacularly in the case of the Department of the Environment, which swallowed Housing, Local Government and the Ministry of Works; but the strategic hierarchy above such mega-departments of which they were supposed to be part, never followed. The amalgamation and name changes were easy; the subsequent step was not.

But there were two other more interesting sources of objection, one derived from strongly held constitutional beliefs about the collegiate nature of Cabinet government, and one from the objections of Her Majesty's Treasury. To consider the constitutional objections, let us take a step back. In war, things are acceptable which are seen to be dangerous in peace. The First World War forced radical modernization of the machinery of British government as it forced change in much else. After Lloyd George replaced Asquith in 1916, an altogether more professional central capability was established around the prime minister, not least to enable him to assert more systematic control over the military. A formal Cabinet Secretariat was established for the first time under Maurice Hankey, and Lloyd George equipped himself with a small but influential policy unit under Professor W. G. S. Adams, Gladstone Professor of Government at All Souls College, Oxford. The unit was known as 'the Garden Suburb' because its staff lived in some huts in the garden of 10 Downing Street. In 1918, a committee under Lord Haldane recommended the permanent establishment of a central analytical capability, using language very like that of the groups established to look at the same subject before 1970.

But the end of the war put an end to all that. Why? The answer was, and remains, the deep suspicion in Britain of 'presidential' leadership. Parliamentary democracy had evolved to limit the powers of the sovereign and diffuse them among Commons and Lords; both Houses felt and feel a deep suspicion of Bonapartist tendencies on the part of the prime minister, whose office had emerged as convener, manager and collegiate head of the Cabinet and not as a democratized version of the monarch (as perhaps had been the objective in the United States presidency). So as soon as the Great War ended, the Garden Suburb was dismantled. Even the policy-neutral Cabinet Secretariat nearly went too: Bonar Law campaigned in 1922 on a ticket of abolishing it.

The pattern in the Second World War was very similar. Churchill had established in the Admiralty when he was First Sea Lord in 1939 a unit under Professor Lindemann to advise him on statistics and science and other matters that fell into his remit as a Cabinet member. He took it with him into No 10 and Lindemann, now Lord Cherwell, became hated and feared throughout Whitehall, as a formidable enforcer for Churchill, along with 'Pug' Ismay, Churchill's military bulldog. Cherwell had a team of about twenty. Note also the point made by Churchill at the Admiralty: it was not just expertise on his own responsibilities he wanted, but advice on how to join in collective discussion led by other departments. Churchill had listened to his friend Leo Amery who had said, 'The one thing that is hardly ever discussed (in Cabinet) is general policy ... there are only departmental policies'. And this was indeed the fundamental point: Cabinet government was founded on the concept of collective discussion, but how was the Prime Minister to equip him or herself to assess departmental policies? And how were other ministers supposed to challenge the expertise of their colleagues on matters which might be crucial to the success of the government as a whole? After all, Lady Sharp, a formidable former permanent secretary, later reported Harold Macmillan as newly appointed prime minister telling her, 'I have now got the biggest job I ever had and less help in doing it than I have ever known'.[10]

Nonetheless, when peace came, the profoundly institutionally conservative new prime minister, Clement Attlee, swept away Churchill's unit, and though he did appoint Edwin Plowden as Chief Planning Officer in 1946, Plowden and his staff were swiftly absorbed into the Treasury. Thus the fear of Bonapartism, doubtless exacerbated by the powerful personalities – and the success – of Lloyd George and of Churchill, restored the doctrine, and the institutional reality, of peacetime prime ministers as chairs of a collegiate cabinet which was collectively responsible to parliament. It is hard to remember now, but when I joined CPRS in 1971 even the existence of Cabinet committees was classified as secret, on the grounds that knowledge that there was a structure of committees would undermine public faith in the singularity of the Cabinet itself as the only proper forum for national decisions, accountable collectively to parliament. At the time of the establishment of CPRS, and of the White Paper, which described its role, it was thought essential to emphasize that the unit was charged with briefing the Cabinet as a whole, not just the prime minister, and that it was not the beginning of a Prime Minister's Department. Britain was not on the way to a White House or an Elysée – God forbid. That is why we were on the 70 Whitehall side of the blue baize door, and had to beg the key from Burke Trend's office if we were summoned to No 10.

Then there is the Treasury. Parliamentarians may watch for signs of Bonapartism, but the altogether more feline opposition of Her Majesty's Treasury (HMT) to any other central capability than itself formed a useful alliance of convenience for such constitutionalists. Then as now HMT saw the growth of such central abilities (other than strictly technical, and sometimes them also) as threats to its chances of success in the perennially difficult task of trying to match resource with expenditure. Prime Ministers, and Cabinets collectively, pressed by vociferous lobbies normally supported in the media, tend to be keen on expenditure in the particular, whatever their alleged views on expenditure in the aggregate. The Treasury, as I know well as a former Chief Secretary, has to work hard to maintain any balance in the other direction. Every expenditure is presented by its sponsor department as 'investment'; every restraint on the growth of expenditure is a cut.

HMT has learnt the skills of guerrilla warfare over the years; that it is normally defeated is shown by the inexorable growth of public spending. Most people think, for example, that Mrs Thatcher slashed state spending; in fact, she left it, on any measure, a bit bigger than she found it. The Treasury's lot is not an easy one even with a philosophically sympathetic prime minister. Thus the establishment of a brand new, powerful central department charged with co-ordinating new strategic plans developed with the help of a prime minister's policy unit staffed by business people and consultants, leaving HMT simply to set and collect the taxes or to issue the bonds to pay for it all must have caused the mandarins of Great George Street acute anxiety.

In the event, HMT won all the critical battles. The Civil Service Department's first permanent secretary was William Armstrong, an archetypal Treasury man, and its role was limited. CPRS as established was excluded from involving itself in fiscal matters, and though it contained in Ridley and Reading and Ross very able economists, it never became involved in macro-economic arguments. Treasury could not quite prevent, to its great annoyance, CPRS sharing its previously unique right to sit on all important cabinet committees and to see all significant Cabinet papers; and this fact did make a dent in HMT's all-encompassing capacity to control such government strategy as there was. I will return to that matter in a moment.

These were the forces, then, which limited the extent of the reforms established in 1970, disappointing the ideological reformers among the younger Conservatives, and perhaps also some of the more open-minded civil service supporters of Fulton, or what Fulton might have proposed had he and his committee been allowed wider terms of reference. But in spite of it all, CPRS was nonetheless a radical peacetime innovation which for a time at least did not entirely fail to cause some salutary trouble for the forces of small 'c' conservatism in the bureaucracy. Robert Wade-Gery, one of the founder members, famously described it as having thrown 'sometimes salutary grit' 'into the smooth running of the Whitehall machine'.[11] I think it did a little better.

In this essay my purpose is not to give a full history of the CPRS. For that, the reader is strongly recommended to return to Blackstone and Plowden. My purpose is to consider some of the continuing issues which surround advice-giving at the centre of Whitehall from the point of view of what I saw as a member of CPRS from 1971 to 1973 and then as the successor to Douglas Hurd as Political Secretary to Edward Heath after I left the civil service in the autumn of 1973, and later as a minister myself.

CPRS work divided itself into two parts: strategy, and specific subject studies. As he was establishing CPRS, Rothschild was also completing a separate high profile report on the organization of government research and development. This report, *The Organisation and Management of Government Research and Development* (published as a Green Paper for discussion in 1971 along with another study by Sir Frederick Dainton in Cmnd 5046, *A Framework for Government Research and Development*),[12] was not a CPRS report as such but a personal study carried out by Rothschild on the basis of his experience of running Shell's large R&D programme. It was highly controversial in the scientific community, though its principles – that where research is applied, rather than curiosity driven, each programme should have a clearly defined customer in a government department, which meant that departments should become intelligent customers for applied R&D and all equip themselves with Chief Scientists – were and remain sensible.

The major controversy surrounding this report did two things. First, it made Rothschild quite famous as a radical policy thinker in the media. Second, it led him to the conclusion that he should be extremely wary in involving CPRS as a unit in high profile and controversial single issue studies, at least if they were to become public. He was well aware that politicians and mandarins alike are always on the lookout for someone else to take the flak for an unpopular set of recommendations which can then be abandoned if the incoming fire becomes too heavy.

This was not how Rothschild wanted the CPRS to be used – and his instinct was in my view shown to be right when, after he left, the unit undertook two pieces of such work – one on the Foreign Office, and one on public expenditure options including radical reform of the Health Service. The first enabled the powerful Foreign Office lobby to inflict considerable damage both on the unit and on two of its most effective members, Tessa Blackstone and Kate Mortimer. The second provided at least part of the excuse for its closure in 1983 when a leaked paper embarrassed the then prime minister – though, if presentation had been handled more carefully, its examination of stark strategic options for the government was well in accordance with the original CPRS remit.

Rothschild was careful – and well connected enough – to maintain close relations with other members of the Cabinet – particularly non-departmental ministers – so that, although the relationship with the prime minister was always the most direct, the doctrine that CPRS served the Cabinet as a whole was not entirely a fiction. In particular, he took trouble when we undertook a study into a particular subject – such as the future of the supersonic airliner Concorde – to ensure that he had support for the work from some other ministers as well as the prime minister, and also from Sir Burke Trend as Cabinet Secretary.

Thus the work was a mixture of the strategic and the particular. Then and now, I believed and believe that the most important work was the strategic. This centred on twice yearly strategy presentations at Chequers in which CPRS presented deliberately provocative papers analysing our view of what the government's medium term objectives were, and how they did or did not fit together. We challenged ministers to tell us that we were wrong and to reformulate their own strategy. The exercise was then repeated for middle and junior ministers. Peter Carey, Robin Butler and I were effectively the team for this activity, which as can be imagined, was wonderfully enjoyable. We well recognized that the purpose of our papers – these were in fact not papers but large charts and visual aids which (I am ashamed to say) Robin Butler and I fixed with drawing pins to the Tudor panelling in the upstairs drawing room at Chequers – were primarily designed to get ministers talking collectively as they had done as colleagues in Opposition but were now prevented by the weight of departmental work from doing as ministers in government. We were determined to prevent ministers simply reading out departmental briefs on these strategy days and invented various ruses for refusing to circulate our material sufficiently far in advance for officials to prepare such briefs. 'Our charts are too big to go in the proper envelopes' was one such ruse, I remember. HMT, for the reasons discussed above, were always the most suspicious of all departments. Nonetheless, we prepared our ground carefully, making friends both of ministers – particularly junior ministers who are often excluded from any proper collective discussion – and forward-thinking officials in departments. Thus it was at least as much the achievement of space protected from departmental crises in which ministers could think about the future collectively and we hoped strategically as it was the actual content of our presentations that was the value of these strategy days. As the political weather darkened from the end of 1972 onwards, the meetings retreated first to No 10 – a much less protected space in terms of departmental and business-as-usual disruption than Chequers – and then became less and less frequent.

Nothing quite comparable has been achieved subsequently, at least by the Conservative governments I served. Mrs Thatcher, genuinely interested in ideas, famously held various kinds of seminars at Chequers – for example on Germany, as recounted in Charles Moore's magisterial biography.[13] But they were for her, not for the Cabinet, and fulfilled a different function as briefing and education for her effectively alone: admirable indeed, but in some degree threatening to her senior ministers in ways which we took trouble to avoid. And of course as they were conducted with outsiders, they leaked. Mr Major held large meetings of officials, experts and ministers on particular subjects – such as his admirable

Citizens' Charter – in No 10 – but they were very formal, and often included sympathetic non-Whitehall participants in front of whom ministers could not speak freely.

In my experience, all good businesses, charities, and other organizations realize the importance of proper 'away-days' when there can be genuine free discussion of the future and the challenges likely to emerge from, for example, changing technology or new competitors. Badly organized and insufficiently prepared, they can waste everyone's time. Well prepared they can help the organization to renew itself and to innovate. That is what we were trying to do in 1971 and the next two or three years at CPRS, and the effort is worth revisiting, I believe, even though we were not able to generate the coherent strategy to take Mr Heath's government through the dark days of 1973 and 1974. We could only provide the forum where such thinking might have been done: we could not, at least when acute crisis came, do the thinking ourselves without the political leadership.

Some other work – on a joint approach to social policy, and on energy policy, for example – had genuine cross-departmental strategic value too. One other piece of work, much mocked and sabotaged by departments then, was in fact thirty years ahead of its time: we proposed an 'Early Warning System' trying to look at troubles ahead (my first draft came back from the all-powerful typing pool headed 'Ear Warming System' which was prophetic). Under Mr Blair, a proper governmental risk register – which is what we were proposing – was finally established, as it would have been long before in any large company.

Let us therefore look at where things stand today. Few, I think, can believe that policy analysis and advice to ministers at the centre of British government or indeed in departments is wholly satisfactory. One general development has been broadly in the right direction, I believe; others not so. The sensible development is in the increase in political advice available to ministers. It was always absurd that, when I succeeded Douglas Hurd as Mr Heath's Political Secretary, I was quite alone, apart from admirable assistants who organized the travel for political visits which the civil service would not handle. Of course the prime minister needs his or her own political advisers. What type these are of will depend on the office holder, but there should certainly be partisan policy thinkers among them as well as speech writers and spin doctors. Mrs Thatcher put that right, and indeed essentially replaced CPRS by the overtly political No 10 Policy Unit. And departmental ministers need their political advisers too.

By the time of writing, in the autumn of 2019, the very large growth of special advisers at all levels in all departments has been shown to create its own problems, if they are thought for example to be providing advice contrary to that at the centre. My own belief is that these spads are now too many, not of uniformly high quality and in many cases engaged solely in doing things which they consider advance the political careers of their masters, rather than helping with the generation of coherent policy. They should be and perhaps are beginning to be, under much tighter control in terms of discipline from the permanent civil servant heads of each department. Otherwise, there is a genuine risk of their introducing issues of conflict of interest – let alone of destruction of necessary confidentiality – which can verge on corruption. But political advisers there certainly should be.

The developments which have not been benign seem to me to be the steady erosion of a sense of Cabinet collectivity. Mr Blair is perhaps most to blame for this; but Mr Cameron is not innocent either. What the press has called 'sofa government' – combined with an over intrusive regime of freedom of information – has in some ways taken us back to the time before Maurice Hankey and the establishment of the Cabinet Secretariat in 1916. Some major items of policy are not discussed collectively at all, and if they are discussed, little is recorded for fear of an immediate and politically driven application under the Freedom of Information Act. This is a recipe for bad decision-taking, as well as for ultimate lack of accountability.

The coherence of government rests on there being coherence at the top: in no successful private sector business that I know of, in spite of the existence of personality cults around some charismatic leaders, is that success truly down to one person. There always has to be a team which can work together. British aversion to Bonapartism is sensible in practical as well as constitutional terms. Thus the subject of policy advice (both political and non-political) for the Cabinet as a collectivity should be reviewed again. Churchill's realization that he was unbriefed on crucial collective issues all those years ago remains as true then as it does today – perhaps even more true now that the growth of political advice in No 10 far outbalances any other political advice available to departmental ministers, and political advice from whatever source is itself not balanced by any corresponding growth of non-political cross-departmental strategic advice, whether derived centrally or departmentally.

It is my belief that the time is ripe for a new Fulton Committee – with terms of reference which allow it to look at the machinery as well as the other issues of central Whitehall governance. Many things will need review in Britain when the issues surrounding Brexit have settled to some form of stability. The machinery of government, and the provision of central advice to ministers, is one among them. If such a committee were to be appointed, I hope they will spend a little time looking at the lessons which can still be learnt from the experience of the CPRS.

## Notes

1    *The Reorganisation of Central Government*, Cmnd 4506.

2    Tessa Blackstone and William Plowden, *Inside the Think Tank: Advising the Cabinet, 1971–1983* (London: Heinemann, 1988).

3    Peter Hennessy, S. Morrison and R. Townsend, *Routine Punctuated by Orgies: The Central Policy Review Staff, 1970–1983* (Glasgow: Strathclyde Papers on Government and Politics, 31, University of Strathclyde, 1985).

4    Blackstone and Plowden, *Inside the Think Tank*, 27.

5    Daniel Bell, *The End of Ideology* (Glencoe, IL: Free Press, 1960).

6    David Osborne and Ted Gaebler, *Reinventing Government: How the Entrepreneurial Spirit is Transforming the Public Sector* (Reading, MA: Addison-Wesley, 1992).

7    Howell, *A New Style of Government* (London: Conservative Political Centre, 1970).

8    David Howell, *Look Where We're Going* (London: Unicorn, 2019).

9    Howell, *Look Where We're Going*, 97.

10   Blackstone and Plowden, *Inside the Think Tank*, 7.

11   William Waldegrave, *A Different Kind of Weather* (London: Constable, 2015), 112.

12   *The Organisation and Management of Government Research and Development*, Cmnd 4814; *A Framework for Government Research and Development*, Cmnd 5046.

13   Charles Moore, *Margaret Thatcher: The Authorized Biography: Volume Three: Herself Alone* (London: Allen Lane, 2019), 528.

# Chapter 10

## ASTROLOGY AND ADVICE AT THE REAGAN COURT

### Colin Kidd

Divination, whether astrological readings of the stars, soothsaying from entrails or other forms of augury, is among the most ancient and long-established forms of political advice; indeed the study of such portents remains a significant feature of advice-giving in some contemporary Asian and African polities. Nevertheless, in Western governments, the court astrologer has been redundant for centuries, an archaism in a post-Enlightenment age which places its trust rather in economists, scientists and other proponents of rational, evidence-based knowledge and techniques. No modern Western ruler would want it known that he or she depended on mystical revelation in the same way that, say, two millennia ago the Emperor Tiberius had placed reliance on his long-serving household astrologer Thrasyllus. Which is exactly why, for purposes of exacting revenge on those who conspired towards – or acquiesced in – his deposition, Donald Regan, an outcast from the Reagan administration, revealed in May 1988 that the incumbent president of the United States had long been under the sway of an astrologer, in due course identified as Joan Quigley, a San Francisco-based medium. According to Regan, 'Virtually every major move and decision the Reagans made during my time as White House chief of staff was cleared in advance with a woman in San Francisco who drew up horoscopes to make certain that the planets were in a favourable alignment for the enterprise.'[1] This embarrassing disclosure punctured the notion – intrinsic to all modern Western regimes – that government was at bottom a rational undertaking.

Regan's kiss-and-tell memoir caused the Reagan administration some momentary discomfiture, not least in its relationship with evangelicals on the Christian Right who regarded astrology as unscriptural and idolatrous.[2] But the damage was limited. Ronald Reagan, serving out the last year of his presidency, was already perceived as a drifty, elderly figure, who exercised little real control over the White House, perceptions which also served handily as the basis of his exculpation from active involvement in the Iran-Contra scandal. First divulged in the fall of 1986, this dominated the two final years of the administration and led to the removal of Regan, Reagan's chief of staff, in 1987. To what extent had a vague and forgetful Reagan connived in the plot by his National Security staff to sell weapons to Iran, in return for release of American hostages in Lebanon, and then to use the funds from the sales to divert military resources to the right-wing Contra rebels in Nicaragua? Moreover, the American public already knew that Reagan was an unconventional politician, with a background in Hollywood moviemaking, where various eccentricities and counter-cultural superstitions were indulged, if not de rigueur. The story of Reagan's astrologer was an immediate media sensation, but it did not seriously affect the president's position.

Nevertheless, the controversy around Reagan's astrologer opens a window onto the subject of political advice. In the first instance it reminds us that even in modern governments, flamboyant and outlandish characters are occasionally to be found in the entourages of political leaders, gaining their trust and sometimes becoming advisers of a sort. Carole Caplin, who dabbled in crystals and other New Age flimflam, was fitness adviser to Tony Blair and style adviser to his wife Cherie, while séances and clairvoyance were White House features, under the auspices of the First Ladies, during the presidencies of Lincoln, Wilson and Harding.[3] Senator Everett Dirksen, the Republican minority leader during the 1960s, is alleged to have had frequent consultations with an astrologer for political advice.[4] Politicians are no more rational than the rest of us, and like their fellow humans sometimes find consolation and reassurance in the occult. This serves as a reminder that at the centre of modern governments arrangements still occur from time to time which bear more direct comparison with the whims of court life in past centuries than with the axioms propounded in our schools of public administration.

This case study also leads us to other questions. What kinds of advice did Quigley offer Reagan? Were her astrological communications a force for ill, which had a negative effect on policy? Or was her advice no more irrational perhaps than the nostrums of supply-side economists, whose work was notoriously mocked by Reagan's rival for the Republican nomination in 1980, later his vice president, George Bush Sr, as 'voodoo economics'? Nor should we forget the role of the president's wife Nancy Reagan at the Reagan court, in this particular instance as the client of Quigley, and more generally as a formidable presence in the White House who meddled in the appointment – and removal – of Reagan's advisers.

As we probe further it turns out that there were other unusual features of advice-giving in the Reagan White House. In part because Reagan was an atypical president with a relaxed-verging-on-cavalier approach to political leadership, the structures of counsel that developed within the White House were themselves decidedly peculiar. These included a non-hierarchical 'troika' of chief advisers – James A. Baker, Mike Deaver and Edwin Meese, the first of whom had been the campaign manager of Reagan's primary rival Bush; the second Nancy's lackey, a PR man, master choreographer and – unusually perhaps in a political adviser – utterly unideological; and the third a loyal Reaganite true believer, but chaotic in his administrative habits. Moreover, there was the recruitment of non-Reaganite Republican opponents, such as Baker, into key advisory positions in an administration which at first appeared to preen itself on its ideological purity. Given Reagan's passive disconnection from the process of government and dislike of confrontation, it is perhaps unsurprising that these ushered in the far-from-uncommon court phenomenon of the overmighty adviser, in an extreme form where the aides exercised so much day-to-day control of policy that they almost forgot the president's existence. More puzzling is the identity of the principal counter-revolutionary usurper who blocked the Reagan revolution: was it Baker, or perhaps the First Lady, via Deaver, or Deaver himself? Peggy Noonan, Reagan's true-believing speechwriter, believed that the president was 'used' by a non-ideological clique of his advisers, led by Deaver, who had themselves effectively picked Baker as chief of staff.[5] Most shocking of all, perhaps, was the indulgence of important subordinates swapping jobs within the administration, on their own – not the president's – initiative. The practices of the Reagan court shine unexpected light, from various angles, on political advice and its supposed modern norms.

*I*

Notwithstanding Don Regan's deliberate suggestion that President Reagan was enthralled to the irrational, he appears to have exaggerated. The advice that Joan Quigley provided to the White House was of a humdrum kind and not substantive, largely concerning the timing of the presidential schedule. According to her memoirs, her advice on timings was also peppered with down-to-earth, commonsensical advice of a very pragmatic kind. Quigley claimed, for instance, to have favoured the superpower rapprochement with Gorbachev, and to have done everything she could to facilitate summit meetings, including providing a positive horoscope of the new Soviet leader.[6] Quigley's advice on timings does seem to have produced heavy demands during the first administration on the chief scheduler, Deaver, who had to rearrange the presidential timetable, often in strangely contorted, impractical ways and at short notice, without being able to explain to staff or the secret service a plausible reason for the changes. Awareness that the schedule was being determined by an astrologer was confined during the first Reagan administration only to Deaver, Baker and Deaver's assistant William Sittman on the president's staff, and to Elaine Crispen (a former employee of Deaver's earlier public relations firm) on the First Lady's;[7] then during the second to Deaver's successor William Henkel and to the new chief of staff, Regan.[8] Although Deaver had no belief in astrology, as a close confidant of the First Lady he was content to allow the whims of Nancy's astrologer to determine the presidential schedule; but the psychological strains imposed on Deaver took its toll, and he succumbed to alcoholism.[9] At the time of Regan's forced resignation from office in 1987, the press was aware of a dispute between the chief of staff and the First Lady over the control of the president's schedule, but at that time it knew nothing of the real backstory: the influence of Quigley.[10] Regan, who did not know the identity of the San Francisco-based astrologer, tried to overcome the logistical headaches involved, with a colour-coded calendar: green for good days, red for bad days and yellow for dubious days. Notwithstanding the chaotic infighting and the burdens on Deaver and Sittman, it seems unlikely that Quigley did any real harm, except, perhaps, in terms of opportunity costs – the loss of time and energy that went into rescheduling.

The reason for Quigley's recruitment was, for all the media scoffing that ensued later, an understandable and heartfelt one. Within weeks of taking office, President Reagan had come very close to death following an assassination attempt on 30 March 1981.[11] Thereafter Nancy Reagan was naturally concerned to do everything possible to protect her husband, including soliciting advice about the most propitious times for his public appearances. Nancy's fears were fanned by a further superstitious coincidence. Every president elected in years ending in a zero, all the way back to Harrison in 1840 – Kennedy in 1960, Roosevelt in 1940, Harding in 1920, McKinley in 1900, Garfield in 1880, Lincoln in 1860 – had failed to survive his term of office; four of those presidents had been assassinated.[12] Was Reagan next? The First Lady's worries were tangible. Reagan's California Governorship (1967–75) had fallen during a period when Martin Luther King and Bobby Kennedy were killed by assassins, and the Southern populist George Wallace, a leading contender for the Democratic nomination in 1972, left crippled after a shooting at a mall in suburban Maryland. Nor had the Reagans been exempt from this violence: the governor's house had been attacked in 1968 and there had been a threat to kidnap Nancy.[13] Within two months of the attempt on Reagan's life in 1981, as Nancy Reagan herself recalls, Pope John Paul II was shot and wounded, and a further five months later President Sadat of Egypt was killed by disloyal extremists during a military parade.[14] Nor was Nancy's worry only the assassin's bullet. She worried that Reagan, inaugurated a few weeks short of his seventieth birthday and at that point the oldest first-term president in American history, might not survive the rigours of office. The president's schedule of meetings and public appearances was not, in the case of an elderly man recuperating from a shooting, a matter of mere routine. In her memoirs Nancy Reagan recounted that Quigley offered the First Lady reassurance, as a 'therapist' would; certainly, she conceded, her relationship with the astrologer 'began as a crutch'.[15]

However, this is not the whole story either, for Reagan had long taken an interest in astrology,[16] and it seems to have been an influence on earlier decisions during his years in California politics.[17] During Reagan's acting days he had consulted an astrologer named Ralph Kraum,[18] and his 1965 autobiography mentioned the Reagans' friendship with the prominent astrologer Carroll Righter and their interest in horoscopes.[19] Possibly, there were further links with another Los Angeles astrologer, Joyce Jillson, who later boasted that she had been involved in the selection of Bush as Reagan's vice-presidential running mate.[20] Such claims carry some credibility. Reagan's 1967 inauguration as governor of California had taken place at the odd hour of ten past midnight, on astrological advice.[21] Furthermore, during the 1960s and 1970s there had been meetings with the astrologer Jeane Dixon at the Mayflower Hotel during the Reagans' trips to Washington, DC.[22] However, the Reagans became disenchanted with Dixon, and in due course turned for occasional consultations to Quigley – a San Francisco socialite – who occasionally appeared on the television chatshow hosted by the Reagans' friend Merv Griffin.

What appears to have cemented the connection with Quigley was the assassination attempt, and in particular Quigley's after-the-fact assessment – communicated via Griffin to Nancy Reagan – that the astrologer could see from Ronald Reagan's charts that 30 March 1981 was a dangerous day for him.[23] Thereafter Quigley's computerized astrological charts determined the president's schedule, and especially the timings of major setpiece events. Quigley only attended the Reagan White House on one occasion, a State dinner for the president of Algeria in April 1985.[24] She had no direct dealings with the president, and communicated by telephone with the First Lady; however, it is worth pointing out that several of these calls lasted for hours, with Nancy Reagan taking copious notes. The longest was a three hour session before the Geneva summit with Gorbachev. Liaison – when Quigley needed to contact the White House outside the normal timetable of conversations – went via Mary Jane Wick, wife of the U.S. Information Agency Director, later via Betsy Bloomingdale, a friend of Nancy's, and occasionally via Nancy's special assistant (later press secretary), Crispen.[25] Billing was carried out by means of various parallel subterfuges.[26]

## II

Initially, when I began to research this piece, I imagined that Quigley's story would provide a case study illuminating the irrational sway that some of the more exotic and outlandish advisers, trusted companions, clairvoyants and healers of various sorts have enjoyed in high places throughout history. However, the environment I uncovered within the Reagan administration provided various other insights into the forms, delivery, content and structure of political advice, some of which were so surprising that they make the role of court astrologer, after all a longstanding presence in pre-modern governments, seem almost pedestrian. Some of the surprises I encountered were very particular to Reagan, but others pertained, in part at least, to structural peculiarities of the American political system, not least the intra-party competitiveness induced by party primaries.

Reagan's 'hands-off' approach to appointing and managing his advisers – a product not only of strangely incurious passivity, but also an implied rebuke to the micromanagerial hyperactivity of his predecessor Jimmy Carter – gave rise to several unusual arrangements, as well as to some lively innovations. Reagan hated to see his advisers – 'the fellas', as he called them[27] – disagreeing. The delivery of advice matters. In part because Reagan was hard of hearing, he seems to have found arguments among his advisers confusing, but also distressing on an emotional level, something that 'paralyzed' him.[28] Yet, there were, of course, ever-present dangers when a president was unable or unwilling to synthesize the range of options presented to him, indeed to prefer something akin to groupthink. So a system of Cabinet Councils was introduced – devised by Meese[29] – after a similar approach used when Reagan had been governor of California; here each Council provided a forum for Cabinet members representing various cognate departments and agencies to resolve policy differences before these came to the attention of the president and the full Cabinet.[30]

Given Reagan's background as a Hollywood actor, he seems to have understood his leadership role as largely one of communicator. He was the star of the White House as he had been in Hollywood, but notwithstanding his star status back then he had been accustomed as an actor to following the leads of producers, directors, and scriptwriters. So too, as president, he would establish the core principles of his presidency which others would tailor to policy realities and implement; moreover, he was happy to deliver lines – written by others – which would promote his message. He saw no diminution in his own status in following the scripts supplied to him. That was what he had been used to, and Reagan remained in an endearing way a modest team player, not in the least unhappy to take direction.[31] While fundamentally incurious and never asking for information from his advisers, he appears to have treated the policy briefings he received as homework, which he tried – within the limits of his dwindling energy and concentration – to complete as assigned.

Notwithstanding its reputation for ideological zeal, the Reagan administration provides a glorious example of the tension that bedevils the field of political advice, between the need for some degree of ideological conformity shared by adviser and advisee, and the practical demands of competence and ability – often in themselves vizier-like and non-ideological – in the ranks of chief counsellors. Reagan's unbudging adherence to a disruptive counter-revolution predicated on anti-statist principles was in part thwarted by his own near-total lack of interest in the mechanics of policy implementation, and by the dishevelled approach to administration of the keeper of the flame, Meese, his true-believing chief strategist. As a result, the administration stood in dire need of Beltway-savvy, mandarin-like support from pragmatic proponents of smooth governance, which it got from Baker and his team.

The ascendancy of James A. Baker, Reagan's principal adviser during his first term, is at first sight bewildering. Not only had Baker been the campaign manager of Reagan's Republican rival George Bush Sr, but he had also been President Ford's chief delegate hunter in his hotly and bitterly contested race for the Republican nomination against an insurgent Reagan in 1976. The 1980 primary race had seen considerable needle between the Bush and Reagan teams, not least during the close-run contest in Texas, which prompted the *Dallas Morning News* to run the headline 'Chance of Reagan-Bush Ticket Slim'.[32] The successful candidate considered that Bush's reference to Reaganite 'voodoo economics' had broken what Reagan referred to as the Eleventh Commandment: 'Thou shalt never speak ill of a fellow Republican'.[33] Indeed, Bush only went on the ticket at the very last minute after the failure of protracted negotiations with former President Ford for a Reagan-Ford ticket, where Ford's hands-on experience, especially on the budgetary matters in which he was adept, would serve to counterbalance Reagan's remoteness from the basic plumbing of governance. Ford, in effect, would be Reagan's chief adviser. However, neither Reagan nor Ford had genuine enthusiasm for the arrangement, which was widely described in the media – much to Reagan's consternation – as a putative 'co-presidency'; thus Bush was reluctantly selected for the vice-presidential nomination at the very last minute, an all-too-evident second choice after the volume of speculation about a Reagan-Ford dream ticket. Both Bush in 1980 and Ford in 1976 had proved intensely irritating to Reagan; and Baker had good claim to be his tormentor-in-chief. How could such a formidable intra-Party opponent become his first chief of staff? As Lou Cannon notes, 'no President had ever chosen his former adversary's campaign manager as chief of staff'.[34]

Although the position of chief of staff has in recent decades become established White House practice, at the time of Reagan's inauguration it had not yet become a permanent fixture. This was in large part because of the overhanging legend of Nixon's disgraced first chief of staff Bob Haldeman, who had become a Watergate ogre. As a result, Nixon's successors, first his appointed Vice President Gerald Ford and then after the 1976 election the Democrat Jimmy Carter, who ran as an anti-Washington outsider, had deliberately tried – and failed – to run their administrations without a formal chief of staff, on what was called a 'spokes of the wheel' arrangement; each spoke of the wheel on the organizational chart connected one of the president's key White House advisers directly to the president without the need of an intermediary gatekeeper in the form of an official chief of staff. Both Ford and Carter had come to abandon the spokes of the wheel, Ford turning to Donald Rumsfeld as chief of staff (later succeeded by Dick Cheney) and Carter to Hamilton Jordan, amidst Carter's advisers first among equals, later formally chief of staff.

There was also a structural dimension to the choice of chief of staff, peculiar to American politics, where party is less important in organizational terms than the personal teams assembled by individual candidates, notwithstanding the party labels which they sport. Helene von Damm, Reagan's loyal, deeply conservative assistant, reflected ruefully later of the liberal Bush gang in the administration, that 'after all, we had married them'.[35] This points to a neglected aspect of American government, and one in which its characteristic patterns of political advice differ, certainly from those in parliamentary systems; namely that presidential campaigns and governments do from time to time marry the internal opposition, thus bringing together the teams of the party nominee with those of a primary rival if that rival is chosen as vice-presidential nominee. Similarly, of course, party rivals can win other favours from the nominee, such as when Hillary Clinton became Barack Obama's Secretary of State. Various kinds of merging take place, whether at the point when the party machine coalesces after the primary season, during the presidential transition, or in government. Indeed, the memoirs of Robert Hartmann, once chief adviser and speechwriter to Gerald Ford, present an embittered account of a most unusual intra-party marriage when the advisers of the former Republican Congressional leader and unelected vice president took office after President Nixon's post-Watergate resignation. Although the former administration had been disgraced, with several of Nixon's key aides serving prison sentences or facing criminal trials, there was still an elbow-bruising clash in the early days of Ford's new administration between entrenched Nixonites, nicknamed pejoratively by Hartmann as 'the praetorian guard' – who thought the White House was theirs and regarded Ford, at least initially, as 'the accidental president' and mediocre interloper – and Ford's most trusted advisers, who suddenly found it difficult to gain access to their boss or even an office in the White House.[36] Not all marriages are happy ones; and teams of political advisers in the throes of marital integration are no less prone to jealous clannishness than other groups.

However, structural factors still do not explain why Bush's campaign manager became Reagan's chief of staff. The story centres on the prime candidate for the job, Ed Meese, who was a notoriously careless and slipshod administrator, utterly unsuited, as even his ideological supporters admitted, for the chief of staff role that he had assumed, after the election, would be his. During the transition, which was nominally headed by Meese, Baker was unexpectedly summoned – unbeknown to Meese – to assume the chief of staff role. This surprising outcome seems to have been the result of a conspiracy involving Nancy Reagan, Reagan's campaign strategist Stu Spencer and the suavely efficient Deaver. Meese, the leading conservative heavyweight within the Californian entourage, was, notwithstanding his legal background and probity as a counsellor, ill-suited to playing the central supporting role to such a detached president-elect. Deaver, in particular, thought that Reagan needed to be guided by someone who knew the ways of Washington, DC.; he felt that his boss's Californian entourage was unable to govern without external assistance. Reagan required to have at his disposal the advice and acumen of a Washington insider, not the naïve fervour of a movement conservative with a Californian background. A different quiver of skills, an entirely different personality, was required in the chief of staff role. Even those most suspicious of the Bush team, and Baker especially, such as the ultra-conservative von Damm, recognized that Meese was a bumbling figure with an ever-messy desk, whose work rhythms were too slow for the frenetic pace at which tasks had to be tackled, or summarily delegated, at the highest levels of government.[37] Moreover, by comparison with Baker – acutely conscious of being an outsider in the Reagan ranks but compensating by forging personal alliances with otherwise uncongenial movement conservatives – Meese lacked guile.[38] As it happens, Baker had struck up a personal rapport with the Reagans when – with the rival primary teams of Reagan and Bush merging for the general election – he had helped to coach Reagan for the presidential debates with Carter and Representative John Anderson, an independent Republican.

From the outset, the shrewd Baker downplayed his own role, and ceded considerable power to his defeated rival Ed Meese and to Mike Deaver, the consummate courtier, who was personally close to the Reagans (certainly to the First Lady, and as close as anyone could get to the notoriously remote, though outwardly genial, Reagan). This triumvirate would share out gatekeeping responsibilities, and no supplicant or counsellor would be allowed to meet the president without at least one member of the troika being in the room. A division of powers obtained from the start of the presidency, initially between Reagan's two principal advisers: Meese was Reagan's chief counsellor, dealing with Cabinet matters, policy development, planning and evaluation, whereas Baker was responsible for staffing, congressional liaison, and communications.[39] Von Damm believes that the troika only emerged properly after the assassination attempt, because from this point onwards public relations with regard to the president's health became crucial, and Deaver – both through his particular skill set (as PR adviser, scheduler and advance man), and his close relationship with Nancy Reagan – came into his own as the third pillar of the triumvirate.[40] As a close relationship developed between Baker and Deaver (a proxy for the First Lady), so Meese's influence – and that of the conservative movement within the administration – waned, and Baker's rose.

The troika of the first Reagan administration was an unusual arrangement for the management of Reagan's advisers, but one which functioned well, possibly because of the temperaments of the triumvirate, who were able to operate with a degree of 'informality' about lines of authority and the ownership of each patch of turf in their respective domains.[41] Moreover, the loose arrangement played to their individual strengths. Baker's role was primarily tactical, Meese's was more strategic and he also served as the president's political conscience. Deaver was the choreographer and stage manager, as well as being the primary conduit and agent of the First Lady. Baker was consummately smooth but with contrived rough edges, tactically astute and agile, knowing when to curse, when to cajole, when to toady (and to whom within court circles). Meese was a concepts man who had an overall plan as well as a blue-sky vision of policy, and, significantly, Baker was on hand to deal with tactics and implementation. Deaver's forte was the planning of domestic arrangements and the choreography of setpiece events which would project the best image of the Reagan presidency in the media. As such he performed a set of roles familiar to historians of court life, an amalgam of lord chamberlain, master of the revels, groom of the stole and chief valet. Unsurprisingly, he was underestimated by many who encountered him, but not by Baker, who saw that an alliance with Deaver was the means to keeping the First Lady on side.

Baker's success as chief of staff owed much not only to his formidable personal qualities, work ethic, people skills and keen judgment, but also to the support he received from his own team of hand-picked advisers, most notably Richard Darman – who controlled the flow of paper to and from the president[42] – and Margaret Tutwiler, Baker's executive assistant. Tutwiler and Darman later accompanied Baker as he moved posts, and he described his two advisers plus his wife as his own 'troika'.[43] Understanding the efficacy of political advice depends not only on appreciating the personalities behind the foremost political players, but the personalities of the further layer of advisers behind the first tier of counsellors.

Within these lower tiers of advisers the administration was not as ideologically driven as its detractors have portrayed it. Pendleton James, Reagan's first head of personnel, put competence above ideology in staffing the ranks of the president's junior advisers.[44] Moreover, Nancy Reagan's secretary Muffie Brandon was a Kennedy Democrat, hired to ensure the First Lady's acceptance into the Eastern social establishment. The First Lady was allergic to ideologues, and, worried about the image of her husband as an extreme right-winger, she contrived to remove some of the hardest right-wingers from the president's team. Lyn Nofziger, assistant to the president for political affairs, soon left the administration because the First Lady found him doubly offensive: too ideological and too slovenly in appearance.[45]

In time a gulf grew between the Baker-Deaver alliance, supported by the First Lady, and the Reaganite true believers led by Meese, who included William Clark, William Casey and Martin Anderson.[46] The Reagan presidency was depicted at the time as ideologically extreme, and as such a departure from conventionally centrist Republican norms. The reality was more complex. Some of the president's closest advisers were true-believing Reaganites, but by no means all of them; and several key positions were held by figures sceptical – and not only privately – of the coherence of Reaganomics. Indeed, there is ironically a harsh Reaganite interpretation of the Reagan Presidency, namely, that a workshy and disengaged president permitted a managerial vacuum to emerge, which was occupied right from the start by anti-Reaganite advisers, and that later under the post-Regan chief of staff, Senator Howard Baker, the regime was entirely co-opted by pragmatist non-Reaganite Republicanism.

By far the strangest aspect of Reagan's advisory team was the utter absence of any management from the very top, with the odd result that his chief advisers plotted behind Reagan's back on two occasions to swap jobs, once unsuccessfully, and on the second occasion to their own personal satisfaction, but not to the smooth functioning of the White House. On the first occasion, in the fall of 1983, when the hardline right-wing Californian William Clark moved from National Security Adviser to head the Department of the Interior, Baker persuaded Reagan that he be transferred from his chief of staff role to become the new National Security Adviser, with his own aide Darman as his Deputy, and Deaver, nominally deputy chief of staff, stepping up into Baker's job. Reagan acquiesced in this round of musical chairs, entirely orchestrated from below, without demur or curiosity, and it was only when Clark himself got to hear of what he perceived as a coup by the pragmatists against the Reaganites that he persuaded the president to stall and the plot fizzled out.[47]

A second coup came in the interstices between the first and second Reagan administration when Baker and Regan, then the Treasury Secretary, decided to swap jobs. Again, Reagan remained inert, and this time the swap proceeded without mishap, though Regan turned out to be temperamentally unsuited to the hand-holding which the chief of staff role involved. The brisk and business-like Regan was oblivious of the courtly pavane of White House life, which necessitated a measure of deference to the First Lady, who, in Regan's strictly managerial mindset, had no assigned role in government. Baker, on the other hand, had possessed an instinctive grasp of people and of the informal power exercised by the First Lady on personnel matters.[48]

This swap initiated from below to serve the interests of advisers, not from above to serve the broader interest of the administration, was in some ways a disaster. Advisers need to develop a rapport with their political leader. Regan was too formal in his dealings with Reagan, too 'linear', with a 'no-nonsense' focus on the bread-and-butter matters in hand, and they never entirely hit it off.[49] Another problem was that Regan inherited the demanding three-headed role of the troika, as Deaver and Meese also left the White House, the former to become a lobbyist, the latter to be attorney general. Nobody seems to have perceived that it was altogether too much to ask of Regan that he operate as a multipurpose Baker-Meese-Deaver-like adviser. Most significantly of all, perhaps, Regan failed to recognize that the White House was more like an ancien régime court than a modern corporation; he had come into political service after a banking career at Merrill Lynch, and lacked political antennae. The absence of Deaver during the second administration was crucial. The exiled Nofziger, indeed, urged Regan to bring in an aide specifically to deal with the demands of the First Lady.[50] In her memoirs Nancy Reagan denounced Regan for attempting to usurp powers that properly did not belong to him. The chief of staff had behaved, she alleges, like a chief operating officer; which was understandable, perhaps, given his business background.

Character is important in chief advisers. While the authoritarian Regan expected deference from those below him in the White House hierarchy, Baker had smoothly indulged those subordinate advisers advising him as chief counsellor to the president, and was content to absorb criticism from his juniors, even when they blew up at him in meetings.[51] The contrasting fortunes of Baker and Regan demonstrate the importance of creating an open, friendly environment in which the give-and-take of advice is welcomed, not necessarily at the very top (for Reagan disliked disagreement), but at least at the second tier of government.

Furthermore, it seems that Regan pandered, unwisely perhaps, to Reagan's unstated but unmistakable preference for unsullied, clear advice. That is not what Reagan had received during his first term, when the squabbles between factions – between the hardline Reaganites, Meese, Clark, Anderson, and the less ideological alliance which favoured competence and the smooth running of the government machine, Baker, Deaver and, behind the curtain, the First Lady – presented Reagan, against his wishes of course, with policy alternatives. Under Regan, Reagan was proffered advice from his counsellors in unison, the form he wanted, not in the contrapuntal strains that the incurious head of government may actually have needed.[52]

Interestingly, Martin Anderson – the most reflective of Reagan's advisers on the topic of political advice – contends in his memoirs that the biggest problem of Reagan's career, the Iran-Contra scandal, occurred because of significant failures in advising processes. In particular, William Casey, the director of the CIA, whose judgment seems to have been affected for some time by an undiagnosed brain tumour, began to confuse the primary advice function of his role – the provision of objective, unspun information – with a broader remit to provide general counsel on foreign and defence policy. Compounding this problem, at this point the president's Foreign Policy Advisory Board – an important source of external advice – had been 'purged' and was largely 'in mothballs'. Moreover, the exiguous staffing of the president's Intelligence Oversight Board meant it was 'woefully unequipped' to winkle out what was going on.[53] As Anderson's account reminds us, the arcane mechanics of the advisory process do sometimes matter as much as the substantive content of policy.

*III*

The Reagan presidency did rely in good part on irrational advice, but it did not come from astrology. It came from the wishful thinking of supply-side economics, or what Bush, his Republican rival and later vice president and an orthodox fiscally strait-laced Republican, had condemned witheringly as 'voodoo economics', 'phony promises' and a 'blueprint for paradise'.[54] For the essential premise of supply-side economics was that by cutting tax rates, one increased tax yields (or at least did not proportionately diminish them),[55] because of the assumed incentives to investment and productivity brought about by the cuts. Its econometric basis was the Laffer curve, famously drawn on a napkin by the controversial supply-side economist, Arthur Laffer: if you tax at 0 per cent you get no tax yield, but equally at 100 per cent the yield is zero because you inhibit all economic activity, in between these zero rates is a curve with a revenue maximization point which precedes the decline in yields which arise from overtaxation. Regardless of the intellectual robustness (or otherwise) of Laffer's model, Reaganite political economy stretched supply-side economics to breaking point, for it included a Cold War pledge to increase military spending against the Soviet Union at the same time as cutting taxes and balancing the budget. Nor did all of Reagan's own team of economic advisers buy into this wishful thinking, divided as they were between supply-side believers, monetarists and old-fashioned fiscally orthodox scoffers, who subscribed instead to the traditional tenets of conventionally balanced budgets.[56]

The chief supply-sider within the administration was the Budget Director, David Stockman, whose late arrival in the Reagan team paralleled James Baker's. Stockman, a former adviser to the liberal Republican Congressman from Illinois, John Anderson, who was running for the presidency against Reagan and Carter in 1980 as an independent, was brought in to help Reagan prepare for his debate with Anderson. Stockman's 'quick mind and mastery of detail' so impressed Reagan and Meese that he was promptly integrated into the heart of the team.[57] His formation as an economist had been a somewhat chequered one, beginning with a period at Harvard Divinity School, during which he shifted into the social sciences. At first supply-side economics functioned as Stockman's faith substitute: in revelations to a journalist which almost cost him his job, he described how 'the whole thing is premised on faith … on belief about how the world works'.[58] Later Stockman himself lost his faith in supply-side mechanisms as a means of filling the growing gaps in the budget between Reagan's tax cuts and Caspar Weinberger's ballooning expenditures at the Defense Department. In the interim various unconvincing makeshifts were deployed which failed to disguise the hole in the nation's finances. Senator Howard Baker, later to be Regan's successor as chief of staff, derisively termed the evasive assurance in Stockman's projections that future deficit problems would be taken care of by unspecified budget reductions as 'the magic asterisk'.[59] Not that Stockman disagreed. By the end of his spell in government he was both disillusioned and disenchanted. Stockman's devastating memoirs puncture the pretension that economic policymaking at the highest levels is a rational affair, or indeed even a process grounded in knowledge, for it depended on hard-to-pin-down jellylike real-time figures for income and expenditure, and unknowable projections.[60] Stockman confessed that with so many different budgets within the federal government, and so many different baselines, the complexity of the overall budget-setting process was such that, 'None of us really understands what's going on with all these numbers ... People are getting from A to B and it's not clear how they are getting there'.[61] At times, it seems, expert advisers themselves do not comprehend entirely the processes that they undoubtedly understand better than the lay citizenry or the political class as a whole.

Notwithstanding the pressures she imposed on schedulers and the tensions she exacerbated within the White House, the Reagans' astrologer otherwise did little or no harm to the administration. Quigley's advice was no more irrational than the incompatible core policy prescriptions of the supply-side Reagan revolution: tax cuts, a balanced budget and a massive military build-up. This inherently unstable package of economic advice resulted in a policy outcome sharply at odds with Reagan's declared anti-Keynesian principles: an unintentional right-wing appropriation of despised left-wing nostrums, a military Keynesianism,[62] in the form of a huge bout of deficit-spending on the armed forces, combined with tax cuts.

Political advice demands the impossible of advisers, not only the assessment of a moving target comprising at any single point innumerable human interactions, but also some attempt to factor in the incalculable: the unintended consequences of policy. At bottom, it seems, the most ideological of Reagan's advisers misunderstood what they were doing, but the stars were with them. Reagan's economic success, at least in unleashing the irrational force of what Keynes himself described as the 'animal spirits'[63] of growth, was something that neither he, nor any grouping of his advisers – not the supply-siders, not the orthodox deficit hawks, not the pragmatists – had actually recommended.

### Notes

1   Donald T. Regan, *For the Record* (San Diego: Harcourt Brace Jovanovich, 1988), 3.
2   George Hackett, 'Of Planets and the Presidency', *Newsweek*, 16 May 1988, 20; Lance Morrow, 'The Five-and-Dime Chorus of Astrology', *Time*, 16 May 1988, 100.
3   Carl Sferrazza Anthony, 'Mediums and Messages', *Washington Post*, 4 May 1988.
4   Joan Quigley, '*What Does Joan Say?' My Seven Years as White House Astrologer to Nancy and Ronald Reagan* (New York: Birch Lane Press, 1990), 163.
5   Peggy Noonan, *What I Saw at the Revolution* (New York: Random House, 1990), 168–9.
6   Quigley, '*What does Joan Say?'*, 122–43.
7   Anne Edwards, *The Reagans: Portrait of a Marriage* (New York: St Martin's, 2003), 297.
8   Lou Cannon, *President Reagan: The Role of a Lifetime* (New York: Public Affairs, 2000), 518.
9   Cannon, *Reagan*, 517–18.
10  Fred Barnes, 'President Nancy', *New Republic*, 23 March 1987, 11–13.

11  Del Quentin Wilber, *Rawhide Down: The Near Assassination of Ronald Reagan* (New York: Picador, 2011).

12  Michael Deaver, *Nancy: A Portrait of My Years with Nancy Reagan* (New York: William Morrow, 2004), 137.

13  Deaver, *Nancy*, 135–6.

14  Nancy Reagan, *My Turn* (New York: Random House, 1989), 45.

15  Reagan, *My Turn*, 47.

16  Joyce Wadler et al., 'The President's Astrologers', *People*, 23 May 1988.

17  Joan Didion, 'Life at Court', *New York Review of Books*, 21 December 1989, 3–10, at 6.

18  Lina Accurso, 'The Reagan Era – Written in the Stars?', in *Astrology and the White House*, ed. Anne Keffer (New York: Diamandis Communications, 1988), 26.

19  Ronald Reagan, *Where's the Rest of Me?* (New York: Duell, Sloan and Pearce, 1965), 249.

20  Richard Reeves, *President Reagan* (New York: Simon and Schuster, 2005), 456.

21  Hackett, 'Planets', 20.

22  Martin Gardner, 'Seeing Stars', *New York Review of Books*, 30 June 1988, 43–5, at 43.

23  Reagan, *My Turn*, 46.

24  Laurence Zuckerman, 'The First Lady's Astrologer', *Time*, 16 May 1988, 41.

25  Quigley, '*What does Joan Say?*', 69.

26  Edwards, *Reagans*, 296; Reagan, *My Turn*, 49.

27  Paul A. Kowert, *Groupthink or Deadlock: When Do Leaders Learn from Their Advisors?* (Albany, NY: SUNY Press, 2002), 56.

28  Kowert, *Groupthink*, 148.

29  Martin Anderson, *Revolution* (San Diego: Harcourt, Brace Jovanovich, 1988), 224.

30  Ann Reilly Dowd, 'What Managers can Learn from Manager Reagan', *Fortune*, 15 September 1986, 33–41, at 40–1.

31  Cannon, *Reagan*, 31–5.

32  Craig Shirley, *Rendezvous with Destiny: Ronald Reagan and the Campaign That Changed America* (Wilmington, DE: ISI Books, 2009), 265–75.

33  Dick Wirthlin, *The Greatest Communicator: What Ronald Reagan Taught Me about Politics, Leadership and Life* (Hoboken: Wiley, 2004), 57.

34  Cannon, *Reagan*, 50.

35  Helene von Damm, *At Reagan's Side* (New York: Doubleday, 1989), 166.

36  Robert T. Hartmann, *Palace Politics: An Inside Account of the Ford Years* (New York: McGraw-Hill, 1980), esp. 220, 279–84.

37  Von Damm, *At Reagan's Side*, 148, 165, 167.

38  Cannon, *Reagan*, 494.

39  Stephen Wayne, 'The United States', in *Advising the Rulers*, ed. William Plowden (Oxford: Basil Blackwell, 1987), 78.

40  Von Damm, *At Reagan's Side*, 195–6.

41  Wayne, 'United States', 77.

42  Reeves, *Reagan*, 16.

43  James A. Baker III, *Work Hard, Study … and Keep Out of Politics* (New York: Putnam/ Penguin, 2006), 210.

44  Lyn Nofziger, *Nofziger* (Washington, DC: Regnery Gateway, 1992), 278.

45  Von Damm, *At Reagan's Side*, 225–6.

46  Edwin Meese III, *With Reagan* (Washington, DC: Regnery Gateway, 1992), 139, 142–3.

47  Cannon, *Reagan*, 373–80.

48  Baker, *Work Hard*, 159.

49  Wirthlin, *Greatest Communicator*, 167–8.

50  Nofziger, *Nofziger*, 289.

51  Patricia Dennis Witherspoon, *Within These Walls: A Study of Communication between Presidents and Their Senior Staffs* (Westport CT: Praeger, 1991), 139–40.

52  Cannon, *Reagan*, 495.

53  Anderson, *Revolution*, 337, 429.

54  Elizabeth Drew, *Portrait of an Election: The 1980 Presidential Campaign* (New York: Simon and Schuster, 1981), 199.

55  A qualification emphasized by Anderson, *Revolution*, 152.

56  For the divisions among right-of-centre economists under Reagan, see Paul Craig Roberts, *The Supply-Side Revolution* (Cambridge MA: Harvard University Press, 1984). See also the revelations of the Chair of the Council of Economic Advisers under Reagan, Murray Weidenbaum, 'The Role of the Council of Economic Advisers', *Journal of Economic Education* 19 (1988), 237–43.

57  Meese, *With Reagan*, 135.

58  William Greider, 'The Education of David Stockman', *Atlantic*, December 1981, 27–54, at 29.

59  Greider, 'Education', 39.

60  David A. Stockman, *The Triumph of Politics* (1986; rev. edn, London: Coronet, 1987).

61  Greider, 'Education', 38.

62  Emma Rothschild, 'The Philosophy of Reaganism', *New York Review of Books*, 15 April 1982, 19–26, at 20.

63  Emma Rothschild, 'Reagan and the Real America', *New York Review of Books*, 5 February 1981, 12–18.

## Chapter 11

# YOU'VE GOT TO ASK THE RIGHT EXPERT: WHO GIVES POLITICAL ADVICE?

## Marius S. Ostrowski

Political advice is not only something that is communicated by advisers to rulers; in the context of modern democracy advice is a more complex phenomenon, flowing from many sources to inform the voting public. A voter, deliberating over which party to vote for in an election, follows discussions of policy proposals in the press, online, or on radio and TV news bulletins; they watch speeches and debates by senior political figures; and they talk about the election with workmates, friends, or family members. A policy adviser in the civil service, tasked with compiling a briefing on the implications of a mooted change in the law, holds consultations with academics and industry specialists; they secure legal opinions from the government legal department or attorney general's office; and they have recourse to the guidance and precedent set by senior colleagues within and beyond their team. A leading cabinet minister, determined to spearhead a new government policy approach that falls within their allotted portfolio, seeks out the recommendations of their special advisers and Permanent Secretaries; they draw on pertinent pieces of party political or think tank research; and they may be more or less susceptible to political lobbying by private corporations and extra-governmental bodies.

Each of these people, in their own way, is getting a range of political advice. Granted, they are doing so for different reasons and different purposes. Casting a ballot, preparing a briefing and devising government policies are all deeply and inherently political activities, but they belong to clearly separate parts of the overall 'domain' of politics. Yet in all cases, this voter, civil servant and minister are looking for political messages that provide them with knowledge and guidance. Further, they are doing so en route to taking political actions that send similar messages to other people in their turn. But why do they refer to these particular sources? What is it about news bulletins, workmates, senior colleagues, think tank researchers, and so forth, that identifies them as worthwhile repositories of political knowledge and guidance? This chapter provides an overview of how political advice-giving works in modern society. It identifies several categories of 'political advisers', or advice-givers, who can be distinguished from one another by their different types of political expertise. The chapter offers a structural explanation for these differences in their expertise, rooted in their various positions within the hierarchy of political discourse. It closes by examining how the recipients of political advice make sense of these different forms of political expertise, along with some remarks about how political advice-giving could be improved in modern society.

*I*

To start with, what is political advice? At its heart, advice is a form of opinion: an epistemological (true/false) or evaluative (right/wrong) judgment on a given matter.[1] As such, advice represents what John Zaller calls a 'marriage of information and predispositions' – it applies particular values and attitudes that link the advice-giver's view (e.g., 'good/bad', 'just/unjust', 'legitimate/illegitimate') to directly or indirectly acquired data about some object of assessment (e.g., things, people, social states).[2] What makes an opinion *advice*, however, is crucially that it is a judgment given, or held, by *someone else*. It is sought out by, or offered to, a person whose own opinion is – in their own or others' view – insufficient for dealing with the object of assessment. It is not just an epistemological or evaluative comment, but a specific recommendation, often designed to encourage the advice's recipient towards decisive action. The information and predispositions that a piece of advice conveys are typically couched in the form of representative cues and valorized micro-indications, which deliver enough evidence and argumentative steer to satisfy the advice's recipient and lead them closer towards forming an opinion of their own. Advice becomes political when its orienting values, attitudes, and objects of assessment are connected to social practices of administration, or coordination, and coercion, or repression, in Louis Althusser's and John Thompson's terms.[3]

In general, all political advice takes this form – informal comments or suggestions, orders or guidelines from superiors, think tank reports or departmental briefings, scholarly journal articles or newspaper opinion pieces. But there are important differences amongst these types of political advice. As it circulates around society's intellectual and communications networks, political advice is not just a chaotic blur of generic political 'noise'. Rather, it can be disaggregated into cues and valorizations transmitted by multiple sources, categorized according to the various roles that subjects can play. The political–scientific tradition tends to assume that most people do not know who originally creates the advice on which they rely. As Zaller puts it:

> To an extent that few like but none can avoid, citizens in large societies are dependent on unseen and usually unknown others for most of their information about the larger world in which they live.[4]

But it would be wrong to infer from this that the actors who give advice about a specific area of political life are anonymous, homogeneous, or nondescript, undifferentiated from the generic networks through which information and predispositions circulate in wider society. They may not be individually known to most people. It should, however, be possible to identify a castlist of figures who generate political information and help to create political predispositions.

As a first step towards establishing this castlist, it should be noted that while sources of political advice are all individual actors, it is not always possible to attribute responsibility to them at a personal level. It can be difficult to locate the starting point for any given piece of political advice, any given political cue or valorization. In some cases, advice originates with individual 'sole' authors; in others, with larger subsets of the population, to whom authorship accrues collectively because it does not belong to any one of them more than any other. The former, paraphrasing Antonio Gramsci, can be called 'influential personalities', while the latter, following political–scientific conventions, are 'reference-groups'.[5] There are some obvious examples of individuals and groups who can be identified as 'prime movers' in directing and operating networks of political advice-giving – party leaders, government ministers, press and broadcast commentators, public intellectuals, state propaganda institutions. But in most instances, their roles are not as obvious, and their personal responsibility can only be hinted and guessed at – as, for instance, in the shadowy shaping of political discourse by certain media proprietors (Rupert Murdoch, the Barclay brothers, Evgeny Lebedev, Lord Rothermere), or the subtle homogenizing effect of peer pressure within offices or friendship groups.[6]

In the case of influential personalities, advice takes the form of political 'opinion-leadership'.[7] This describes the role of government spokespeople, media commentators, or senior judges but also, as Michel Foucault suggests, academia, in particular its occasional tendency to lionize the role of individual canonical 'great' thinkers and 'foundational' theories.[8] Meanwhile, with reference groups the same processes constitute a political 'opinion-climate', to use Elisabeth Noelle-Neumann's phrase.[9] This represents two related situations: (1) receiving advice that exhibits a prevalent pattern implies that its individual sources share the same prevailing political conditions, and hence a prevailing experience which explains the similarity of opinions amongst them; and (2) subjects feel surrounded by sources of advice because the cues and valorizations they receive come from multiple sides. This happens whenever subjects respond to their work environment, adopt the herd mentality of a political protest, adapt to family expectations – or, as Pierre Bourdieu and Edward Bernays both note, when they 'look up to' the social circles in which they aspire to move.[10]

With this observation, it becomes possible to identify in greater detail the individuals and groups who are overwhelmingly responsible for transmitting advice to others. Again, Zaller tentatively characterizes the political actors in question:

> The 'others' on whom we depend, directly or indirectly, for information about the world are, for the most part, persons who devote themselves full time to some aspect of politics or public affairs – which is to say, political elites. These

elites include politicians, higher-level government officials, journalists, some activists, and many kinds of experts and policy specialists.[11]

Such full-time devotion to politics and public affairs is the basis of political expertise. Expertise, in general terms, is the result of high and growing specialization of roles through the division of labour in modern society. Expertise can be defined in terms of two related claims: (1) on the nature of people's interaction with their environment – through the social roles they play, people are situated in a specific context, which limits the aspects of overall society with which they engage; expertise makes this interaction disproportionately frequent, consistent, or intense, and gives these people a greater experience of the phenomena (events, other people, objects, etc.) in their immediate context; and (2) on the horizon of people's perceptual attention and awareness – through their social roles, people are oriented towards specific focuses, which limit the aspects of overall society that are typically of concern or relevance to them; expertise makes this awareness disproportionately close, extensive, or sensitive, giving these people a better perspective for registering phenomena within their horizon.

Political expertise accrues to the people in those roles/occupations that are disproportionately engaged, and concerned, with the parts of society associated with administration/organization and coercion/repression – i.e. the political domain. While Zaller's list is a useful starting point for outlining which roles fit this definition, he is wrong to group all of them together into an 'elite' categorization. Such a characterization wrongly implies that political expertise necessarily bestows a quality of 'eliteness' on individuals and groups, in the sense of a maximal position of class power underpinned by the greatest available share of social resources, and the most privileged, advantageous possible status within social hierarchies. People have *some* (any) political expertise if, and when, they specialize in *some* (any) occupation within the political domain, regardless of how powerful this makes them within political structures and institutions. By brushing over this distinction, and eliding political advice-giving with having political power, the political–scientific tradition panders unwittingly to populist rhetoric around an aloof yet pervasive political 'establishment'.[12]

Nevertheless, Zaller's list shows a way to classify and differentiate the individuals and groups from whom subjects may receive political advice. In broad terms, these categories comprise the following political advisers, or advice-givers: (1) members of political elites; (2) members of the political masses; (3) co-members of political peer groups; (4) actors belonging to the political intelligentsia; and (5) 'heroic' political actors with disproportionate influence for their political position (see Figure 1). Together, individually and as groups, people in these categories take the lead in providing others with guidance about the political conditions beyond the horizons of their personal experience, and thus shape how these others form and express political opinions and make political decisions. These categories are far from monolithic, and the individuals and groups that each one comprises are both highly diverse and distinct. Yet what unites each category is the structural basis on which the individuals and groups within them give political advice to others.

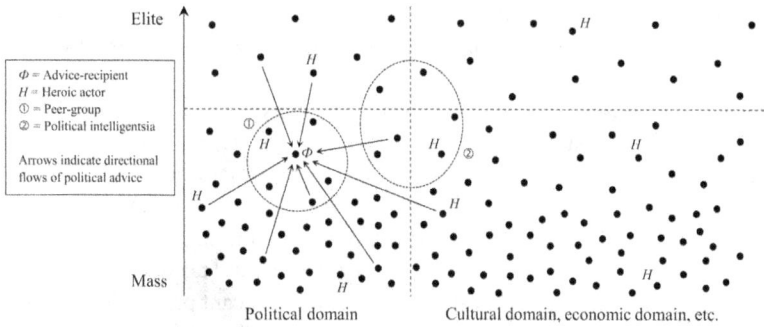

**Figure 1** Sources of political advice

## II

In politics, individuals and groups can have different shares of political resources at their disposal – e.g. government buildings and other physical assets, public transport and infrastructure, machinery, technology, weaponry, and sovereign territory. They also have different levels of advantage or privilege through their relative position in political hierarchies – e.g. executive, legislative, bureaucratic, or judicial–legal institutions, police/defence organizations, and other public/ third-sector bodies. These differences give political actors varying amounts of political power: when they control, or have access to political resources, they gain a particular political capacity to act; when they are favoured by a certain arrangement of political relations, they gain a particular political status compared with others.[13] These resource and relational differences align with the various political roles that people can hold and perform: elected and appointed officials, cabinet ministers, parliamentary representatives; employees of the state bureaucracy; members of the police and security services; the diplomatic corps; the judicial branch; as well as the wider population of 'political subjects' (citizenry, *demos*, electorate). Individuals and groups who share the same roles, or roles that convey broadly similar political power, can be gathered together into political strata, or classes – the political equivalent of economic classes based on wealth, income, or position in employment relations.

One of the effects of such stratification is that people in different political roles/ occupations and classes are active on vastly different scales within the political domain. Individuals and groups whose occupations place them into a higher political class – e.g., national or supranational officials, commissioned officers, judges, departmental secretaries – have more resources under their control, and hold a more advantageous status than those whose occupation places them in a lower class – e.g., local officials, NCOs/rank-and-file, low-grade clerks and civil servants. In their political activity, the power that higher-class actors wield typically goes further. Taking into account the scope for variation across individual actors in the same category, their actions have a more extensive or intensive impact, and their consequences are further-reaching, longer-lasting, or more significant. When they mobilize their resources or leverage their status, they usually do so to greater decisive effect on political life.

Political elites are those individuals or groups who on average have the greatest political impacts.[14] By virtue of their larger arena of action, elites have more expansive, 'Olympian' experiences and perspectives than people who are subordinated to them through their political roles. Their high level of control of resources and privileged status – owning offices or buildings as assets, holding capital for public investment, determining regulations and tax and spending levels, being at the top of chains of command – places a significant proportion of political structures and institutions within their reach. This allows elites to experience a greater range of phenomena frequently, or consistently, as part of their everyday activity than people in subordinate political roles. Moreover, the nature of their political responsibilities means that their attention and awareness is oriented towards a 'big-picture' or 'global' perspective, and their work involves 'taking charge' and 'staying on top of' the workings of (e.g.) legislatures and departments. This allows them to register closely and sensitively a larger range of phenomena in their perceptual horizons. This gives elites far-reaching coverage of the conditions associated with the political domain, where their expertise derives from overview, or surveillance knowledge of political activity. As such, elites' class situation makes them vital macroscopic contributors to the networks of political advice-giving, on which other people, especially those in subordinate roles, rely for guidance about political areas beyond their narrower expertise.[15]

By contrast, political masses are the individuals and groups who exercise a comparatively insubstantial level of political power. Individually, the members of the political masses may not possess many resources or an exalted status, and their influence on the political domain may be limited. However, it is through their collective efforts – on aggregate if not necessarily in harmony – that large-scale mass action becomes possible, and that politics is ultimately constituted as a quasi-autonomous domain in society. Numerically, there is a stark asymmetry between the political masses – which, in conventional usage, encompass many if not most of the political stratifications below the elite – and the elite itself. Even if political life is not structured, formally or informally, into anything as rigid or simplistic as pyramidal hierarchies, there are quite simply vastly greater numbers of people to be found among the political masses. Thanks to the growing division of political labour in complex modern societies, there is increasing diversity among the types of lower-level political occupations as well. These include junior researchers, policy advisers, and clerks, office assistants, temporary/part-time staff, interns, trainees and volunteers, working for state bodies, political parties, or in the wider public policy world – as well as ordinary voters.

What unites all the people in 'mass' roles and occupations is their smaller scale of action, and the densely clustered, 'cog-in-the-machine' political experiences and perspectives they have as a result. Their access to resources is specific and circumscribed, and their status carries little privilege – limited decision-making power, non-permanent employment, dependence on company/departmental office space and resources – so only a restricted, partial share of the political domain lies within their frame of action. The members of the political masses only experience a small set of phenomena frequently, consistently, and intensely in their everyday context. Further, given the narrow remit of their political roles, only a small segment of political life receives their sustained attention and awareness – the cases and briefs their team works on, the needs and interests of MPs and party figures, or immediate strategic objectives. As a result, they closely, extensively and sensitively register a smaller range of phenomena in their perceptual horizon. Even though, taken together, the masses achieve a coverage of political conditions that is (at least) as far-reaching as that of elites, individual members' coverage is far more limited, and the expertise they acquire is one of intimate, or frontline familiarity with political activity. From their class situation, then, people in 'mass' political roles make crucial granular contributions to political advice-giving, on which other people in either more elevated or parallel but unrelated roles rely.

### III

The advisory role of peer groups is another effect of the resource and relational differences between people, consolidated by their stratification into classes. People in the same political class, and especially the same or equivalently powerful political occupations/roles, have broadly the same access to political resources, and enjoy a comparable political status. The pertinent contrast here is with the members of other political classes, whose share of resources or status is (quantifiably or qualitatively) higher or lower than their own. Members of the same occupation and class undertake the same, or at least closely related political activities, and do so on broadly analogous scales. When they exercise their political power, its effects are of equivalent, if not strictly equal, decisiveness and importance to the political domain as a whole.[16] This gives them a basic alikeness, or affinity to one another; in respect of their political tasks, or functions, at least, it makes them one another's 'peers', in the sense of companions, fellow associates, or members of the same group of contemporaries. Examples of such peer groups can be found in all areas of political life: work colleagues; fellow citizens/nationals/'locals'; family members; fellow members of a religious community, especially in the same congregation.[17]

Through their similar political roles and activities, the members of peer groups such as these have political experiences and perspectives that strongly resemble one another – or at least significantly overlap. Their political actions are not just on similar scales, but also typically take place in shared or analogous contexts, whether spaces or institutions, and are geared towards generally similar ends. By using the same kinds of resources and enjoying a status of more-or-less equal (dis)advantage and (dis)privilege – being physically in the same space or workplace, having the same job description/title, 'working for' or 'answering to' the same superiors – peer groups have the same (narrow) set of political conditions in their immediate proximity. Their members frequently, consistently experience the same contextual phenomena – whether greater (elite) or smaller (mass) in range. Likewise, since they have the same political responsibilities, members of peer groups are attentive to, and aware of, the same part of political life – they work on the same sources of information, purchase and deploy the same goods and services, and attend the same meetings. Thus, they closely, sensitively register the same phenomena – again, greater (elite) or smaller (mass) in number – in their horizons. As a result, peer groups replicate, and to a degree reinforce, their members' coverage of their particular subset of political conditions. The nature of their expertise is that individual political actors' familiarity with their activity is broadly comparable to that of others in their group. Peer groups thus contribute valorized cues that corroborate people's own (narrow) area of direct expertise with networks of political advice-giving.[18]

## IV

In contrast, the advisory role of the political intelligentsia does not stem directly from their political power or the scale of their political activity. Instead, their function in political discourse comes about through the discursive domain – the domain of ideation and communication. 'Intelligentsia' here should be understood in a broader sense than its conventional definition, which typically groups together professional academics and journalists, and should also include people in social roles that have *ex officio* discursive influence – parents, teachers, propagandists and lobbyists, advertisers and public relations firms, or legal and religious authorities. Just as political actors are stratified in their involvement with – or subjection to – social processes of administration and coercion, the social conditions of discourse also create asymmetric differences between people in how they think and express themselves. As in politics, individuals and groups who participate in social discourse can have greater or fewer discursive resources available to them – psychological, biological, and technological tools, media, mechanisms, and modes of thought and expression – and find themselves holding a more or less privileged discursive status, depending upon whether they participate in formal academic research or more casual reflection, critical theorizing, apologism, or dogmatic exposition; and whether their communication takes the form of public speaking, personal correspondence, literary writing, art, or broadcasting.

Through specialization, social discourse becomes systematized and, in part, professionalized to create the set of discursive roles and occupations that make up the intelligentsia. This process has two effects that are particularly relevant here. First, different areas of discourse become siloed off from one another as they focus on different societal activities – economics, politics and law, religion, education – and mirror the prevailing divisions between them.[19] This creates a distinct political intelligentsia, which includes political theorists, policy researchers, pollsters and (e.g.) war or foreign affairs journalists. Second, discursive professionalization places individuals and groups in these roles at the cutting edge of new developments in political thinking and communication – new theoretical models and approaches, new databases of experimental evidence, the latest publications, new media outlets, or new apps and messaging platforms.[20] This enables academics, journalists, and other influencers to disseminate political discourse that is in general more complex, sophisticated and rigorous than that of people who only think or express views about politics in an *ad hoc*, informal way. When they weigh in on political debates with their superior analytical methods and media access, from their elevated position as professional thinkers or 'talking heads' – their ideas and statements have greater impact, and weightier consequences than those of 'ordinary' people. Generally, when members of the intelligentsia put their minds to, or speak out about, a pressing political issue, they do so to greater effect and with higher importance for social (especially political) discourse.

Conceptually, the elite status of the political intelligentsia is different from that of governmental or military leaders, senior civil servants, or senior judges. Yet in practice, discursive stratifications may align to a significant extent with the internal stratifications of the political domain which political academics and journalists specialize in covering. Members of the political intelligentsia often enjoy close links to political elites, which may confer on them an occupational or class presence in their own right within their specialist activity. There is also extensive osmosis of personnel between the two categories, with academics and journalists being hired as policy researchers, special advisers, speechwriters, strategists, or spin doctors by politicians, think tanks, and parties, and often going into politics themselves. This, ultimately, allows Zaller to elide the shared higher-class situation of journalists and policy specialists with that of politicians and higher-level government officials when categorizing people with expertise in the political domain.[21]

Through their more complex, sophisticated discursive engagement with politics, members of the political intelligentsia acquire more refined experiences and perspectives than people whose intellectual or communicative engagement is more ad hoc. The silo effect shrinks and reshapes the context of their intellectual and communicative activity until their environment narrows to, and is defined by, the proximate political conditions which they experience ('research', 'study', 'cover', etc.), and to which they are expected to respond most frequently and consistently. This specialization can be determined by disciplinary divisions within academia, special journalistic foci (business, home affairs, foreign affairs), or research and investigation opportunities.[22] Meanwhile, the nature of their specialization allows them more even attention to, and awareness of, the particular political conditions towards which they are oriented, and to register ('address', 'focus on', 'report on') related political phenomena more closely and sensitively – not least by dedicating time to extensive research or investigation. This experience gives people in the intelligentsia a thorough and systematic familiarity with political activity. The cues and valorizations that they feed into networks of political advice-giving add precision to the contributions of other categories of advisers, complementing the macroscopy of elites, the granularity of the masses and the corroboration of peer groups.

*V*

The final category in the castlist of political advice-givers is conceptually different from all the others. Political discourse, especially in an era of mass communication, often focuses on select cases of 'heroic' individuals and groups. These 'heroic' political actors are chosen for the express purpose of being generally lauded, admired, or acclaimed by political audiences for the qualities and achievements ascribed to them. As a result, they are often cast in the roles of central characters or protagonists in public narratives about political events – whether in notionally factual news coverage or social studies, or fictionalized through forms of political art. Heroic political actors' distinction from their political surroundings can manifest in two ways, which echo the 'elite-mass' distinction outlined above. First, in a strong-willed 'agonal' way that is superhuman or above and beyond the call of duty, whereby their heroism is a corollary of their atypical strength, courage, ability, or other exceptional qualities. Thus they may appear in the guise of celebrities – star businesspeople (Warren Buffett, Bill Gates, Gina Rinehart, George Soros, Mark Zuckerberg), 'colourful' politicians (Rob Ford, Pim Fortuyn, 'Amma' Jayalalithaa Jayaram), sportspeople, actors and comedians, TV judges and doctors, chefs and musicians. Second, by being representatively average and relatably human in their performance of political tasks, where their sheer 'ordinariness' makes them a perfect encapsulation of the notionally typical degree of ability, bravery, or insight that might be attributed to the general population. Such 'man of the people' tendencies can be seen in the fetishizing of 'normality' and 'popularity' in contexts as diverse as the eliciting of 'vox pop' views by print and broadcast media, 'normcore' tastes in music and fashion, or the high level of attention to reality TV contestants (Big Brother, the X Factor, Britain's Got Talent, I'm A Celebrity Get Me Out Of Here).[23] Heroic political actors of both types are elevated to a kind of sociocultural semi-divinity.

The advisory role of heroic political actors is unrelated to their political power or their scale of political activity. Indeed, their impact on political discourse may be radically misaligned with their actual political role, or the comparative location this gives them within political class stratifications. They may be asked to comment on topics whose subject matter or scale lie well beyond their formal expertise, or have their views broadcast to a far greater audience than they would usually enjoy. Yet in contrast with the roles and occupations that belong to the intelligentsia, even under the broad conception adopted above, heroic political actors' advisory role does not depend on them holding *prima facie* any permanent place within society's discursive elite. Their disproportional discursive power, and their unusually high access to discursive resources and privileged discursive status compared to others in their position is an exceptional social construction – a 'one-off' endowment, either in the sense of being time-limited or contingent, or uniquely reserved for them (as opposed to others similarly qualified). It is in no small part due to the tendency of mass-media political discourse to rely on individualized human interest stories and illustrative case studies to make large, abstract themes more tangible to audiences. This picking out of select 'influential personalities' and 'opinion-leaders', and their elevation into a highly personalized advisory role goes explicitly against the norms of prevailing political and discursive stratifications. Whether in their agonal or 'representatively average' conception, heroic political actors think and above all articulate their political conditions in a way that is extraordinary, because they achieve – or rather, have bestowed on them – an uncharacteristically heightened focus on their political and discursive activities.

Fundamentally, however, in their ordinary social existence, heroic political actors lie somewhere between political elites and masses on the stratification spectrum, and may be members of some political peer groups, or have some more-or-less formalized discursive role. They may be politicians, lawyers, pollsters, academics, journalists, *as well as* highly visible stalwarts of wider public life. Heroic individuals may have more refined, more expansive, or more densely clustered experiences and perspectives than other people in their peer groups, but nonetheless superficially resemble them, since they are influenced by the same proximate set of political conditions – the same information sources, goods and services, workspaces, meeting schedules, and/or employment relations.[24] This means that their expertise is characterized by largely the same kind of familiarity with 'their' part of the political domain as would characterize the political advice of anyone else in their social position. The main difference – and, in fact, the entire point of the special elevation of 'heroic' political actors – is that their expertise is also necessarily inflected with their subjective, or personal familiarity with political activity. On that basis, the cues and valorizations that heroic actors transmit into networks of political advice-giving have a microcosmic tenor. They add a measure of humanizing colour to the otherwise sometimes overwhelmingly grey impersonal 'wall' of macroscopic, granular, corroborative, or precise information and predispositions that confronts the general public.

## VI

Together, political elites and masses, peer groups, the intelligentsia, and heroic actors drawn from among these other categories of advisers create an intricate, ever-shifting ecosystem of reference groups (and occasional stand-out influential personalities) from whom the public receives political advice. But how do the recipients of political advice encounter this ecosystem? Certainly, they do not necessarily perceive political advisers as falling neatly into such discrete categories. The categories may overlap considerably, and individual advice-givers may bridge them through their personal collection of political roles: politicians who are regular newspaper columnists, academics who are drafted in as special advisers, celebrities-turned-politicians, and so on. The voting public is also unlikely to get political advice in any systematic, ordered, or sequential way; rather, ordinary individuals get it – sought-after or unprompted – constantly and from all over the place: at work, at home, in the street, when they are politically 'switched on', when they are relaxing or doing other things. Advice is also not necessarily 'labelled' as coming from a particular category of political advice-giver, and it is often left up to advice-recipients to establish where a particular piece of advice originally came from and hence the type of political expertise it reflects. Advice is characterized by competing simultaneous tendencies towards credentialism and anti-credentialism: signalling its provenance and quality via academic or official titles versus the subversive 'anti-elitism' of would-be populist political leaders or 'insurgent' media spokespeople.

However, the point of highlighting the conceptual distinctions between different members of the castlist of political advice-givers is to identify and structurally explain the major potential faultlines between the different kinds of political advice that people can receive. Each reference group tries to create its own opinion climate; each influential personality seeks to lead opinion in a particular direction. The political advice given by members of each might not always be internally consistent, whether within or across categories. Indeed, it often is not: members of different parties, politicians from different parliamentary chambers or 'tiers' of government, senior and junior workers in the same department, and academics in different fields, may all provide different information and predispositions about the same object of political judgment. This is ultimately because no reference group as a whole, and certainly none of their individual members, has a truly comprehensive or universal experience of, and perspective onto the political domain. They cannot transcend the contexts in which they are situated, and the foci towards which they are oriented, because of their political or discursive roles. This makes the expertise they offer when they give political advice vitally useful, but also – crucially – partial and limited. Elites' political opinions are too 'Olympian' to give a complete account of the workings of the political domain, those of the political masses too 'cog-in-the-machine' to 'see the wood for the trees'. The opinions within peer groups resemble each other too much to accommodate the existence of radically contrary views. The judgments of the intelligentsia may be too refined to offer the general public straightforward and conclusive political guidance. And the contingent assessments of heroic political actors may be simply too distinctively idiosyncratic to be like-for-like transferable to other people's political contexts. The recipients of political advice are left, in the end, with a wealth of political recommendations of varying calibre, as well as the need to draw their own conclusions.

Against this backdrop, the tendency has been for different categories of political advice-givers to compete for primacy, and for the various reference groups to identify their own particular opinion climate as 'the' (pervasive, prevailing) 'public opinion' on political matters. Central to this competition have been strategies of exaggerating or lionizing the credibility of one's own judgments – their authenticity, earnest good intention, or calibre – while delegitimizing or denigrating those of one's rivals – their corruption, ulterior motive, or sheer wrong-headedness. Many internecine political clashes in recent years have not only involved internal divisions and differences of opinion within political elites via partisan contestation, but have also pitted different categories of political advice-giver and their type of expertise against one another. The technocratic insights of scientists and economists have been a particularly prominent recent target, dismissed by politicians, journalists, and celebrities on topics such as climate change, vaccines, or the economic consequences of Britain's departure from the European Union. These competitive strategies have borne fruit, in that different sections of the population have become increasingly reliant on – or, conversely, hostile to – certain categories of political advice-giver. Perhaps the most extreme example of this is the growing hostility towards 'mainstream' press and broadcast media among consumers of cable and online/digital news outlets. This has led to a situation beyond mere ideological polarization, which could more accurately be described as epistemological and evaluative fragmentation, produced by growing schisms in the societal networks through which political advice circulates. In plainer terms, people today are operating in increasingly partial, mutually incongruous and hostile political 'realities'.

It is not easy to arrive at a solution to this. But any meaningful attempt must start by pushing back against the tendency to see different sources of political advice as competing with one another. On one level, this means that both political advice-givers and advice-recipients must recognize the benefits of complementarity. If no subjective expertise – no matter how macroscopic, granular, corroborative, precise, or microcosmic – is ever going to be enough to fully engage with a political issue, then the best strategy for transcending this partiality lies in receiving and comparing advice from a wider variety of sources. People in general, and political experts in particular, must learn to become accustomed to epistemological and evaluative uncertainty. They need to acknowledge that nothing that might pass for a 'full picture' of a political issue may even be available, and that certain political questions may not be completely answerable, and some political decisions may not be wholly final. In the last analysis, they need to accept that for political matters, there is no one single 'right expert' to ask. Given the ever-greater proliferation of political roles in complex modern societies, pluralism in political experiences and perspectives is ever more inevitable. And any attempts to base political opinions and decisions on isolated pieces of political advice are increasingly doomed to inadequacy.

## Notes

1   Vincent Price, *Public Opinion* (London: Sage, 1992), 6; Slavko Splichal, 'Introduction: Public Opinion and Democracy Today', in *Public Opinion & Democracy: Vox Populi – Vox Dei?*, ed. Slavko Splichal (Cresskill, NJ: Hampton Press, Inc., 2001), 6.

2   John R. Zaller, *The Nature and Origins of Mass Opinion* (Cambridge: Cambridge University Press, 1992), 51.

3   Louis Althusser, *On the Reproduction of Capitalism: Ideology and Ideological State Apparatuses*, tr. G. M. Goshgarian (London: Verso, 2014 [1971]), 39–43, 125–9, 239–45; John B. Thompson, *The Media and Modernity: A Social Theory of the Media* (Cambridge: Polity, 1995), 13–18.

4   Zaller, *Nature and Origins of Mass Opinion*, 6.

5   Edward Bernays, *Propaganda* (Brooklyn, NY: Ig Publishing, 2005 [1928]), 73–6; Antonio Gramsci, *Selections from the Prison Notebooks*, ed. Quintin Hoare and

Geoffrey Nowell-Smith (London: Lawrence & Wishart, 2005 [1935]), 194; Robert E. Lane and David O. Sears, *Public Opinion* (New York, NY: Prentice Hall, 1964), 34, 40–1, 70; Zaller, *Nature and Origins of Mass Opinion*, 41.

6  Antoni Calvó-Armengol and Matthew O. Jackson, 'Peer Pressure', *Journal of the European Economic Association* 8, no. 1 (2010): 62–89; Mark Day, 'The Proprietorial Model', *Media International Australia* 157, no. 1 (2015): 28–33; Rawley Z. Heimer, 'Peer Pressure: Social Interaction and the Disposition Effect', *Review of Financial Studies* 29, no. 11 (2016): 3177–209.

7  Edward Bernays, *Crystallizing Public Opinion* (Brooklyn, NY: Ig Publishing, 2011 [1923]), 88; Gramsci, *Selections from the Prison Notebooks*, 194–5; Tom Hoffman, 'Democratic Theory and the Intellectual Division of Labor in Mass Electorates', in *Public Opinion & Democracy*, ed. Splichal (Cresskill, NJ: Hampton Press, Inc., 2001), 127, 137; Zaller, *Nature and Origins of Mass Opinion*, 45–6.

8  Michel Foucault, 'What Is an Author?', in Foucault, *Language, Counter-memory, Practice: Selected Essays and Interviews*, ed. Donald F. Bouchard (Ithaca, NY: Cornell University Press, 1977).

9  Floyd H. Allport, 'Toward a Science of Public Opinion', *Public Opinion Quarterly* 1, no. 1 (1937), 18; Elisabeth Noelle-Neumann, *The Spiral of Silence: Public Opinion - Our Social Skin* (Chicago, IL: University of Chicago Press, 1984), 28, 124, 169; Elisabeth Noelle-Neumann, 'The Theory of Public Opinion: The Concept of the Spiral of Silence', in *Communication Yearbook 14*, ed. James A. Anderson (Newbury Park: Sage, 1991), 269; Price, *Public Opinion*, 67.

10 Bernays, *Propaganda*, 38, 54, 73–6; Bernays, *Crystallizing Public Opinion*, 124, 130–3, 161–2; Pierre Bourdieu, *Distinction: A Social Critique of the Judgment of Taste*, tr. Richard Nice (Abingdon: Routledge, 2010), 5–8, 73–80, 262, 280–93.

11 Zaller, *Nature and Origins of Mass Opinion*, 6.

12 Cas Mudde and Cristóbal Rovira Kaltwasser, 'Populism', in *The Oxford Handbook of Political Ideologies*, ed. Michael Freeden, Lyman Tower Sargent and Marc Stears (Oxford: Oxford University Press, 2015); Michael Serazio, 'Encoding the Paranoid Style in American Politics: "Anti-establishment" Discourse and Power in Contemporary Spin', *Critical Studies in Media Communication* 33, no. 2 (2016), 181–94.

13 Hannah Arendt, *The Human Condition* (Chicago, IL: University of Chicago Press, 1958), 199–207; Michel Foucault, *Discipline and Punish: The Birth of the Prison* (New York, NY: Pantheon, 1977), 88; Michel Foucault, *Power/Knowledge: Selected Interviews and Other Writings 1972-1977*, tr. Colin Gordon (Hemel Hempstead: Harvester Wheatsheaf, 1980), 119, 122, 138, 142, 186, 207; Thompson, *Media and Modernity*, 13; Max Weber, 'Politics as a Vocation', in *From Max Weber: Essays in Sociology*, ed. Hans-Heinrich Gerth and C. Wright Mills (Oxford: Oxford University Press, 1946), 78; Max Weber, *Economy and Society: An Outline of Interpretive Sociology*, ed. Guenther Roth and Claus Wittich (Berkeley, CA: University of California Press, 1978 [1922]), 926–7.

14 Althusser, *On the Reproduction of Capitalism*, 194–9, 266–70; Bernays, *Propaganda*, 147–8; Bernays, *Crystallizing Public Opinion*, 88, 94, 124–33, 161–2; Zaller, *Nature and Origins of Mass Opinion*, 6–22.

15 Amanda H. Goodall, Lawrence M Kahn, and Andrew J. Oswald, 'Why Do Leaders Matter? A Study of Expert Knowledge in a Superstar Setting', *Journal of Economic Behavior & Organization* 77, no. 3 (2011), 265–84; Fred O. Walumbwa, Bruce J. Avolio, William L. Gardner, Tara S. Wernsing and Suzanne J. Peterson, 'Authentic

Leadership: Development and Validation of a Theory-based Measure', *Journal of Management* 34, no. 1 (2008), 89–126; Gary A. Yukl, *Leadership in Organizations* (New York, NY: Prentice Hall, 2010).

16   Richard Breen, 'Foundations of a neo-Weberian Class Analysis', in *Approaches to Class Analysis*, ed. Erik Olin Wright (Cambridge: Cambridge University Press, 2005), 32–43; Erik Olin Wright, 'Foundations of a neo-Marxist Class Analysis', in *Approaches to Class Analysis*, ed. Wright, 23–7.

17   Rachel Dyson, Gail C. Robertson and Maria M. Wong, 'Brief Report: Peer Group Influences and Adolescent Internalizing Problems as Mediated by Effortful Control', *Journal of Adolescence* 41, no. 1 (2015), 131–5; Vernon Henderson, Peter M. Mieszkowski and Yvon Sauvageau, *Peer Group Effects and Educational Production Functions* (Ottawa, ON: Economic Council of Canada, 1976); Gail Barbara Stewart, *Peer-group Pressure* (London: Simon & Schuster, 1991).

18   Michael A. Campion, Gina J. Medsker and A. Catherine Higgs, 'Relations between Work Group Characteristics and Effectiveness: Implications for Designing Effective Work Groups', *Personnel Psychology* 46, no. 4 (1993), 823–47; International Labor Office, *International Standard Classification of Occupations: ISCO-88* (Geneva: ILO, 1990 [1968]), 5; Nancy Morse and Robert Weiss, 'The Function and Meaning of Work and the Job', *American Sociological Review* 20, no. 2 (1955), 191–8.

19   Althusser, *On the Reproduction of Capitalism*, 74–81, 103–39, 142–7, 218–31, 242–6; Noam Chomsky, *Media Control: The Spectacular Achievements of Propaganda* (New York, NY: Seven Stories Press, 1997); Göran Therborn, *The Ideology of Power and the Power of Ideology* (London: Verso, 1980), 84–92.

20   Asa Briggs and Peter Burke, *A Social History of the Media: From Gutenberg to the Internet* (Cambridge: Polity, 2010); Jane L. Chapman, *Comparative Media History: An Introduction* (Cambridge: Polity, 2005); Bill Kovarik, *Revolutions in Communication: Media History from Gutenberg to the Digital Age* (New York, NY: Continuum, 2011); David Rowe and Kylie Brass, 'The Uses of Academic Knowledge: The University in the Media', *Media, Culture & Society* 30, no. 5 (2008), 677–98.

21   Zaller, *Nature and Origins of Mass Opinion*, 6.

22   Andrew Delano Abbott, *The System of Professions: Essay on the Division of Expert Labour* (Chicago, IL: University of Chicago Press, 1988); Andrew Delano Abbott, *Chaos of Disciplines* (Chicago, IL: University of Chicago Press, 2001); Daryl E. Chubin, 'The Conceptualization of Scientific Specialties', *The Sociological Quarterly* 17, no. 4 (1976), 448–76; Jerry A. Jacobs and Scott Frickel, 'Interdisciplinarity: A Critical Assessment', *Annual Review of Sociology* 35, no. 1 (2009), 43–65.

23   Scott Allison, *Heroes: What They Do and Why We Need Them* (Oxford: Oxford University Press, 2010); Katherine Brooks, 'The Real Meaning of Normcore, the Fashion Trend That Went Oddly Viral', *Huffington Post*, 6 March 2014. http://www.huffingtonpost.com/2014/03/06/normcore_n_4912788.html. Accessed 8 December 2019; Su Holmes and Deborah Jermyn (ed.), *Understanding Reality Television* (London: Routledge, 2004); Susan Murray and Laurie Ouellette (eds.), *Reality TV: Remaking Television Culture* (New York, NY: New York University Press, 2009).

24   Laura Grindstaff, 'Just Be Yourself – Only More So: Ordinary Celebrity', in *The Politics of Reality Television: Global Perspectives*, ed. Marwan M. Kraidy and Katherine Sender (London: Routledge, 2011), 44–58; Murray and Ouellette, *Reality TV*.

# Chapter 12

## ADVICE IN A TIME OF BELIEF: CIVIL SERVICE IMPARTIALITY IN TWO REFERENDUMS

## Jim Gallagher

*'The people of this country have had enough of experts', Michael Gove, June 2016*

The UK has held two existential referendums in recent years, on Scottish independence and on leaving the European Union. Both split the relevant electorate down the middle. The result of the second has paralysed UK politics for over three years and (in this writer's view) destroyed the country's reputation for good governance. It is, at the time of writing, leading to significant constitutional and economic change. As a result, it is quite possible that the Scottish referendum could be repeated, with potentially even more profound consequences. Each of these choices engaged deep, emotionally resonant, issues of identity, as well as complex economic, legal, and social questions which required expertise and analysis, inside government as well as more widely. This has challenged the UK civil service, with its long-standing commitment to 'objectivity', basing advice on evidence and analysis, and political impartiality. Official advice percolated into both referendum campaigns and subsequent discussions. In the Brexit referendum, it has, however, been perceived as supporting one side. Civil service advice on economics, like the consensus of external experts more generally, pointed up the risks; official experience of implementation issues suggested serious problems, many of which have eventuated; it was, however, dismissed as tainted by sections of the electorate and of the Conservative party, including some in office at the time of writing.

This chapter frames the challenge of advice-giving with respect to two main themes. First of all, there is the UK civil service's long-standing commitment to political impartiality and objectivity (broadly speaking, reliance on evidence), and how it has in the past coped with radical changes of priorities, following political changes inside Westminster, and the different sort of change from Westminster politicians running Whitehall to devolved politicians running new administrations. None of these changes has been painless, but the underlying impartiality and objectivity of the civil service has not been challenged in the same way as by the

Brexit referendum. To shed some more light on why, this chapter reviews how the civil service and government addressed the policy questions thrown up by the possibility of Scottish independence and of Brexit.

Secondly, we need to consider the nature of identity-based politics and the claims of nationalism (whether Scottish or English/British) and the challenge which they, using the referendum as a device, present to the idea of basing policy choices on evidence at all. The more populist these movements, the greater the challenges. Brexit is an obviously populist nationalism, and left the UK in the position that, three years after the referendum, it was still not clear if the UK was definitely going to leave, and that four or five years after it the UK's future relationship with the EU remains unclear. Might different use of official evidence and analysis have mitigated these problems? And, if so, are there any lessons if another Scottish referendum is held?

*I*

All states need public officials to run them. Form follows function, so civil servants in developed, democratic countries tend to be quite similar. The UK civil service nevertheless has some particular characteristics. Going back to the Northcote-Trevelyan report of the nineteenth century, it is appointed on merit, not on spoils or patronage, even at the most senior levels. In part due to the influence of the Fulton Report of the late 1960s, it has a commitment to professional expertise (contrasting not only with the idea of the gifted amateur, of which it is often accused, but also that of the party hack chosen for loyalty). It remains a long-term, permanent, career, contrasting with 'inners and outers' in, say, the United States. So its most senior staff tend to be experienced, if not lifelong, public servants, though with a significant admixture of political advisers directly appointed by ministers.

This approach of having government departments staffed from top to bottom by officials obliged to serve any government and pursue its objectives with the same commitment as another's is long-standing. The principles which underlie it have over time become codified and more public (in an age of greater official secrecy, explanation was less necessary). Today they are set out in the Civil Service Code, a document which evolved from a set of terms and conditions of employment into a definition of the constitutional role of permanent officials. There the values of the civil service are defined as:

> 'integrity', putting the obligations of public service above your own personal interests
> 'honesty', being truthful and open
> 'objectivity', basing advice and decisions on rigorous analysis of the evidence
> 'impartiality', acting solely according to the merits of the case and serving equally well governments of different political persuasions.[1]

It is the latter two we will be concerned with here.

In offering evidence-based advice, permanent officials should have one advantage over even unbiased temporary advisers: they are, or should be, deeply knowledgeable about how the tools of government can actually be used to achieve political objectives, i.e. implementation or 'delivery'. This might range from a relatively narrow technical expertise, say effective legislative drafting, to the management of large public organizations, like the NHS or the prison service. The UK civil service has struggled with management.[2] In response, the 'Next Steps' programme of the 1980s and 1990s sought to separate 'delivery' from 'policy', by splitting departments into Executive Agencies and policy cores. But whatever the detail of its structure, a strong institutional link between those who advise ministers on policy and those who implement it on the ground is a strength of the system. It should allow for a real connection between the development of government strategy and its execution. Permanent officials can be expected to discuss with authority what will work, and much of the evidence which they bring to bear is drawn, not from research or study, but from experience of managing the system, running services, operating regulatory frameworks or (highly relevant in the Brexit case) negotiating with foreign governments.

The idea of permanent officials serving politicians with radically different political values is not self-evidently right. How can they be expected to share the passions of one party one week, and the opposite the next? Even if dutiful in implementing ministers' instructions, how can they develop policies and programmes which are guided by values and beliefs they do not share, and may not really understand? And (the insight of the public choice economists, caricatured so brilliantly in *Yes, Minister*) will they as a permanent institution not have interests or objectives of their own which will conflict with ministers', whether it be control, influence, career aims, or objectives such as managing ministers towards 'the common ground'?[3] Finally, there is the human dimension. Do officials who must be prepared to devise and implement one set of policies one week and another the next not become jaded and cynical? Can ministers learn to work with and trust those who were very recently committed and loyal to their opponents?

And yet, it has been made to work, across some very radical changes. Perhaps the most profound of the last half century was Mrs Thatcher's arrival in 1979. She saw herself (rightly) as the agent of a profound change in British society and state. Deeply suspicious of civil servants from her period as Education Secretary in the Heath government ('I was not among friends')[4] she regarded many of the Permanent Secretaries she inherited as negative and opposed to change. In essence, however, her concern was about attitude. She wanted commitment to getting things done rather than detachment or what she saw as defeatism. She shrunk the civil service along with the wider public sector and introduced more external appointments to senior positions. But such appointments were often aimed (with variable success) at injecting management expertise into operational activities like defence procurement or NHS management rather than completely supplanting civil service advice.

1997 witnessed a less radical shift than 1979. The Blair government represented a break from its tired Conservative predecessor, but adopted many of its market-driven changes, seeking to harness them for progressive aims. It was less negative about the public sector in itself, though often dismissive of official analysis and impatient of official distaste for 'presentation'. But it was hungry for evidence and analysis ('what matters is what works'). The Blair government was heavy with political advisers, two of whom were given formal powers to direct officials (one was himself a former FCO official) and sometimes (but not always) neglectful of the formal systems of Cabinet government, which enabled official advice to be brought systematically to bear on the issues ministers were concerned about. The coalition government of 2011, by contrast, needed machinery of Cabinet government, supported by official advice, to manage itself, and in general worked well with officials serving both parties.

None of this was painless. There were those around Mrs Thatcher who thought the civil service second only to the trades union movement in its responsibility for the national decline they sought to reverse. Some New Labour apparatchiks were contemptuous as well as distrustful of officials. So were various ministers of all parties: individual officials, including at the most senior level, were sidelined, dismissed or retired. Nevertheless the basic model of permanent Whitehall officials giving advice based on analysis and evidence has shown remarkable durability.

The transition to devolved administrations in Wales and Scotland tested the model in a different constitutional environment. Official–ministerial relations were constrained to be on the UK model, as the civil service was reserved to Westminster in the devolution legislation, substantially drafted by Scottish Office officials. New politicians, however, had not been socialized to expect their relations with officials to be on a Whitehall model and many thought the civil service represented the unsatisfactory aspects of Westminster government which devolution was to replace. Nevertheless the first Labour-Liberal administrations' working methods presaged 2011 in Whitehall, with orderly official processes supporting coalition Cabinet decisions. Even Scottish nationalist ministers from 2007 accepted the basic relationship. They adopted gratefully, for example, officials' evidence-based 'Scotland Performs' management framework. Despite changes from the closeness of political supervision (many more devolved ministers, and much more parliamentary involvement) the nature of the relationship in Edinburgh would be recognizable to a civil servant of the 1970s.

*II*

The question which these official–ministerial relationships have addressed themselves to is, broadly speaking, 'what should we do?', whether about reversing national economic decline, harnessing the marketplace to promote social justice, improving the efficiency and effectiveness of public services, developing new devolved governance, or similar matters. But the questions posed by nationalism, in the two recent referendums and their aftermath, are of a different sort: 'who should we be'? They are not ordinary public policy issues, but existential and emotional choices, emerging from the nature of nationalism itself.

For the avoidance of doubt, Brexit is a nationalist project, probably best described as English nationalism. English, not because Scotland and Northern Ireland voted differently in the referendum, but because England has never wholly distinguished English and British identity, and it is plain that those who support Brexit are in general prepared to prioritize England's leaving the EU over its relationship with Northern Ireland and even Scotland. Brexit and Scottish nationalism show the characteristics of all nationalist projects documented in the literature.[5] The essence of the proposition is that the nation exists, is different and unique from others, and must be sovereign with the minimum restrictions on its freedom of action. Hence there must be an 'us' and a 'them', nationals and foreigners, but perhaps also true nationals and those who do not belong or reject nationalism. There must be national myths and stories to distinguish and burnish national identity as, without uniqueness, the 'imagined community' of the nation cannot be built or sustain its claim to sovereignty. And there must be borders.

These characteristics of nationalism, especially in a referendum, present real challenges for the kind of evidence and analysis which the civil service machine (and indeed academic, and other policy communities) is accustomed to resort to in advising ministers. Evidence calling into question the wisdom of the nationalist project identifies its provider as one of 'them', not one of us: someone or some institution which does not belong. Second, national myths are emotionally powerful, and strengthen the feelings of belonging, indeed of self-worth, of those who believe them. Scottish Nationalists, for example, think Scotland is intrinsically more communitarian (essentially virtuous) than the rest of the UK. Supporters of Brexit appeal to a less precise image of England standing alone, defiant, with its back to the wall – but ultimately triumphant. No hard evidence, of course, backs these images up, but that is not the point; analytical material addressing itself to risks, detailed economic forecasts, complex implementation questions about borders or currency regimes cannot match their emotional power. To the extent that such data questions these images, it is threatening, hard to accept and easy to dismiss.

Scottish nationalism and Brexit make many of the same arguments and harness some of the same resentments. For example, in 2014 Scottish independence gained the support of about two-thirds of people in the poorest neighbourhoods; Brexit similarly was voted for by about sixty per cent of the least well off. Scottish nationalism has been consistently crowd-pleasing, but, with a creditable aspiration to be 'civic' rather than ethnic, has so far avoided explicitly populist approaches. Brexit is newer, less well-developed ideologically, and much less domesticated. It is explicitly populist, more so since the referendum outcome. The nature and implications of this populism are discussed later.

## *III*

This is the environment in which the civil service, under the direction of ministers, addressed itself to bringing evidence to bear on an existential choice about identity. It did so first in the Scottish independence referendum. The Scottish government, assisted by its civil servants, produced a white paper setting out what it claimed independence would mean. This was of course highly political, and issued in the name of SNP ministers, making the nationalist case for Scotland to be a separate state. It was not a heavily analytical document. It had, for example, only a single table of one year's tax and spending projections for an independent Scotland. It was, however, a bulky tome, and sought to answer as many questions as possible about the implications of creating a new state. (*Frequently Asked Questions* included whether Scotland's time zone would change, and whether it would enter the Eurovision Song Contest.) It nevertheless clearly drew on civil service policy knowledge, and on official implementation expertise, e.g. in setting out plans for how independence might be negotiated, and the necessary changes to the machinery of government.

The UK government's Scotland Analysis programme[6] had a different look and feel. It too had a political purpose, to identify the risks of independence and the advantages of remaining in the UK, but it contained much more analytical material. Papers dealing with currency or trade made political points, but heavily backed up by data and analytical material on, for example, the fiscal implications of currency union or potential border effects on trade. Over a dozen substantial volumes were produced, on subjects such as the legal implications of separation, economics, defence, welfare and pensions, and international affairs (including, ironically enough, EU membership). These were informally peer-reviewed by external academics and others and, despite their clear political positioning, read like pieces of civil service policy analysis, drawing on internal and external evidence. Although they were, generally speaking, written for a non-specialist readership they were not aimed at the ordinary voter, but rather at campaigners and commentators, and to provide the backup for political speeches, and one widely distributed pamphlet.

Scotland then voted to remain in the UK, and it must have seemed to David Cameron's government that the Scotland Analysis programme contributed to this success, because they commissioned a similar series of publications in the European referendum.[7] Chancellor George Osborne, heavily involved in the Scotland series, and apparently convinced that its message of risk had won the day, took the lead. Indeed, not only did the government repeat the process, covering much of the same ground, but it also reprised two basic themes from the Scottish referendum. First, there was a strong emphasis on the economic risks of separation. Secondly, the papers repeated a slogan heavily used in the 2014 campaign: Scotland had been said to have the 'best of both worlds', as devolution offered many of the opportunities of independence while pooling economic and social risks with the

UK. Similarly, the UK was said to have the 'best of both worlds' in the EU, by virtue of membership and its opt-outs, notably from the Euro.

On the face of it, this must have seemed like a reasonable idea. After all, both referendums were about leaving unions; both carried significant economic consequences; in both cases the government could say that the risks and downsides of change were significant; and in both it could claim that concerns were recognized by the special status of devolution or UK opt-outs. But there were actually significant differences, helpfully brought out in an interesting paper by Megan Morrison of the University of Glasgow.[8]

## *IV*

While some basic arguments were similar, the material revealed quite profound differences between the unions being defended. Breaking up the UK would have involved Scotland setting up the institutions of a new state, with risks to institutions that mattered in voters' daily lives, like pensions or benefits. It required a new foreign and defence policy, armed forces and so on. Such risks were obviously largely absent from the EU analysis: security issues, for example, were largely confined to threats to antiterrorism cooperation. Similarly, since the UK is a currency and fiscal union, it was straightforward to present the economic risks of Scottish independence in terms which resonated with the public. The major risks identified included 'losing the pound' (supported by analysis of optimum currency areas) and big cuts in public spending from the end of UK fiscal transfers to Scotland. Similarly, the welfare union of the UK – exemplified by demographic risk sharing in old age pensions – was a strong card in the Scotland Analysis series.

Drawing attention to such risks was characterized as 'project fear' by nationalist campaigners, but undoubtedly had a campaign impact, as tangible and emotionally relevant issues were at stake. The EU series, however, relied on the thinner gruel of the economic downside of trade reductions from exiting the single market and customs union and its knock-on effects on incomes and the resources available for public spending. While the border effect of independence on trade had featured in the Scotland Analysis, these arguments were hardly at its centre. Currency featured in the EU analysis only as the risk of Euro membership avoided, and fiscal arguments were largely absent from the government's case. (Indeed the Leave campaign put them, inaccurately, on the side of their bus.) Overall, the EU analysis series identified risks which, while real, were more abstract, and less emotionally engaging than the pound in your pocket or the security of your old age pension.

Morrison's paper, however, identifies a more profound difference. Even though the Scotland Analysis papers are self-consciously analytical and evidence driven, the government's language about Scotland had a strong emotional overtone. The papers speak of shared identity, common history and emotional connection, and not merely shared transactional interests. The union between Scotland and the rest of the UK is presented throughout as undeniably a good thing. By contrast, the language in the EU papers is uniformly utilitarian. The advantages the UK was said to obtain from its EU membership were economic or the fruit of practical cooperation. The 'best of both worlds' did not speak of the advantages of being both British and European, but rather of the alleged downsides of EU membership which the UK's opt-outs had avoided. Nowhere in the series is membership of the EU presented as an unequivocal good.

This, of course, reflected the deep ambivalence in the Conservative party about relations with Europe which led to the EU referendum in the first place. Taken together with the greater difficulty in identifying the risks which would impact on ordinary people, this ambivalence undermined the effectiveness of the EU Referendum Series. The government was trying to replicate what it saw as the success of its Scottish Referendum Analysis Series. But it made only rather abstract, utilitarian arguments, and could not find a positive word to say about the European project.

## V

Another important difference between the Scottish and European cases is that civil servants were on both sides in the Scottish referendum. The civil service as an institution supported two sets of ministers and was therefore not identified as on one side of the argument or another. There is a rather engaging sense of British fair play about this. It is not immediately obvious that it is proper for devolved civil servants, who work for ministers whose ministerial competences are defined by law and do not include campaigning for independence, should be involved in supporting their politicians in doing so. Internally in Edinburgh, the argument was made that since considering changes to the devolution settlement was within ministers' powers, so too was considering independence. No-one in Whitehall was disposed to make an issue over that figleaf. Having civil servants working up the case for independence may have left some residual resentments in the minds of Scottish opposition politicians, but in present political circumstances these may be a theoretical rather than a real problem.

By contrast, civil service resources and expertise were available to the government in the EU case, but not to the Leave side, even though there were ministers in the Leave campaign. No official resources were devoted to thinking through how a Leave vote might be put into practice. The government offered the population the choice, but no plan to implement it. One consequence was that Leave campaigners' claims did not have even the limited grounding in reality offered by the Scottish government's independence White Paper. As a result, the outcome of the vote paralysed the UK government. Another was that the civil service was made to seem aligned not merely with the views of the government of the day, but with the views of one (then, but no longer, dominant) faction inside the Conservative party.

## VI

How does this leave the civil service looking? Subsequent developments have exacerbated the problems of perception. Mrs May's sustained failure over three years to find a way forward on Brexit may stem in large measure from the mess she inherited, and her own political choices – calling an election which reduced her parliamentary room for manoeuvre, failing to seek consensus with opposition parties, and setting 'red lines' which so restricted her policy scope as to render her position unmanageable. But it also resulted from her accepting the civil service analysis of Brexit's economic downside, and of the problems it would create for Northern Ireland, and trying to mitigate the damage.

The nature of the advice matters. Some of it is drawn from well-established economic theory – restricting trade with the EU will make the UK worse off. Here departmental advice chimes with the consensus of external experts. Much, however, is drawn from officials' practical knowledge and experience, which only the civil service can offer. How can borders be set up and managed in practice? Nobody in Britain knows more about that than the Border Agency of the Home Office. How might the EU respond to the UK's leaving, and what is it likely to agree or reject? The Foreign Office and the Cabinet Office are the experts. What are the UK's international obligations on Northern Ireland, and how might its population and political system react to changes? Ask the Northern Ireland Office. It is pretty clear that official advice has contained unwelcome truths. Imaginary technology cannot make an EU border work. Sir Ivan Rogers was eased out for explaining accurately how the EU would react. And the international obligations of the Good Friday agreement which officials will have set out left Brexiteers feeling the Irish tail was waving the British dog. As for the longer term, agreeing and implementing a new long-term relationship with the EU, that is still to be negotiated, on a timetable and with objectives that officials may struggle to find plausible: messengers may again be shot.

Taken together, these issues present an immediate and continuing challenge to relations between officials and ministers who now seek to deliver Brexit. They are starting with a deficit in trust, larger than might be expected on a change of government. But there is also a wider problem of the Civil Service's reputation for political impartiality with a substantial section of the population.

## VII

Brexit was earlier described as a nationalist project. It is also a populist one. Populism is a term easier to throw around than to define, as few movements nowadays would describe themselves as populist, even when they are. I use the term as Mudde and Kaltwasser do,[9] to mean a political approach which is ideologically light, that is to say not necessarily left- or right-wing, nor focused on one or other social group's interest, as in the past it has been for agricultural populations. It is probably always nationalist, but has only two key concepts. First, a demand for popular sovereignty, which is not the same as liberal, representative democracy. (It differs notably in relation to minority rights, and shows a preference for the plebiscite over the election.) Second, it makes a distinction between the (true) people and the (corrupt) elite. On this description, President Donald Trump ('I love stupid people') is undoubtedly a populist, as is Prime Minster Orban of Hungary, although his elite are in Brussels. The description fits Brexit well. Those Brexiteers who talk of the 'will of the people', as against the hesitations of Parliament, are on any view populist, as are those elements of the press which can refer to judges as 'enemies of the people'.[10]

Two distinct problems arise from this. The first is how evidence and analysis of any sort feeds into debates about identity dominated by populist approaches. Most of us do not enjoy being presented with evidence which contradicts our beliefs, and will subject it to more rigorous scrutiny than confirmatory material. The more important and emotionally resonant the belief, the greater the likely resistance. This was evident during the Scottish referendum campaign. Evidence about, e.g., Scotland's fiscal position (published by the Scottish government itself) was regularly questioned by independence campaigners, as were official forecasts of North Sea oil revenues. But in the more populist atmosphere of the Brexit campaign, uncomfortable facts were dismissed outright, or replaced by fake news. Attempts to correct them, as in the notorious '£350 million for the NHS' written on the side of the campaign bus, seem merely to have drawn attention to the misinformation. Some US evidence on how correcting misinformation affects voter behaviour is similar. The so-called backfire effect[11] suggests that presenting voters with factual rebuttals can compound ignorance. In one study, conservatives presented with factual information which corrected their misperception 'doubled down' and became more sure of it. That attitude was certainly evident in the Brexit debate, not just from ordinary voters, but campaign leaders (perhaps best exemplified in the quotation at the head of this chapter).

Of more immediate concern for the future of the civil service, however, is its identification with a 'Remainer elite'. This has been more evidently a problem after the vote rather than during the campaign, as the three-year paralysis of the May government allowed resentment by Leave voters, in an increasingly febrile environment fanned by a Brexit-supporting press, to fester. Judges, 'experts', business leaders and civil servants were presented not merely as an elite, but a Remainer elite conspiring to thwart the will of the people. There was both a social class (the better off versus the left behind) and a geographical (London versus the North of England) division to this. But this deliberately populist labelling could undermine the legitimacy of a politically impartial civil service, with a substantial proportion of the population and a number of politicians taking the view that the civil service is not impartial on the biggest political question of the day.

## VIII

Fundamental upheavals like Scottish independence or leaving the EU can be expected to create constitutional aftershocks. Perhaps unexpectedly, one principle shaken up turns out to be the political neutrality of the civil service. Since the Scottish people decided against independence, its aftershocks for officials have been muted. In any event, the involvement of civil servants on both sides made the idea of political neutrality easier to defend. The Scottish independence campaign produced its share of dismissal of evidence, official and otherwise, and (largely on the fringes) naming of Quislings etc., but the civil service as an institution was not a target.

The Brexit referendum and its aftermath felt quite different. The Cameron Government chose to have a referendum in order to fix a problem inside the Conservative party and save it from a populist challenger. In part, they were following Harold Wilson's 1975 example, though without his campaign dexterity. Taking their lead from the Scotland Analysis programme, they used civil service expertise to point out the risks of leaving the EU. The material was less persuasive, and ultimately ineffective, but it was seen (accurately enough if not formally) as supporting the policy, not of the whole government, but of the pro-EU faction inside the Conservative party. Civil service analysis, in a populist campaign, was seen as not neutral but aligned with one side. This got worse after the vote. Mrs May's undeliverable compromise, derived from accepting civil service analysis of risks and some spectacularly inept political advice, allowed increasingly populist campaigners and press to paint the civil service as part of a conspiracy against the will of the people. In a febrile and rather leaky atmosphere it was easy, and perhaps not always unjust, to blame officials for presenting the problems of delivering the undeliverable. The effect on individual officials and the morale of Whitehall is tangible, and the threat to the idea of a permanent, impartial and objective, civil service is real also.

This was in part unavoidable. Permanent officials will tend to be institutionally, if not politically, conservative. They know how the present system works, and inevitably to some degree are invested in it – they understand it and are inclined to defend their own positions in it. They are good at identifying risks and problems, and at marshalling evidence to explain why simple, appealing political ideas turn out to be much more complex in practice (in the words of the onetime Labour Chancellor Hugh Dalton, 'congenital snag-hunters'). So it is hard to imagine them advising ministers that leaving the EU would mean the 'easiest trade deal ever' or that the problems of the Irish border could be solved by yet-to-be-invented technical solutions. But the choices of the Cameron government, followed by the paralysis of the May government, brought backroom advisers into the frontline, so populist campaigning has been able to paint bureaucratic caution and professional advice as resistance to the will of the people.

These problems might have been mitigated by a different approach to civil service expertise. Had the Cameron government not decided to harness the power of the state to solve the Conservative party's problems, it might have chosen to allow official resources to be used to set out not merely the problems of leaving the EU, but alternatively what would have to be done to put a Leave decision into practice, thus better informing the public to some degree (and maybe grounding the Leave campaign too). As in the Scottish referendum, supposedly impartial civil servants might not then have been perceived as only on one side of the question. It might even have been possible for officials to work on summaries of the arguments for and against to be presented to the voters (as in Switzerland). Even the sketch of a Leave plan might have helped Mrs May escape gridlock. But the practice of using the referendum for tactical political, rather than constitutionally mandated, reasons obviously appealed to Cameron. This was the second referendum he had promoted in which he opposed the change he offered to the population (the first being on electoral reform, during his coalition with the Liberal Democrats.) At least the SNP actually wanted the change on which they sought a referendum.

Numerous lessons can no doubt be drawn. The simplest might be, don't (perhaps Mrs Thatcher was right to describe the referendum as the 'device of … demagogues') or at least develop a set of constitutional rules and expectations about how referendums can be held and organized. One of those, drawing on the reflections here, might be that if the public are to be offered a highly divisive choice, then public officials should be seen to be working on the case for neither side of the argument or for both. Otherwise their impartiality will again be challenged.

It may be, depending on how politics develops, that the next referendum that the UK faces will be on Scottish independence once again. It seems likely that Scottish Nationalists will seek to learn some of the lessons from the winning Brexit campaigners, for example on how to dismiss evidence and analysis, and thus adopt a distinctly more populist tone than last time. It may be easier to identify post-Brexit England as different and 'other', and to portray the UK's governance as by a corrupt elite, contrasted with the true people of Scotland. It would be ironic, but not necessarily undesirable, if a post-Brexit UK government sought to impose on such a referendum some of the constraints which might have led to a more reasonable, evidence-based debate in 2016.

Meantime, it could yet get more difficult for officials, as there may be further unwelcome realities ahead for Brexiteers. Advising that trade negotiations could take longer and produce worse outcomes than presented to the public, or setting out the demands that the EU might make of the UK, may well be true, but is unlikely to produce gratitude. The only course open to officials is to continue to give their best advice, and to do so in complete privacy. This will be hard for officials, as morale will start from a low base, and the human factors referred to above will be tangible. Nevertheless civil service advice is for ministers, not for partisan consumption, and for ministers to accept or reject. Whether this enables the present and next generation of Whitehall officials to gain the trust of their political masters remains to be seen. It depends on the integrity of officials, and the attitude taken by politicians, but also on how divided the UK remains after Brexit.

## Notes

1    Civil Service Code, HM Government, 2015, at www.gov.uk/government/publications/civil-service-code/the-civil-service-code

2    See, for example, Leslie Chapman, *Your Disobedient Servant* (London: Chatto and Windus, 1978), or Michael Coolican, *No Tradesmen and No Women: The Origins*

*of the British Civil Service* (London: Biteback Publications, 2018), for the tension between the highflying policy generalist at the centre and the hard-working delivery staff.

3   As suggested in the 1980s by the Permanent Secretary Sir Anthony Part.

4   Geoffrey K. Fry, *The Politics of the Thatcher Revolution: An Interpretation of British Politics* (Basingstoke: Palgrave Macmillan, 2008).

5   Anthony D. Smith, *Nationalism: Theory, Ideology, History*, 2nd edn (London: Polity Press, 2010).

6   www.gov.uk/government/collections/scotland-analysis

7   www.gov.uk/government/topical-events/eu-referendum

8   Megan Morrison, 'Repeating History: The Second Time as Failure: Government Analysis in the Scottish and EU Referendums' (2019). www.uofgschooloflaw.com/blog/2019/7/30/repeating-history-the-second-time-as-failure-government-analysis-in-the-scottish-and-eu-referendums

9   Cas Mudde and Cristóbal Rovira Kaltwasser, 'Populism', in *The Oxford Handbook of Political Ideologies*, ed. Michael Freeden, Lyman Tower Sargent and Marc Stears (Oxford: Oxford University Press, 2013), 493–512.

10  *Daily Mail*, 4 November 2016. The headline was only tepidly criticized by the Brexit-supporting Secretary of State for Justice Truss; the article's author went on to work as a spokesman for Prime Minister May.

11  Brendan Nyhan and Jason Reifler, 'When Corrections Fail: The Persistence of Political Misperceptions', *Political Behavior* 32 (2010): 303–30.

# Chapter 13

## ADVISING TRUMP

### Rob Goodman

Political theory is full of bad advice. I'm not referring to Plato's counsel that the first step towards an ideal city is expelling everyone over the age of ten, or Hobbes's prescription that the university politics curriculum should consist of *Leviathan*, full stop, or any number of other canonically bad ideas. Rather, I'm claiming that bad advice is one of political theory's favourite problems. The flatterer, the demagogue, the Machiavel, the wicked counsellor, the lying courtier, the power behind the throne – all of these are familiar figures in the history of political thought, and it is worth asking why.

Of course, political theory lives on problems. There is simply more to say – more need, we reasonably assume, for our own advice – when something has gone wrong than when something has gone right. All of us, even political theorists, want to be useful; and there seems to be more use in identifying and proposing defences against the flatterer or the demagogue than in identifying and celebrating the wise counsellor.

And yet I think it is also the case that good advice is scandalous in a way that bad advice is not. Good advice, counsel that performs a necessary and salutary role in the political system of which it is a part, is a permanent reminder of the insufficiencies and shortcomings of those who receive it – that is, of those who rule. The problem is not so much the personal flaws of rulers as it is the structural flaws of their regimes. Rulers have needed advisers because the qualities that make them rulers – those that are selected for under a given regime – are frequently separate from, and sometimes even exclude, the qualities needed to rule well. To put it another way, the qualities that legitimize power are often quite different from the qualities required for its exercise. Good advice lives in that awkward gap.

To say so is necessarily to paint with a very broad brush, but that gap is evident across a wide range of historical cases, with a wide range of legitimation criteria. Take the case of hereditary monarchy, in which competence was famously something of an anti-qualification. 'The princes who peaceably inherit the sceptre of their fathers', wrote Edward Gibbon, 'claim and enjoy a legal right, the more secure as it is absolutely distinct from the merits of their personal characters'.[1] If personal merit had been the criterion of the sovereign's legitimacy, any subject with more merit would have had a better, and destabilizing, claim to rule. Making legitimacy heritable privileged stability at the risk of competence. Legitimacy-rich but often competence-poor, hereditary monarchs were obliged to import competence into their courts in a variety of forms.

Or take the opposite case of direct democracy. In the Athenian democracy, the assembled *demos* was sovereign because it comprised the entire citizen body, or at least an approximation of it. But because the *demos*-in-Assembly was a multitude, it was also functionally mute – or at least capable of a radically restricted vocabulary. An assembly can vote, cheer, hiss, and grumble, but can only deliberate with help. Recently, Matthew Landauer has convincingly argued that the orators who addressed the Athenian Assembly saw themselves, and were seen by the public, as advisers to the sovereign – and that the form of speech we often refer to as 'deliberative rhetoric' is perhaps better rendered as 'advisory rhetoric'.[2] As in the case of the hereditary monarch, the quality that made the *demos* the legitimate sovereign – its multiplicity – mandated its dependence on advice from an outside source: in this case, members of the *demos* who temporarily stood outside the *demos*, and in doing so recovered the full range of their voices.

Or take, last, the 'audience democracy' that is American presidentialism.[3] Is it surprising that the ability to project charisma and the ineffable presidential mien to a mass audience have only a loose correlation with technocratic knowledge, or managerial skill, or ideological fluency? Sometimes, to be sure, these qualities coincide; 'but success in a lottery', as Walter Bagehot characterized the Lincoln administration, 'is no argument for lotteries'.[4] It is a telling tic of language that presidents and would-be presidents are commonly urged not to lead but to 'show leadership': the American system selects above all for the display of leaderly qualities.[5] And if Americans believe that this criterion misses the point in important ways, they are in good historical company.

My argument, then, is that we cannot understand political advice without understanding legitimacy – in particular, the limits of what gets legitimized. This has been a roughly sketched and stylized account, but I hope you will agree with me on this much: when advisory institutions are stable and functional, the principal and the adviser each offer something the other needs and lacks. The adviser helps to fill the gap between legitimacy and good governance. And the principal has access to legitimate power in a way that the adviser does not. At its best, the relationship is a symbiotic one.

## I

But what does any of that have to do with the notoriously badly advised Donald Trump? A student of political advice in the Trump years needs to be fluent in firings-by-Twitter, the phenomenon of the self-incriminating lawyer, the literally baroque Cabinet meetings in which high officials take turns offering escalating homage to the president's superlative greatness, and the definition of the word *kakistocracy*. How, except by the *via negativa*, can a theory of good advice help us approach this president?

It can, I think, if we begin from the premise that Trump is quite possibly a 'new prince' in Machiavelli's sense of the term. He is new because he is – in self-presentation, and in reception by the public – visibly out of continuity with his predecessors. He claims power on terms other than theirs. The vocabularies, signs and rituals that legitimize him are essentially new ones. And Trump's newness has some radical implications for his relationship with advice.

But am I overstating this newness? Formally, of course, Trump is president because he received a majority of Electoral College votes, like the great bulk of his predecessors; like all of his predecessors but one, he is a white man. Substantively, what is perhaps most surprising about Trump is how little he has deviated from conservative Republican orthodoxy, cutting upper-income tax rates, slashing regulations and appointing Federalist Society-approved judges. But those facts, on their own, tell an incomplete story.

The more complete story would account for events like Trump's first address to Congress, on 28 February 2017. That evening, after promising 'a great, great wall on our southern border' and 'new roads, bridges, tunnels, airports, and railways gleaming across our very, very beautiful land', he turned to memorialize William Ryan Owens, a Navy SEAL killed in Yemen, the first combat death of the Trump presidency. 'Ryan died as he lived', read Trump, gesturing to Owens's widow in the balcony, 'a warrior and a hero, battling against terrorism and securing our nation'.[6] A ninety-second standing ovation ensued, and on the CNN broadcast following the speech, Van Jones, a Democratic commentator and generally a harsh critic of Trump, singled out that moment as pivotal: 'He became president of the United States in that moment, period.'[7]

Once you have paused to reflect on how queasy-making Jones's claim is – particularly its implication that killing and dying by proxy makes presidents, no matter how covert the war or unclear its aims – recognize, too, that it is basically correct. A president is not simply made by an election, but rather by a series of gestures that confirm a claim on power: touring the wreckage of shootings and hurricanes, presiding at egg hunts and tree lightings, standing behind decorated podiums to firmly utter the correct sentiments, and, yes, memorializing the uniformed dead. All political offices have these legitimating signs, but the American presidency is defined by them more than most, given that it knows no firm line between its roles as head of government and head of state, and given that its institutional power, as political scientists have long argued, is essentially the power to persuade.[8] If there is something wrong with Jones's argument, it is not that pronouncing appropriately sober words in an appropriately regal setting makes one president, but rather his implication that the ritual works once and for all; on the contrary, as in all rituals, 'getting it right is doing it again and again and again'.[9] What is so striking about the behaviour that Jones singled out, then, is its rarity. For Trump, anodyne commander-in-chiefly conduct is a stunning departure from form.

Whatever their other failings, modern presidents, Trump excepted, have been conventionally 'presidential' as a matter of course. In Trump's case, 'presidential' conduct is so surprising as to deserve special notice. Trump is as likely to feud with the loved ones of killed service members as to honour them. He has drawn a political rival into an extended debate on penis size, railed against 'shithole countries', and posed next to an orphaned baby – his parents murdered in the August 2019 mass shooting in an El Paso Walmart – with an uncanny smile and thumbs-up.[10] To read the news in the Trump years is to be treated to one or another of these minor outrages every week. In fact, one of the longer-running disputes among Trump's antagonists is between those who see his presidency's harms mainly in its flagrant unpresidentialism, its coarsening of American public discourse, and those who see his public conduct as a distraction, intentional or otherwise, from the true harms. I am convinced that the latter are mostly right; the former are generally those for whom a cheapening of the discourse is the very worst thing they can suffer under this president. Nevertheless, I agree with them that Trump's words and gestures matter profoundly – not so much because they plumb new depths of incivility, but because they amount to a new legitimizing language. Trump commands the support of a sizeable minority not despite them but because of them, because of the ways in which they convey contempt for the 'establishment' and its established means of authorizing power. Hence the newness of his power – one of the few things in his life that Trump has *not* inherited.[11]

From the moment he entered presidential politics – with a record as a reality TV star and promoter of the 'birther' conspiracy theory, but none in previous office – to his televised invitations of foreign interference in American elections, Trump has unsettled Americans' notion of what makes a president. His relationship with his advisers has hardly been the sole casualty of this unsettling, but it has been an important one – and a misunderstood one. When Trump's critics blame his propensity for flattery or firings on his personal shortcomings, they are too quick to moralize. Instead, it is more illuminating, both of the current presidency and of the Trumpian figures to come, to think in terms of the instability of Trump's position as a would-be pioneer of new modes of legitimacy, and of the ways in which this instability infects everything around him.

## II

Recall that in the model of advice I proposed at the outset, there is an essential division of labour between principal and adviser: the former controls access to legitimate power, and the latter offers counsel on its exercise. When this model is in equilibrium, we could think of principal and adviser as engaging in a mutually beneficial exchange. But when it is unsettled, that mutual benefit is no longer so clear. One of the main things that might unsettle this model is the accession of a 'new prince' – in other words, a change in what counts as legitimate power, an overturning of the established qualifications. In such conditions, the adviser might conceive of new ambitions – why not, when the conditions of authority seem to be up for grabs? In turn, the principal might have new reason to fear and mistrust the adviser, to demand increasingly elaborate displays of loyalty. Further, it is not simply the case that the old language of legitimacy has been destabilized, in the passive voice – rather, the principal is the one who has actively destabilized it. And if this implies that the principal has won power through some outstanding quality, why solicit and accept advice at all? When advisory relationships are as deeply troubled as they appear to be in the Trump White House, we should look not merely to the personalities in play, but to the ways in which modes of authority have become uncertain.

Situating Trump and his circle in this framework can help us untangle the contradictions that appear, at first glance, to define their relationship. On the one hand, Trump, for all his bluster, is a deeply impressionable figure. For instance, the gatekeeping function of the White House staff – a matter of strict and unremarkable protocol in most administrations – has swollen in political importance, given that 'Trump tends to echo the words of whomever last spoke to him, making direct access to him even more valuable.'[12] But on the other hand, Trump's impressionability co-exists with intense bouts of imperiousness: he has berated subordinates in Cabinet meetings; set records for turnover in Cabinet secretaries and White House staff; and on occasion, especially in the international realm, has made unilateral decisions against the vehement advice of the military brass and foreign policy establishment.[13] He is, by turns, an empty space and an autocrat. And yet what appears to be a series of mood swings is, I would argue, better understood as the effect of the Trumpian newness I have described here.

We can begin with Trump's malleability – or, to put it differently, the unusually assertive role that his advisers have claimed to shape his politics in their image. It is an old commonplace that an insecure ruler should fear those closest to him, those in proximity to power who aim to 'take away his state from him.'[14] One thinks, for instance, of Sejanus in the court of Tiberius, whom 'the senators and the rest looked up to … as if he were actually emperor.'[15] And in fact, it was reported in 2018 that administration officials seriously considered invoking the Twenty-Fifth Amendment to the Constitution to remove Trump from power on grounds of incapacity. Trump's more enduring concern, though, is not that members of his circle will literally deprive him of office, but rather that they will substitute their judgment for his, usurping his role in fact if not in name. This is precisely where Trump's uncertain legitimacy matters. If Trump's accession was so improbable, who is to say which other improbable claims on power might be borne out? Moreover, the meaning and politics of Trumpism remain unclear and fluctuating. Especially in the early days of his presidency, Trumpism might have been anything from unalloyed white nativism to *Herrenvolk* welfare-statism to oligarchy-plus-culture-war to undisguised self-enrichment. With varying results, Trump's advisers have rushed into that vacuum of meaning.

One of the first into the breach was Steve Bannon, Trump's chief political strategist. The former editor of the far-right *Breitbart* site, Bannon ended the 2016 election campaign as one of the most influential figures in Trump's orbit and began 2017 dubiously honoured on the cover of *Time* magazine as 'the great manipulator' (whether of the public or of the president was left ambiguous).[16] In his comments to the press during the administration's transition period, Bannon had no qualms about casting himself, rather than the president or the Republican Party, as the primary driver of policy:

> The conservatives are going to go crazy. I'm the guy pushing a trillion-dollar infrastructure plan ... Shipyards, ironworks, get them all jacked up. We're just going to throw it up against the wall and see if it sticks. It will be as exciting as the 1930s, greater than the Reagan revolution – conservatives, plus populists, in an economic nationalist movement.[17]

Bannon's words are a remarkably candid statement of a widely held view in Trump's circle – the president had enabled a 'revolution', while remaining a virtual blank slate as to that revolution's content. Needless to say, Bannon overestimated himself. No massive public works spending ensued, and Bannon himself did not last a year in the White House. Nevertheless, the nationalist component of 'economic nationalism' outlasted him, and indeed became a defining theme of the Trump presidency. The travel ban on visitors from seven Muslim-majority countries, written by Bannon in January 2017 and upheld in modified form by the Supreme Court in June 2018, was the first demonstration that Trump's animus against Muslims would inform policy as well as rhetoric. Erstwhile allies of Bannon, such as Stephen Miller, continue to shape the president's nativist impulses into policy. Trump demands an alligator-filled moat on the Mexican border; Miller, like a translator working freely but with a deep fealty to the source text, renders this as the revocation of Temporary Protected Status for 59,000 Haitian earthquake victims, or the denial of visas to immigrants who fail to report adequate income.[18]

Operating in a less self-consciously disruptive vein, but with a similar faith in the president's malleability, is the informal clique of 'adults in the room'. Figures including Trump's first and second chiefs of staff, Reince Priebus and John Kelly; his second national security adviser, H.R. McMaster; his first secretary of defense James Mattis; and former economic adviser Gary Cohn have all been numbered among the 'adults'. They share a background in the party, defence, or economic establishments, and they more or less openly defined their role as protecting the public from Trump's worst impulses – impulses which were understood as ranging from the heterodox (on trade wars: 'Good and easy to win')[19] to the *very* heterodox (on hurricanes: 'Why don't we nuke them?').[20] That the 'adults' could co-exist with the travel ban, the border wall and the separation of migrant families suggests that punitive white nativism did not rank especially high on their list of concerns.

Like the nationalists, the 'adults' were a by-product of Trump's ideological fungibility. Observing the phenomenon of their more or less open contempt for their principal, the political theorist Corey Robin drew an important contrast between Presidents Trump and Reagan. When Reagan took office, it was as the head of a long-germinating ideological movement with a set of clearly defined goals. As a result, he was able to staff his administration and the federal bureaucracy with a group of disciplined loyalists; even when the president's directives were unclear or absent, they could generally act with reference to a pre-existing set of conservative principles. On the other hand, there is no shared understanding of Trumpist ideology – or even a set of parameters within which recognizably Trumpist arguments can take place – and there is only ever one Trumpian in good standing at all times. That fact placed the president in the unusual situation of staffing his administration with critics, sceptics, and outright enemies, simply for lack of more reliable options. Their attitude toward the president was evident in news leaks – for instance, the disclosure that Kelly and Mattis had agreed that one of them would remain on American soil at all times, in case the president attempted something drastic – and, above all, in the remarkable 2018 op-ed. that gave the clique its name, 'I Am Part of the Resistance Inside the Trump Administration.'[21]

Writing in the *New York Times*, the anonymous author self-identified as one of the 'adults in the room', with unmistakable implications about a child-in-chief. The author described senior officials 'working diligently from within to frustrate parts of his agenda' and 'to insulate their operations from his whims', resulting in a 'two-track presidency' in which staffers and appointees quietly make their own policy among more conventional lines. And yet, the 'adult' narrative relied on a rhetorical sleight-of-hand, which the author rather carelessly gave away in describing Trump, in one breath, as 'anti-trade and anti-democratic'. The former sentiment, even if it is wrong, is well within the mainstream of American political debate; the latter is something else entirely. It was never entirely clear what the 'adults' did to defend democracy from the president – but it is entirely reasonable to suspect that they harvested credit for doing so in order to offset their defence of their party's generally unpopular economic and foreign policy priorities. If we knew what outrages they had foiled, we were promised, we would be grateful that they had remained at their posts, thankful that they had taken on the burden of apparent complicity in order to stymie a mad king. But we would have to take their word for it. Even America's greatest anti-democratic institution, the Supreme Court, feels compelled to make arguments and show its work. In their professed inability to do so, the 'adults' made claims that are unverifiable because they themselves withheld the evidence needed to verify them – as when members of the Bush administration assured the public that its torture and surveillance programs had foiled untold numbers of unnamed terrorist plots. Arguments like these are as dubious as they are well-worn – though it is striking that the purportedly foiled plots are now said to be originating not in an Afghan cave, but in the White House.

Incidentally, the reader may have noted that I have referred to the 'adults in the room' in the past tense, largely because, with the departures of most of the president's initial appointees, culminating in Mattis's resignation in December 2018, their influence is held to be in eclipse, freeing 'Trump to be Trump'. I will return to that thought at the end of this essay.

First, though, a discussion of Trump as an empty space for others to fill would not be complete without accounting for his relationship with Fox News. Journalists like Matthew Gertz and Alvin Chang have documented dozens of instances in which commentary from Fox, especially its morning show, 'Fox & Friends', is tweeted out verbatim by Trump. On 11 January 2018, for instance, a 'Fox & Friends' chyron asked 'DID FBI USE INTEL TOOL TO INFLUENCE ELECTION?': a reference to the 'deep state' conspiracy theory in which federal law enforcement agencies attempted to undermine Trump in the 2016 election. The president, twenty-seven minutes later, tweeted this in response: 'Disproven and paid for by Democrats "Dossier used to spy on Trump Campaign. Did FBI use Intel tool to influence the Election?" @foxandfriends Did Dems or Clinton also pay Russians? Where are hidden and smashed DNC servers? Where are Crooked Hillary Emails? What a mess!'[22]

Fox personalities, in turn, are well aware that they are advising the president on live TV, not simply reporting on him. Chang found a marked increase in their use of phrases such as 'We need to', 'We are going', and 'We have got' in the months following Trump's election.[23] Frequently, Fox hosts have appealed to their most important viewer directly. Sometimes, their advice is couched in the plausible deniability of the third person, as when Ainsley Earhardt discussed the president's firing of FBI director James Comey in May 2017: 'He is the boss. And he gets to decide who works for him. Someone who works for him who is not supportive of him, he gets rid of them. He has the ability to do that.'[24] At other times, their advice is couched in nothing at all, as when judicial analyst Andrew Napolitano looked directly into the camera and said, 'Mr. President, this is not the way to go.'[25] Trump's days, which generally begin with Fox & Friends, often end with a late-night phone conversation with Sean Hannity, the Fox evening host who has become something of an informal communication director for the president.[26]

Trump entered public life with only a handful of political commitments. A 'law-and-order' celebration of the death penalty, economic protectionism and the (oddly specific) demand that allies pay for the presence of American troops overseas are the handful of documented Trumpian preoccupations with pre-presidential roots. As for the rest, the obsessions of Fox News – voter fraud, the migrant 'invasion', the machinations of the deep state – have become the obsessions of the president, in a way that the rest of us can follow in real time. Now, modern presidents have always developed messages and policies collaboratively, and they or their staffs have long coordinated media coverage with friendly outlets. But until Trump, they studiously maintained the fiction of the president's authorship: the president ultimately set policy, and his advisers helped carry it out; the president made news, and the media reported it. In Trump's unsettled circle, on the other hand, the old fiction no longer applies. Not only does Fox claim the power to make policy, to govern the president's judgment and perception of the world. It does so openly. The act of advising a certain type of ruler – the fawning and wheedling on one side, the arbitrary fits of compliance or defiance on the other, of the kind one imagines has been going on in the courts of powerful men from time immemorial – is visible in a way it has rarely ever been.

On the side of Fox and its hosts, literally broadcasting their influence over the president speaks, again, to the dominant attitude with which Trump's advisers relate to him. It is the attitude shared by Bannon and Mattis, by the white nationalists and the 'adults', by Secretary of State Mike Pompeo, who has risen in Trump's esteem while taking such ingratiating steps as branding the State Department 'the premier agency delivering on behalf of the President of the United States'.[27] It is the attitude that advisers will almost always take to a principal with a weak claim on legitimacy: contempt. It is one thing to flatter a ruler. It is another thing to flatter that ruler in public, to display his manipulability on a daily basis.

That Trump, for his part, effectively allows all of this to be so visible might almost bespeak a certain kind of cockeyed humility, or a vanity so superhuman that it transcends vanity and becomes its own opposite. He is, in effect, the constant butt of his advisers' joke – but then, he has never really objected to being the butt of jokes, provided that they are constant. The historian Roberto Calasso understood how the same dynamic was at work in the Soviet Union. 'Excessive ridicule – its relentless, daily production – can lead to the total neutralization of its destructive power', he observed. 'And perfection is reached when anti-Soviet stories become a part of the regime.'[28] Trump's regime is strengthened by industrial-scale mockery of Trump, by the display of both flattery *and* his susceptibility to it, by the openness with which he parades the ugliness of power.

He has to: in a world in which power were not widely perceived to be ugly, he would not be president. So if prior presidents drew their legitimacy from 'the pleasing illusions, which made power gentle and obedience liberal', Trump draws his from the flagrant, performative destruction of illusions.[29] In this legitimizing story, Trump is no better or more suited for power than any other contender, whether within his circle, among his own party, or from the opposition, with one important caveat: Trump broadcasts his unfitness and his ugliness more openly and forthrightly than they do. But as a result, he is committed to a permanent series of outrages, demonstrations of unfitness and invitations to mockery – and, because the public can build up a tolerance for outrage, he is committed to permanent escalation.

Needless to say, this is not a stable or comfortable way to be president. The imperious side of the Trump presidency, his sporadic efforts to centralize power in himself, is a response to that inescapable discomfort. His tirades against staff and subordinates, his carousel of hirings and firings, his vesting of an unprecedented degree of influence in members of his family, his establishment of parallel and informal White House 'departments' – such as the communications operation led by Hannity, or the foreign policy operation led by his personal lawyer, Rudy Giuliani – can all be seen as reactions to the dynamic of advisory contempt that I have described here. Like most aspiring strongmen, Trump prizes loyalty above all. But the instability of his regime means that his search for it is permanent: it is premised on the unlikely existence of an adviser who can look at Trump and see something other than hollowness.

Trump's relationship with his advisers is said to have a destination. After enough firings, he will arrive at a staff compliant enough that it may as well not be there at all – a staff that will finally 'let Trump be Trump'. Trump himself has endorsed this view, and even some of his firees have echoed it, too, as when John Kelly claimed that he predicted Trump's impeachment if the president failed to hire staffers willing to check his instincts.[30] Sure enough, as I write this, Trump does appear to be heading for impeachment, and he has issued a number of decrees, such as the abandonment of America's Kurdish allies in Syria, over the objection of virtually everyone with an opinion on the matter.

But it would be wrong to conclude that 'letting Trump be Trump' is simply a matter of getting the staffing 'right' once and for all. No set of hirings and firings can change the dynamics that make advising Trump so fraught, because those dynamics are fundamentally not personal – as much as the spectacle of Trump's personality would lead us to believe otherwise. Trump has always been free to be Trump. But the question is whether he can bring a critical mass of others along with him. No one, not even a despot, can govern alone.[31] And Trump is likely to discover that whatever is left of his presidency will not be marked by freedom, but by the repetition of the same infuriating patterns. He simply has too little to offer his advisers in exchange for their compliance – in a way that this most transactional of presidents would surely appreciate if it were happening to anyone else.

If Trump ever succeeds in breaking those patterns, it will not be because of a change in staffing, but because of a change in the basis of his presidency, a successful attempt to bring about the political realignment that stabilizes his claim on power, renders his newness familiar, and, as a side effect, brings his advisory relationships into the kind of equilibrium that has so far evaded them. Trump is either a founder or a mistake – and our dim awareness that those are the stakes must surely account for much of the vitriol in which his presidency swims.

## Notes

1    Edward Gibbon, *The History of the Decline and Fall of the Roman Empire*, vol. 2 (1781; repr., New York: Penguin, 1994), 1072.

2    Matthew Landauer, *Dangerous Counsel: Accountability and Advice in Ancient Greece* (Chicago: University of Chicago Press, 2019), 6.

3    Bernard Manin, *The Principles of Representative Government* (Cambridge: Cambridge University Press, 1997), 218.

4    Walter Bagehot, *The English Constitution* (1867; repr., Oxford: Oxford University Press, 2001), 24.

5    One recent instance: Andy Slavitt, '2020 Democrats, you're doing it wrong on health care. Stop arguing and show leadership', *USA Today*, 8 October 2019. www.usatoday. com/story/opinion/2019/10/08/america-falls-behind-health-how-would-2020-democrats-fix-column/3892653002.

6    'Trump's Address to Joint Session of Congress, Annotated', *National Public Radio*, 28 February 2017. www.npr.org/2017/02/28/516717981/watch-live-trump-addresses-joint-session-of-congress.

7    Jason Kurtz, 'Van Jones on Trump: "He became President of the United States in that moment, period"', *CNN*, 1 March 2017. www.cnn.com/2017/03/01/politics/van-jones-trump-congress-speech-became-the-president-in-that-moment-cnntv/index.html.

8    Richard E. Neustadt, *Presidential Power and the Modern Presidents*, rev. edn (New York: Free Press, 1990), 29.

9    Adam B. Seligman, Robert P. Weller, Michael Puett and Bennett Simon, *Ritual and Its Consequences: An Essay on the Limits of Sincerity* (Oxford: Oxford University Press, 2008), 24.

10   On penis size: Gregory Krieg, 'Donald Trump defends size of his penis', *CNN*, 4 March 2016. www.cnn.com/2016/03/03/politics/donald-trump-small-hands-marco-rubio/index.html. On 'shithole countries': Lauren Gambino, 'Trump pans immigration proposal as bringing people from "shithole countries"', *The Guardian*, 12 January 2018. www.theguardian.com/us-news/2018/jan/11/trump-pans-immigration-proposal-as-bringing-people-from-shithole-countries. On thumbs-up: Edward Helmore, 'Anger as grinning Trump gives thumbs-up while Melania holds El Paso orphan', *The Guardian*, 9 August 2019. www.theguardian.com/us-news/2019/aug/09/trump-el-paso-melania-orphan-baby-thumbs-up.

11   If anything can be said to have justified Trump's stylistic break from the past in the eyes of his partisans, it was most likely to be the example of his predecessor, Barack Obama. Obama observed the existing forms of the presidency quite scrupulously – but as a black president, broke what was, in the eyes of Trump's base, the most important form of all. For this reason, Ta-Nehisi Coates called Trump the 'first white president': not literally, of course, but because 'he is the first president whose entire political existence hinges on the fact of a black president'. Coates, *We Were Eight Years in Power: An American Tragedy* (New York: One World, 2017), 344.

12   Robert Costa, 'Trump and advisers remain split on how far to move toward middle', *Washington Post*, 27 August 2016, www.washingtonpost.com/politics/trump-and-advisers-remain-split-on-how-far-to-move-toward-the-middle/2016/08/26/e94f5eb4-6ba1-11e6-ba32-5a4bf5aad4fa_story.html. Amber Phillips, 'Want to change Trump's mind? Be the last one who talks to him', *Washington Post*, 14 April 2017. www.washingtonpost.com/news/the-fix/wp/2017/04/14/want-to-change-trumps-mind-on-policy-be-the-last-one-who-talks-to-him.

13   On berating subordinates: Josh Dawsey and Nick Miroff, 'The hostile border between Trump and the head of DHS', *Washington Post*, 25 May 2018. www.washingtonpost.com/politics/were-closed-trump-directs-his-anger-over-immigration-at-homeland-security-secretary/2018/05/24/4bd686ec-5abc-11e8-8b92-45fdd7aaef3c_story.html. On turnover: Tamara Keith, 'Trump Cabinet turnover sets record going back 100 years', *National Public Radio*, 19 March 2018. www.npr.org/2018/03/19/594164065/trump-cabinet-turnover-sets-record-going-back-100-years; Keith, 'White House staff turnover was already record-setting. Then more advisers left', *National Public Radio*, 7 March 2018. www.npr.org/2018/03/07/591372397/white-house-staff-turnover-was-already-record-setting-then-more-advisers-left.

14   Niccolò Machiavelli, *The Prince*, trans. W. K. Marriott (1513; London: J.M. Dent & Co., 1916), 143.

15   Cassius Dio, *Roman History*, vol. 7, trans. Earnest Cary (c. 220; Harvard: Harvard University Press, 1924), 195.

16   David von Drehle, 'Is Steve Bannon the second most powerful man in the world?', *Time*, 2 February 2017. time.com/4657665/steve-bannon-donald-trump.

17   Michael Wolff, 'Ringside with Steve Bannon at Trump Tower as president-elect's strategist plots "an entirely new political movement"', *The Hollywood Reporter*, 18 November 2016. www.hollywoodreporter.com/news/steve-bannon-trump-tower-interview-trumps-strategist-plots-new-political-movement-948747.

18   Jacqueline Charles, 'Feds ask appeals court to reverse TPS ruling so administration can deport Haitians', *Miami Herald*, 19 September 2019. www.miamiherald.com/

news/nation-world/world/americas/haiti/article235276197.html (the decision is still under appeal as of this writing). Daniel Trotta and Mica Rosenberg, 'New Trump rule targets poor and could cut legal immigration in half, advocates say', *Reuters*, 12 August 2019. www.reuters.com/article/us-usa-immigration-benefits/new-trump-rule-targets-poor-and-could-cut-legal-immigration-in-half-advocates-say-idUSKCN1V219N.

19  Thomas Franck, 'Trump doubles down: "Trade wars are good, and easy to win"', *CNBC*, 2 March 2018. www.cnbc.com/2018/03/02/trump-trade-wars-are-good-and-easy-to-win.html.

20  Jonathan Swan and Margaret Talev, 'Scoop: Trump suggested nuking hurricanes to stop them from hitting U.S.', *Axios*, 25 August 2019. www.axios.com/trump-nuclear-bombs-hurricanes-97231f38-2394-4120-a3fa-8c9cf0e3f51c.html.

21  Anonymous, 'I am part of the resistance inside the Trump administration', *New York Times*, 5 September 2018. www.nytimes.com/2018/09/05/opinion/trump-white-house-anonymous-resistance.html. The op-ed. was later expanded into a full-length book, titled *A Warning* and published in November 2019.

22  Matthew Gertz, 'I've studied the Trump-Fox feedback loop for months. It's crazier than you think', *Politico Magazine*, 5 January 2018. www.politico.com/magazine/story/2018/01/05/trump-media-feedback-loop-216248. Gertz, *Twitter*, 11 January 2018, twitter.com/MattGertz/status/951437980945866752/photo/1?ref_src=twsrc%5Etfw%7Ctwcamp%5Etweetembed%7Ctwterm%5E951439214645833730&ref_url=https%3A%2F%2Fwww.mediamatters.org%2Ffox-friends%2Fexecutive-timehail-live-tweeter-chief.

23  Alvin Chang, 'We analyzed 17 months of Fox & Friends transcripts. It's far weirder than state-run media', *Vox*, 9 February 2018. www.vox.com/2017/8/7/16083122/breakfast-club-fox-and-friends.

24  Chang, 'We analyzed 17 months of Fox & Friends transcripts. It's far weirder than state-run media'.

25  Gertz, 'Executive time: Hail to the live-tweeter in chief', *Media Matters*, 11 January 2018. www.mediamatters.org/fox-friends/executive-time-hail-live-tweeter-chief?redirect_source=/blog/2018/01/11/executive-time-hail-live-tweeter-chief/219036.

26  Olivia Nuzzi, 'Donald Trump and Sean Hannity like to talk before bedtime', *New York*, 14 May 2018, nymag.com/intelligencer/2018/05/sean-hannity-donald-trump-late-night-calls.html.

27  Susan B. Glasser, 'Mike Pompeo, the Secretary of Trump', *New Yorker*, 19 August 2019. www.newyorker.com/magazine/2019/08/26/mike-pompeo-the-secretary-of-trump.

28  Roberto Calasso, *The Ruin of Kasch*, trans. Richard Dixon (1983; New York: Farrar, Straus and Giroux, 2018), 43.

29  Edmund Burke, *Reflections on the Revolution in France* (1790; repr., London: John C. Nimmo, 1887), 332.

30  Colby Itkowitz and Josh Dawsey, 'Kelly says he warned Trump he'd be impeached if he hired a "yes man" as chief of staff to replace him', *Washington Post*, 26 October 2019. www.washingtonpost.com/politics/john-kelly-says-he-warned-trump-hed-be-impeached-if-he-hired-a-yes-man-as-chief-of-staff-to-replace-him/2019/10/26/e4d5d028-f827-11e9-8cf0-4cc99f74d127_story.html.

31  'Even the tyrant, the One who rules against all, needs helpers in the business of violence', in *On Violence*, ed. Hannah Arendt (San Diego: Harcourt Brace Jovanovich, 1969), 41.

## Chapter 14

## MANAGING THE GROWING TENSION BETWEEN POLITICS AND GOVERNANCE: HARD CHOICES AHEAD FOR WHITEHALL AND WESTMINSTER

## Martin Donnelly

UK politics have moved into a period marked by greater disruption and less consensus. Questions are being asked not just about policy outcomes but also the scope and legitimacy of the governmental process. This chapter considers the underlying issues involved in defining the balance between political and administrative layers of government, specifically the new choices facing the UK national civil service at a time when its existence as a neutral permanent body is under sustained challenge. Brexit has been the most recent challenge to a national consensus on how government should function. However, it comes in a wider context of social and economic dispute over the future structure of the UK, including concern about the continued impact of austerity since 2010 on deprived communities and more strongly ideological politics on both left and right. The emergence of a more divisive political culture across the UK inevitably has implications for how government can sustainably function.

*I*

The current structure of the UK civil service, with its strong separation of politicians and administrators, arose in the mid-nineteenth century for very practical reasons. In his novel *Little Dorrit* (1857), Charles Dickens describes a fictional government department he calls the Circumlocution Office. It is staffed by the Barnacle family, who attach themselves tightly to the ship of state. They defend the status quo, not interested in efficiency, innovation, or anything other than a quiet, well-paid life for themselves and their relations. This description was all too close to reality in the 1850s. It was becoming clear to many in parliament that political patronage and outright corruption in appointments, the lack of coordination between government agencies, and a failure to adjust to the growing complexity of managing an industrial society necessitated urgent change.

The second half of the nineteenth century saw steady progress away from public jobs for the 'unambitious, the indolent or incapable' in the blunt terms of the 1854 Northcote-Trevelyan report towards competitive examination and permanent appointment of officials by the independent Civil Service Commission. This led over time to a unified home civil service – the Treasury was the last department to join – with a shared structure, criteria for entry and promotion, and unified permanent leadership. It also meant that senior officials across government departments had a high degree of permanence, whatever ministerial changes took place.

Equally important was the Gladstonian focus on financial rectitude and transparency in the management of public funds. The senior official of each department, the Permanent Secretary, became the Accounting Officer, directly responsible to parliament for the propriety of all public funds spent. Ministers could ultimately direct their officials to spend money, but if the department and ultimately the Permanent Secretary considered this spending to be improper – outside the legal powers granted by parliament, novel, or in some way contentious – the Accounting Officer required a written Direction from the relevant minister before proceeding.

The system of Accounting Officer letters and Ministerial Directions, automatically reported to the House of Commons Public Accounts Committee, to the Comptroller and Auditor General of the National Audit Office, and then made public, still works as a serious brake on misuse of taxpayers' money. In my own experience as a civil servant, the existence of this system continues to prevent a significant amount of politically tempting but poor value for money spending from taking place. The Permanent Secretary has a strong personal incentive to ensure that all departmental spending is properly controlled, since the National Audit Office publishes regular detailed reviews of whether such spending, even if legal, is actually providing genuine value for money to the taxpayer.

The final element of this system was and is the Public Accounts Committee – the PAC – which holds regular hearings on reports prepared by the National Audit Office. At its best, this provides rigorous public scrutiny of spending decisions by the department. Traditionally, the PAC was chaired by a member of the Opposition who had served as a Treasury Minister, and therefore had relevant experience of managing government money. When Commons parliamentary committee heads became elected, this tradition was lost. Not all recent PAC Chairs have had relevant financial experience inside or outside government. Over time the analysis of public spending has become more political and less forensic. The Permanent Secretary and supporting officials are often left with the difficult job of defending government policy choices against political attack, rather than focusing on the efficiency of implementation of policy choices which have already been approved by parliament.

Tensions around the role of parliamentary committees, in particular the PAC, towards civil servants in recent years reflect this lack of agreement about their respective roles. A low point was reached in 2011 when the then Chair of the PAC insisted a permanent official swear an oath before giving evidence to the

Committee, a practice which was subsequently judged to have been an abuse of parliamentary process and has not been repeated. But damage was done to the relationship of mutual respect between elected parliamentarians and civil servants that is required to deliver genuinely effective scrutiny.

The PAC, with its element of cross-examination theatre, now available on the Parliamentary TV channel, highlights a wider issue concerning the boundaries of responsibility of permanent officials for the policies agreed by their ministers and at least implicitly supported by a majority in parliament. Can this distinction between the political and the administrative be fully maintained in the face of modern online scrutiny? And should it? The UK civil service model of open recruitment on merit, political neutrality and permanence of appointment has had a good run for the last century and a half. In its favour it has proved flexible at serving very different national governments through the extension of the electoral franchise, wars, global economic depression, the end of empire and the collapse of communism, membership of the European Union and devolved government in Scotland, Wales and Northern Ireland.

The strengths of this system include continuity of administration through rapid political change at elections, the development of expertise and managerial experience in the various businesses of government, and clarity of responsibilities. A shared system of appointments and promotion helps to develop a culture of professional trust between officials, based on a shared public service ethos, and often many years of working closely together. Having an agreed framework for cooperation helps to manage conflict over resource allocation between priorities, or decisions on responsibility between departments, and even changes of government, without any discontinuity of public service – a uniquely effective feature of the British system.

*II*

But challenges have been growing, externally and internally. Essentially, these are making it more difficult to combine trust with provision of relevant knowledge. Ministers and their advisers need to have confidence that the expertise offered to them by the civil service is not influenced by hostility to their own political priorities. Otherwise they will look elsewhere, preferring optimism and a sense of urgency to technical knowledge and professional caution. Officials need a similar confidence that offering rigorous analysis, telling it like it is to ministers, drawing on civil service experience of what works and what does not, will not prove career limiting, or leave them shut out of subsequent decision making. If politicians do not like the trade-offs they may face in the real world, they can have an understandable tendency to look for advisers willing to offer more palatable advice.

However, if elected politicians in government and parliament are not prepared to accept that advice can be impartial and constructive, even if it challenges the practicability of their political priorities, what is the point of recruiting and retaining an impartial service? The option of self-censorship – officials aiming not to offer more reality in their advice than the political market will bear – is ultimately not sustainable, though increasingly tempting to permanent officials faced with sceptical or even hostile ministers.

The issue of Brexit has brought these challenges more vividly into focus, but it did not create them – the stresses were already apparent. Advice on policy options must take a view about what is likely to happen under different scenarios. It is of course not possible to predict future outcomes with complete reliability. Faced with a policy change with a large potential impact, government officials, like other professionals, tend to err on the side of extrapolation from the past. And this approach tends to produce cautious conclusions.

Some of those making the case for the UK to leave the European Union argued that such conservatism was essentially a defence of the status quo, designed to put any radical change in an unfavourable light. They stressed the uncertainty attached to any change, and the upside potential which necessarily goes with uncertainty. Was, for example, the absence of evidence that Brexit could have a positive economic effect the same as evidence that such positive impact was necessarily absent? What if the very process of leaving the political and regulatory structures of the European Union produced a step change in UK firms' commitment to become more competitive? Faced with a chasm between the assumptions being made by the two sides, the normal civil service response of drawing firm policy conclusions from an imperfect evidence base has proved to be unsatisfactory to politicians who disagree with those conclusions. In this way, trust in the competence of those drawing the supposedly apolitical conclusions becomes eroded or even lost entirely.

Beyond Brexit there is a range of factors which in my experience have made building that combination of trust and frank competent advice more difficult in recent years. Some are technical; others represent wider societal trends away from consensus about legitimate policymaking procedures. First, the shift from a formal, recorded process of government to a more real time informal culture of political decision making with less analysis written down, and limited private space for policy debate. Freedom of information and a 24-hour media increasingly constrain private advice on managing conflicting priorities within government. We can see this in the contrast between the frank private written advice provided to ministers on sensitive political issues from the 1980s and 1990s now being released in the Public Records Office, and current political communication where social media is often used to provide a commentary on government decision making while it is taking place.

Until the end of the last century, ministers in each department would normally be briefed on policy options in writing by their officials. Advice from a junior official would be approved formally by a senior civil servant of Assistant Secretary rank who would occasionally add a comment to the note, which would also be copied to a range of interested colleagues across the department. Where issues crossed departmental borders there would be correspondence about the arguments between officials in the departments concerned, seeking to pull together evidence on the relevant facts, and the range of available outcomes which could then be put to ministers for final decision.

This process could take place over some weeks, allowing for any legal or financial consequentials to be highlighted and clarified, and for further detailed fact-finding to take place. If further discussion were needed, the Cabinet Office, always copied into correspondence between departments, would organize a meeting between departments and circulate a record of the results including follow-up actions. The cloak of government confidentiality meant that in practice these discussions remained private within Whitehall, and would not necessarily be visible to ministers until officials considered they were in a final form. Ministers accepted that such discussions led to a fuller range of realistic options for them to consider, and did not seek to anticipate or limit the scope of their conclusions.

Notes of this kind reviewing the advantages and drawbacks of policy options, including their negotiability, could not be written and circulated in today's Whitehall, because they would sooner or later, usually sooner, become public. Freedom of information legislation has frequently proved to be no respecter of internal government communication. But the eradication of a safe space to lay out policy options, including discussion of the management of dissenting ministers, parliament or external stakeholders, makes honest discussion around complex issues much harder to achieve.

Regardless of legislative constraints it is unrealistic to expect to go back to a more closed environment of private, deliberative policymaking. We live today in a world of social media and tweets going viral in real time. But in parallel to the arrival of digital media there has been a loosening of political discipline within and across government. Normal debates between ministers, including arguments about resourcing with the Treasury, are increasingly carried out through the media. There have always been leaks, but they risk now becoming part of the normal process of government, reducing further the scope for confidential discussion before decisions are reached.

It may be relevant that the end of the Cold War in the early 1990s removed the clear military/security need for continuity of the state during and after armed conflict. Throughout the post-war period departments maintained contingency plans kept up to date on their responsibilities during and after conflict, including in relation to the system of regional government that might be required after nuclear war. There was a shared sense between politicians and officials of a national interest which transcended party politics, even while the choices of the UK's defence policy stance was on occasion a seriously divisive issue in parliament. The necessary confidentiality required for a range of national security discussions also provided the discipline needed for private discussion of government issues within Whitehall. Inevitably it also led to excessive secrecy in areas which should have been more open to public debate, and allowed the executive to escape legitimate scrutiny. A new balance between open evidence-based discussion and some private assessment of conflicting public priorities within government has yet to be found.

A third factor is the issue of the growing complexity of government decision making, blurring the lines between political and technical issues. In particular, as the European Union has extended its range of regulatory activity it has become harder for the civil service to take account of the divisive domestic politics surrounding apparently technical issues within its remit. Over the last two decades devolution, with the growth of separate political and administrative cultures within UK nations, has also complicated decision making in Westminster and Whitehall. The culture of central government is still essentially to look to national decision-making and see devolved interests as something to be managed after the event. Since the devolution of powers within the UK, the Sewel Convention has set out the understanding that the Westminster Parliament would not legislate in areas of devolved responsibility, even if it retained the formal right to do so across the entire UK. After the Brexit referendum the Government decided that EU-related issues including fisheries policy should all be negotiated with Brussels on a UK-wide basis. This unilateral undermining of the understanding that devolution was a fixed commitment seriously eroded the trust between Westminster and the devolved administrations needed for devolution to function.

A fourth dimension relates to a significant shift in UK political culture in recent years, which reflects wider societal moves to value trust in groups of like-minded individuals sharing the same outlook, and often the same prejudices, over technical knowledge provided by impersonal experts. Similarly a new generation of politicians sees a prior commitment to the political goals of the administration, or even the individual minister, as the precondition for engagement on policy and its delivery. Some believe that within the civil service there is a bureaucratic self-interested culture with its own interests to defend which can obstruct political choices; and consider that those who do not share a political outlook should not have authority over its choices or implementation, because they do not understand or commit to why it is being done. The Brexit debate serves to bring many of these tensions into sharper relief. But they already existed.

In parallel, a lack of trust within government between an increasingly powerful centre and less trusted departmental ministers has weakened collective Cabinet responsibility and focused more decision making within the prime minister's team, reducing transparency and public accountability. Unelected aides with a position inside No 10 Downing Street can and do set the agenda for entire government departments, marginalizing the ministers with formal responsibility for those policies before parliament. There is often some uncertainty about what the prime minister's views on any specific issue may be. But officials in other departments have to take the latest pronouncement from one of the aides within No 10 as an authoritative decision until told otherwise.

### III

This new political centralization can be seen in the growing size of the centre. During Mrs Thatcher's time in No 10 the Prime Minister's Office was around 70 strong; today it numbers some 200. Within that total, political advisers working directly for the prime minister have doubled from 20 when Tony Blair came to power in 1997 to 40 today. A group of this size provides a separate source of advice and policy planning to the wider government machine, and leaves both officials and ministers struggling to know what new initiatives are being planned or even announced by the centre. Essentially No 10 has begun to operate increasingly separately from the dispersed expertise contained within separate government departments, and sometimes in rivalry to them.

Within government departments ministerial appointments no longer bring an automatic authority. They are often in practice used to help maintain a parliamentary majority. We currently have 23 full Cabinet ministers and another 6 ministers who attend Cabinet; there are over 100 ministers in total, not counting around 25 Whips in parliament. By comparison the French system works with 16 Cabinet minister equivalents and only around 20 junior ministers. French senior ministers have *cabinets* – their personal executive staff, usually a mix of seconded civil servants and external experts – of 9 to 11 members; at less senior levels the French Europe Minister in 2018 had 8 advisers, and the junior health minister a *cabinet* of 5. It is worth remembering that these are not adviser posts in the way that special advisers function in the UK. French *cabinet* members have full responsibility for policy and its implementation, and will replace their minister to deliver official speeches; notes are commissioned from permanent officials by *cabinet* members who then put the analysis they are satisfied with under their own private cover note to the minister. *Cabinet* members also seek to coordinate policy across government on behalf of their minister. The French system is of course hard to compare with the UK because the majority of *cabinet* members are officials on secondment from the department or elsewhere in the civil service; usually graduates of the Ecole Nationale d'Administration, as indeed are many ministers. This provides an element of shared professional education and therefore builds the trust which allows government to access the knowledge and expertise needed to function effectively from within its own ranks.

Westminster has over one hundred political appointees across government, and at least one senior minister recently appointed five political advisers. Despite those special advisers not having formal executive responsibilities, they do have significant power over decisions. They provide an alternative network for political coordination working alongside and sometime entirely separately from formal governmental coordination, which still works through the appointed junior ministers in each department.

So the Westminster political superstructure has grown significantly, reflecting a trend towards greater trust of the politically committed rather than the professionally neutral. This change has made it harder for Whitehall to provide ministers with a fair analysis of the issues, drawing on the technical competence of the permanent civil service to tell it like it is while also seeking to take forward the government's agenda. At senior level, a lot of time has to go into building relationships, which can mean limiting or suppressing advice which would be unwelcome and seen as off message.

*IV*

This requirement for greater focus on trust-building with political appointees, and the erosion of well-tried structures of governmental coordination comes at a time of massive and rapid external change in the wider economic environment, which poses its own challenges to government. The digital revolution has both social and economic consequences which need urgent attention. A coherent pathway to more digital government, including service delivery, was set out ten years ago in the 2009 Smarter Government report commissioned by Gordon Brown when Prime Minister. Many of the ideas in the report were subsequently implemented under the Coalition Government from 2010 to 2015. But inevitably the pace of change lagged behind wider changes to the global economy.

The impact of the digital revolution has become even more rapid and profound in recent years, not just in the UK but globally. Out of a total world population of 7.7 billion, nearly four billion of us are regular internet users. Over one billion are already subscribers to broadband, the new global infrastructure which determines what news people access and what they believe to be true; as well as how they communicate, work and enjoy their leisure. Global interconnectedness floats on a rising tide of data. Ninety per cent of the world's data is less than two years old. One point seven megabytes of data are being created every second for every person on earth. So the growing role of machine-learning algorithms to control and manage this data is now critical to our economy, wider society, and therefore how government functions.

At the same time public sector statistics struggle to capture how the digital economy works. Digital value creation is hard to localize and therefore hard to tax. Estimates of national economic growth are substantially revised over time. National trade figures do not sum to zero; at present separate US and UK trade data suggests that each country runs a surplus with the other, which cannot be true at the same time. Faced with this massive shift towards an increasingly digital economy, and data of increasingly limited reliability to describe the change, there is a temptation to oversimplify reality. Seeking to explain complex and uncertain issues seems to be less successful politically than populist identity politics. These communicate simply about the nation with a shared view of its history and place in the world. They encourage trust in familiar narratives, offer personal leadership and an upbeat view of the future.

But such narratives have little useful to say about how best to manage the complex interdependence of modern economies, investment and trade. Achieving the shared regulation of environmental, labour or safety standards required to open markets; safe food production and farming; visa access for skilled workers and those needed to deliver health or social care; agreed procedures to resolve trade disputes are all issues requiring serious analysis and often difficult trade-offs. Identity politics is not well equipped to deliver these decisions, and permanent officials cannot do so without political readiness to take responsibility for necessary but unpopular consequences.

Short-term populist politics also struggles to deal with longer-term decisions which influence global competitiveness. Maintaining modern transport infrastructure and expanded housing stock requires a willingness to accept criticism from those who dislike the local impact, or who would prefer all to remain unchanged. Significant investments in digital infrastructure are costly, and often slow to produce the needed improvements. Encouraging appropriate immigration is key to maintaining a productive, growing economy in countries with otherwise static or declining populations, and ensuring a world-leading research base. These all require significant funding, and strategic political leadership to explain, often against entrenched resistance, why such long-term change is needed. Experience shows that soundbites or popular tweets are not a substitute for such leadership.

*V*

Faced with these challenges, what are the options available for Whitehall and Westminster now? The first is to carry on maintaining the basic administrative rules of the road – political neutrality, continuity of officials in senior posts, financial responsibility to parliament and support for Cabinet government – while hoping that current pressures diminish over time, and that politicians return to a more managerial role within which the technical expertise of their advisers is genuinely valued. But in today's febrile political environment this option may be seen as a failure to accept that new political and societal realities together with the rapidly changing digital economy have undermined much of the implicit trust needed for officials to function effectively across traditional government departments. There is no point pretending that Cabinet government remains a reality in a political world focused on 10 Downing Street; nor that politicians who choose to take most of their advice from people they know and who depend on them are going to turn to impartial expert advisers when in government. Even legal advice risks becoming politicized in the context of majoritarian government run by the prime minister and focused on maintaining a parliamentary majority.

An alternative is to accept, however reluctantly, the reality of the move in recent decades towards a permanent group of political advisers around key ministers, and in particular the prime minister, who together form a layer of effective decision-makers across government, and at least seek to codify it. This would imply that the UK moved formally towards a continental style *cabinet* system, with advisers accepted as having some delegated authority on behalf of their ministers. Arguably this has already been the case for several decades in No 10 Downing Street where advisers are seen as representing the prime minister, whatever their formal position as temporary civil servants. A note or call from a No 10 Adviser is seen within Whitehall as normally being authoritative and to be actioned – although conflicting messages coming from different parts of the No 10 internal bureaucracy have not been uncommon in the past.

If other advisers are to take on this authority, they will also need to be the sole channel of briefing to the ministers. This in turn implies a change in the responsibilities of officials, no longer directly engaged with ministers but instead working to and briefing advisers. In turn these advisers would be expected to play a more significant role in front of parliamentary committees, justifying publicly their role in taking policy and management decisions, while officials focus on providing objective technical analysis, which would be made publicly available.

A final significant change concerns control of financial and other resources. This is the area in which political advisers have until now had least impact in the UK. Typically spending reviews are managed by the Permanent Secretary working directly with the Secretary of State, since ultimately the Permanent Secretary has to justify all spending directly to parliament under the control of the National Audit Office and the Public Accounts Committee. It is not possible to separate policy decisions from the resources needed to deliver them. At present the Permanent Secretary is responsible for approving all departmental spending. This would no longer be practical moving to a *cabinet* system, which would therefore require a fundamental adjustment to the way in which public money is controlled and spent.

A more radical option is to look not to Europe but across the Atlantic to a US-style system, in which all domestic senior public service posts are open to nomination by the administration, as well as ambassadorial positions abroad. This assumes that a better result is achieved through political commitment rather than experience in the job, while ensuring a regular input of new challenge as to how things are done. It also, however, reduces morale and lessens the expertise accumulated within a permanent public administration. The US government regularly experiences considerable disruption at the beginning and end of a presidential tenure as senior posts become, or remain, vacant for considerable periods of time. Coordination across government becomes even more difficult as new appointees have no shared culture or administrative structure to work within when resolving disputes or setting priorities. Finally this approach makes effective executive administration much harder. Agencies need continuity of leadership, and their Boards require a mix of skills which cannot be delivered effectively through political patronage, as UK experience shows.

## VI

My own view is that we should start from a clear recognition that the current UK system has considerable advantages – honest, merit-based, capable of adjustment, proven to be loyal to different political persuasions when in government. But it requires a shared understanding of who does what and why with politicians and their advisers. There are signs that this understanding is diminishing. We need to understand why this is the case. If this change reflects a permanent, more ideological commitment by politicians to trust only those who are known to be committed to their party or even personal political viewpoints within a particular faction or wing of a party, then there is less space for a neutral set of advisers to be effective. Replacing them with politically acceptable substitutes would, however, mean less coherent and less expert administration, with a short-term tactical focus. It should at least be accompanied by increased transparency, including on the decision-making role of the Prime Minister's Office.

Irrespective of the political choices made, there is an urgent need for governmental structures to become more technically competent and more flexible, adjusting to our digital society and economy. This in turn requires politicians not to seek a hands-on managerial role in areas such as IT or infrastructure development for which they have no technical preparation. It also requires more discipline in changes to governmental structures – merging or creating new departments – which distract from efficiency and confuse responsibility for outcomes.

There is no off-the-shelf model for modern administrative excellence. All governmental structures reflect their national political culture and history. The French system has since 1945 relied on graduates of the Ecole National d'Administration to provide the majority of both ministers and senior officials. In recent years France has seen growing opposition to the concentration of power in the hands of a small technocratic elite. In contrast the UK's current political adviser class have no shared skills base beyond political loyalty, and even less legitimacy than do ENA graduates, who must all spend several years working for the French administration before making other career choices. Moreover, any changes to UK political structures would have to ensure clear lines of responsibility for decision-taking which include clarity to parliament over how public money is spent.

The evidence remains overwhelming that good governance is best provided through a meritocratic, politically neutral permanent civil service focused on providing a professional service for ministers seeking to govern and carry out the business of public administration effectively. The precise skill set required of officials can and should change over time. And policy officials like others in managerial positions need to keep up with the times, in particular with the requirements of a digital economy. So too do politicians.

This in turn requires close relations between government systems and innovative firms, researchers in data and digital trends, and a willingness to seek out disruptive new solutions – recognizing that these will not always be successful on first trial. Such creative innovation cannot be imposed centrally, as recent experience has shown, but requires scope for flexible change within departments and agencies. However, this neutral administrative model only functions with a group of politicians who, while disagreeing about priorities and use of resources, accept that their goals will be better achieved through cooperation with permanent officials bringing independent judgement, continuity and objective analysis to decision-making. The argument in favour of this model needs to be made and won across the political spectrum, and our wider society, not as an abstract but in comparison with the available alternatives.

If it is not won, the most likely next step for the UK would be an increase in explicit political patronage over senior civil service posts, meaning less cohesion, continuity, and expertise within the administrative machine. But if professional expertise without political commitment stops being enough to gain a trusted place in the Westminster room where it happens, then the meritocratic, politically neutral Whitehall we have taken for granted will no longer have legitimacy. Instead politics will take over the official space, and loyalty will be valued over technical competence or independent analysis. That change should not be made lightly, because it will be very hard to reverse.

# FURTHER READING

Aaron, Henry J. *Politics and the Professors: The Great Society in Perspective*. Washington, DC: Brookings, 1978.

Alanbrooke, Lord. *War Diaries: 1939–1945*, ed. Alex Danchev and Dan Todman. New edn. London: Weidenfeld and Nicholson, 2002.

Bacon, Francis. 'Of Counsel', in *The Essayes or Counsel, Civill and Morall*, ed. Michael Kiernan. Oxford: Clarendon Press, 1985.

Baker, James A., III. *Work Hard, Study … and Keep Out of Politics*. New York: Putnam/Penguin, 2006.

Balogh, Thomas. 'The Apotheosis of the Dilettante: The Establishment of Mandarins', in *The Establishment: A Symposium*, ed. Hugh Thomas. London: Anthony Blond, 1959.

Benn, Tony. *The Case for a Constitutional Civil Service*. Nottingham: Institute for Workers' Control, 1980.

Benveniste, Guy. *The Politics of Expertise*. 2nd edn. San Francisco: Boyd and Fraser, 1977.

Blackstone, Tessa, and Plowden, William. *Inside the Think Tank: Advising the Cabinet, 1971–1983*. London: Heinemann, 1988.

Blaydes, Lisa, Grimmer, Justin, and McQueen, Alison. 'Mirrors for Princes and Sultans: Advice on the Art of Governance in the Medieval Christian and Islamic Worlds', *Journal of Politics* 80 (2018), 1150–66.

Blick, Andrew. *People Who Live in the Dark: The History of the Special Adviser in British Politics*. London: Politico's, 2004.

Blick, Andrew, and Jones, George. *At Power's Elbow: Aides to the Prime Minister from Robert Walpole to David Cameron*. London: Biteback, 2013.

Boroujerdi, Mehrzad (ed.). *Mirror for the Muslim Prince: Islam and the Theory of Statecraft*. Syracuse, NY: Syracuse University Press, 2013.

Brown, Jack. *No. 10: The Geography of Power at Downing Street*. London: Haus, 2019.

Colclough, David. *Freedom of Speech in Early Stuart England*. Cambridge: Cambridge University Press, 2005.

Colville, John. *The Fringes of Power: Downing Street Diaries 1939–1955*. London: Hodder and Stoughton, 1985.

Crossman, Richard. *Diaries of a Cabinet Minister*. London: Hamish Hamilton/Jonathan Cape, 1975.

Crowther-Hunt, Norman. 'Mandarins and Ministers', *Parliamentary Affairs* 33 (1980): 373–99.

DeLeon, Peter. 'The Historical Roots of the Field', in *The Oxford Handbook of Public Policy*, ed. Robert E. Goodon, Michael Moran and Martin Rein. Oxford: Oxford University Press, 2008.

Dickinson, Matthew J., and Tenpas, Kathryn Dunn. 'Explaining Increasing Turnover Rates among Presidential Advisers, 1929–1997', *Journal of Politics* 64 (2002): 434–48.

Donoughue, Bernard. *The Heat of the Kitchen: An Autobiography*. London: Politico's, 2003.

Donoughue, Bernard. *Downing Street Diary: With Harold Wilson in No. 10*. London: Jonathan Cape, 2005.

Donoughue, Bernard. *Downing Street Diary Volume Two: With James Callaghan in No. 10*. London: Jonathan Cape, 2008.

Ferguson, Niall. *Kissinger 1923–1968: The Idealist*. London: Allen Lane, 2015.

Fisher, Frank, and Forester, John (eds.). *The Argumentative Turn in Policy Analysis and Planning*. Durham, NC: Duke University Press, 1993.

Goldhamer, Herbert. *The Adviser*. New York: Elsevier, 1978.

Guy, John. 'The Rhetoric of Counsel in Early Modern England', in *Tudor Political Culture*, ed. Dale Hoak. Cambridge: Cambridge University Press, 1995.

Guy, John. *Politics, Law and Counsel in Tudor and Early Stuart England*. London: Routledge, 2000.

Haines, Joe. *The Politics of Power*. London: Jonathan Cape, 1977.

Halberstam, David. *The Best and the Brightest*. 1972; New York: Modern Library, 2001.

Harris, Robert. *Good and Faithful Servant: The Unauthorized Biography of Bernard Ingham*. London: Faber and Faber, 1990.

Hartmann, Robert. *Palace Politics: An Inside Account of the Ford Years*. New York: McGraw-Hill, 1980.

Heclo, H. Hugh. 'Policy Analysis', *British Journal of Political Science* 2 (1972): 83–108.

Hennessy, Peter et al. *Routine Punctuated by Orgies: The Central Policy Review Staff, 1970–1983*. Glasgow: Strathclyde Papers on Government and Politics, 31, University of Strathclyde, 1985.

Hennessy, Peter. *Whitehall*, rev. edn. London: Pimlico, 2001.

Janis, Irving L. *Victims of Groupthink: A Psychological Study of Foreign-Policy Decisions and Fiascoes*. Boston: Houghton Mifflin, 1972.

Johnson, Richard T. *Managing the White House*. New York: Harper and Row, 1974.

Jones, G. W. 'The Prime Minister's Aides', in *The British Prime Ministers*, ed. Anthony King. 2nd edn. Houndmills: Macmillan, 1985.

Jones, Nicholas. *Sultans of Spin: The Media and the New Labour Government*. London: Gollancz, 2000.

Kavanagh, Dennis, and Seldon, Anthony. *The Powers behind the Prime Minister*. London: HarperCollins, 1999.

Kellner, Peter, and Crowther-Hunt, Norman. *The Civil Servants: An Inquiry into Britain's Ruling Class*. London: Macdonald and Jane's, 1980.

Kowert, Paul A. *Groupthink or Deadlock: When Do Leaders Learn from Their Advisors?* Albany, NY: SUNY Press, 2002.

Landauer, Matthew. *Dangerous Counsel: Accountability and Advice in Ancient Greece*. Chicago: University of Chicago Press, 2019.

Lasswell, Harold et al. *The Policy Sciences*. Palo Alto: Stanford University Press, 1951.

Lasswell, Harold. *The Decision Process*. College Park, MD: University of Maryland, 1956.

Lasswell, Harold. 'The Emerging Conception of the Policy Sciences', *Policy Sciences* 1 (1970): 3–14.

Lasswell, Harold. *A Pre-view of Policy Sciences*. New York: American Elsevier, 1971.

Lowe, Rodney. 'Grit in the Oyster or Sand in the Machine? The Evolving Role of Special Advisers in British Government', *Twentieth Century British History* 16 (2005): 497–505.

Machiavelli, Niccolò. *The Prince*, ed. Quentin Skinner and Russell Price. Cambridge: Cambridge University Press, 1988.

MacRae, Duncan Jr. and Whittington, Dale. *Expert Advice for Policy Choice*. Washington, DC: Georgetown University Press, 1997.

Mapstone, Sally. 'The Advice to Princes Tradition in Scottish Literature, 1450–1500'. Oxford, University of. D. Phil. thesis, 1986.

Marlow, Louise. 'Surveying Recent Literature in the Arabic and Persian Mirror for Princes Genre', *History Compass* 7 (2009), 523–38.

Moore, Charles. *Margaret Thatcher The Authorized Biography: Volume Three Herself Alone*. London: Allen Lane, 2019.

More, Thomas. *Utopia*, ed. George M. Logan and Robert M. Adams. Cambridge: Cambridge University Press, 1989.

Mulgan, Richard. 'Truth in Government and the Politicization of Public Service Advice', *Public Administration* 85 (2007): 569–86.

Palmer, Alasdair. *The Return of Political Patronage: How Special Advisers Are Taking Over Our Civil Service and Why We Need to Worry about It*. London: Civitas, 2015.

Paul, Joanne. *Counsel and Command in Early Modern English Thought*. Cambridge: Cambridge University Press, 2020.

Plowden, William (ed.), *Advising the Rulers*. Oxford: Royal Institute of Public Administration/Basil Blackwell, 1987.

Plutarch. 'How to Tell a Flatterer from a Friend', in *Moralia*, vol. I, trans. Frank Cole Babbitt. Loeb Classical Library, 197, Cambridge, MA: Harvard University Press, 1927, 264–395.

Radin, Beryl A. *Beyond Machiavelli: Policy Analysis Reaches Midlife*. 2nd edn. Washington, DC: Georgetown University Press, 2013.

Reinhardt, Nicole. *Voices of Conscience: Royal Confessors and Political Counsel in Seventeenth-Century Spain and France*. Oxford: Oxford University Press, 2016.

Rose, Jacqueline (ed.), *The Politics of Counsel in England and Scotland, 1286–1707*. Oxford: Oxford University Press for the British Academy, 2016.

Sackville, Thomas, and Norton, Thomas. *Gorboduc or Ferrex and Porrex* (1565), ed. Irby B. Cauthen jr. London: Edward Arnold, 1970.

Sorensen, Theodore. *Decision-Making in the White House; The Olive Branch or the Arrows*. 1963. New York: Columbia University Press, 2005.

Stone, Deborah. *Policy Paradox: The Art of Political Decision Making*. 2nd edn. New York: W. W. Norton, 1997.

Tetlock, Philip. *Expert Political Judgment: How Good Is It? How Can We Know?* Princeton, NJ: Princeton University Press, 2005.

Whipple, Chris. *The Gatekeepers: How the White House Chiefs of Staff Define Every Presidency*. New York: Crown, 2017.

Wildavsky, Aaron. *Speaking Truth to Power: The Art and Craft of Policy Analysis*. Boston and Toronto: Little, Brown and Co., 1979.

Wilson, Harold. *The Governance of Britain*. London: Weidenfeld and Nicolson, 1976.

Witherspoon, Patricia. *Within These Walls: A Study of Communication between Presidents and Their Senior Staffs*. Westport, CT: Praeger, 1991.

Worden, Blair. 'Oliver Cromwell and the Council', in *The Cromwellian Protectorate*, ed. Patrick Little. Woodbridge: Boydell, 2007.

Yong, Ben, and Hazell, Robert. *Special Advisers: Who They Are, What They Do and Why They Matter*. Oxford: Hart Publishing, 2014.

Zuckerman, Lord. *Advice and Responsibility: The Romanes Lecture 1975*. Oxford: Clarendon Press, 1975.

# INDEX

www.ingramcontent.com/pod-product-compliance
Lightning Source LLC
Chambersburg PA
CBHW070407270326
41926CB00014B/2734